First World War
and Army of Occupation
War Diary
France, Belgium and Germany

17 DIVISION
Divisional Troops
77 Field Company Royal Engineers
14 July 1915 - 23 May 1919

WO95/1993/1

The Naval & Military Press Ltd
www.nmarchive.com
Published in association with The National Archives

Published by

The Naval & Military Press Ltd

Unit 10 Ridgewood Industrial Park,

Uckfield, East Sussex,

TN22 5QE England

Tel: +44 (0) 1825 749494

www.naval-military-press.com

www.nmarchive.com

This diary has been reprinted in facsimile from the original. Any imperfections are inevitably reproduced and the quality may fall short of modern type and cartographic standards.

Contents

Document type	Place/Title	Date From	Date To
Miscellaneous	WO95/1993/1 17 Div 1915 July-1919 May 77 Field Coy RE		
Heading	17th Division 77th Field Coy R.E. Jly 1915-May 1919		
Heading	17th Division 77th F.C.R.E. Vol. I from 14 Jly to 31 Aug 15		
War Diary	Southampton Havre	14/07/1915	30/08/1915
War Diary		27/08/1915	31/08/1915
Heading	17th Division 77th F.C.R.E. Vol II Sept. 15		
War Diary			
War Diary	Map 28.0.3.6	02/09/1915	04/09/1915
War Diary	Map 28.1.33	05/09/1915	16/09/1915
War Diary	Map 28.13.1.C	17/09/1915	23/09/1915
War Diary	Map 28.1.33.a	24/09/1915	29/09/1915
Heading	17th Division 77th F.C.R.E. Vol 3 Oct 15		
War Diary		01/10/1915	06/10/1915
War Diary		05/10/1915	05/10/1915
War Diary		06/10/1915	26/10/1915
War Diary		06/10/1915	30/10/1915
Miscellaneous	Field Return.	01/10/1915	01/10/1915
Miscellaneous	In the field	01/10/1915	01/10/1915
Miscellaneous			
Miscellaneous	Perforated Sheet giving detail of personnel and horses wanting to complete. shown on Army Form B. 213		
Miscellaneous	Field Return.	08/10/1915	08/10/1915
Miscellaneous			
Miscellaneous	Field Return.	08/10/1915	08/10/1915
Miscellaneous	Perforated Sheet giving detail of personnel and horses wanting to complete, shown on Army Form B. 213		
Miscellaneous	Field Return.	15/10/1915	15/10/1915
Miscellaneous			
Miscellaneous	Field Return.		
Miscellaneous	Perforated Sheet giving detail of personnel and horses wanting to complete, shown on Army Form B. 213		
Miscellaneous	Field Return.	22/10/1915	22/10/1915
Miscellaneous	In the field	22/10/1915	22/10/1915
Miscellaneous			
Miscellaneous	Perforated Sheet giving detail of personnel and horses wanting to complete, shown on Army Form B. 213		
Miscellaneous	Field Return.		
Miscellaneous	In the field	29/10/1915	29/10/1915
Miscellaneous			
Miscellaneous	Perforated Sheet giving detail of personnel and horses wanting to complete, shown on Army Form B. 213		
Heading	17th Division 77th F.C.O. R.E. Nov Vol 4 Nov 15		
War Diary		01/11/1915	09/11/1915
War Diary		02/11/1915	19/11/1915
War Diary		09/11/1915	30/11/1915
Heading	17th Div 77th F.C.R.E. Vol 5		
War Diary		02/12/1915	31/12/1915
Miscellaneous	Field Return.	04/12/1915	04/12/1915

Miscellaneous	In the field	03/12/1915	03/12/1915
Miscellaneous			
Miscellaneous	Perforated Sheet giving detail of personnel and horses wanting to complete, shown on Army Form B. 213		
Miscellaneous	Field Return.	10/12/1915	10/12/1915
Miscellaneous	In the field	10/12/1915	10/12/1915
Miscellaneous			
Miscellaneous	Perforated Sheet giving detail of personnel and horses wanting to complete, shown on Army Form B. 213		
Miscellaneous	Field Return.	17/12/1915	17/12/1915
Miscellaneous	In the field	17/12/1915	17/12/1915
Miscellaneous			
Miscellaneous	Perforated Sheet giving detail of personnel and horses wanting to complete, shown on Army Form B. 213		
Miscellaneous	Field Return.	24/12/1915	24/12/1915
Miscellaneous	In the field	24/12/1915	24/12/1915
Miscellaneous			
Miscellaneous	Perforated Sheet giving detail of personnel and horses wanting to complete, shown on Army Form B. 213		
Miscellaneous	Field Return.	31/12/1915	31/12/1915
Miscellaneous	In the field	31/12/1915	31/12/1915
Miscellaneous			
Miscellaneous	Perforated Sheet giving detail of personnel and horses wanting to complete, shown on Army Form B. 213		
Heading	77th F.C.R.E. Vol. 6 Jan 16		
War Diary		01/01/1916	31/01/1916
Heading	77th F.C.R.E. Vol. 7		
War Diary		01/02/1916	29/02/1916
War Diary		19/02/1916	19/02/1916
Heading	77th F.C.R.E. Vol 8 17 Div		
War Diary		03/03/1916	31/03/1916
War Diary		02/03/1916	29/04/1916
War Diary	Lille Post	00/04/1916	00/04/1916
War Diary	Leith Walk	00/04/1916	00/04/1916
War Diary	Support Line 68.S	00/04/1916	00/04/1916
War Diary	Chards Farm	00/04/1916	00/04/1916
War Diary	Support 69S & 70S	00/04/1916	00/04/1916
War Diary	Head Quarter Walk	00/04/1916	00/04/1916
War Diary	Trench Tramway	00/04/1916	00/04/1916
War Diary	Mushroom & F. Trench	00/04/1916	00/04/1916
War Diary	73.S	00/04/1916	00/04/1916
War Diary	Port Egal Avenue		
War Diary	Port Egal Avenue Stop		
War Diary		01/05/1916	30/05/1916
War Diary		01/05/1916	19/05/1916
War Diary		01/06/1916	30/06/1916
War Diary		08/06/1916	30/06/1916
War Diary		01/06/1916	31/07/1916
War Diary		02/07/1916	24/07/1916
War Diary		03/07/1916	31/07/1916
Heading	17th Divisional Engineers 77th Field Company R.E. August 1916		
War Diary	Becordel	01/08/1916	11/08/1916
War Diary	Dernancourt.	12/08/1916	14/08/1916
War Diary	Gezaincourt	15/08/1916	15/08/1916
War Diary	Neuvillette	16/08/1916	18/08/1916

War Diary	St Amand	19/08/1916	22/08/1916
War Diary	Souastre	23/08/1916	31/08/1916
War Diary		02/08/1916	31/08/1916
War Diary	Souastre	01/09/1916	21/09/1916
War Diary	Grenas	22/09/1916	22/09/1916
War Diary	Remaisnil	23/09/1916	23/09/1916
War Diary	Neuilly-Le-Dien	24/09/1916	30/09/1916
War Diary		01/09/1916	30/09/1916
War Diary	Neuilly-Le-Dien	01/10/1916	01/10/1916
War Diary	Barly	02/10/1916	02/10/1916
War Diary	Halloy	03/10/1916	03/10/1916
War Diary	Souastre	04/10/1916	05/10/1916
War Diary	Sailly	06/10/1916	14/10/1916
War Diary	Souastre	15/10/1916	18/10/1916
War Diary	Milly	19/10/1916	20/10/1916
War Diary	Talmas	21/10/1916	21/10/1916
War Diary	Ville	22/10/1916	26/10/1916
War Diary	Citedal	27/10/1916	29/10/1916
War Diary	Carnoy	30/10/1916	31/10/1916
War Diary		03/10/1916	29/10/1916
War Diary	Carnoy & Longeval	01/10/1916	11/10/1916
War Diary	Meaulte	12/10/1916	15/10/1916
War Diary	Argoeuves	16/10/1916	16/10/1916
War Diary	St Pierre	17/10/1916	19/10/1916
War Diary	Fourdrinoy	20/10/1916	30/10/1916
War Diary		01/11/1916	30/11/1916
War Diary	Meaulte	16/11/1916	22/11/1916
War Diary	Bernafay Wood	23/11/1916	27/11/1916
War Diary		03/12/1916	26/12/1916
War Diary		03/11/1916	03/11/1916
War Diary	Fourdrinoy	01/12/1916	11/12/1916
War Diary	Corbie	12/12/1916	13/12/1916
War Diary	Meaulte	14/12/1916	15/12/1916
War Diary	Bernafay Wood	28/12/1916	31/12/1916
War Diary		02/01/1917	31/01/1917
War Diary	Bernafay Wood	01/01/1917	15/01/1917
War Diary	Meaulte	16/01/1917	25/01/1917
War Diary	Combles	26/01/1917	19/02/1917
War Diary	Mansel Camp	20/02/1917	20/02/1917
War Diary	Franvillers	21/02/1917	28/02/1917
War Diary		04/02/1917	28/02/1917
War Diary	Vadencourt	01/03/1917	12/03/1917
War Diary	Gezaincourt	13/03/1917	13/03/1917
War Diary	Bernatre	14/03/1917	14/03/1917
War Diary	Labroye	15/03/1917	19/03/1917
War Diary	Fillievres	20/03/1917	20/03/1917
War Diary	St Pol	21/03/1917	31/03/1917
War Diary	Vadencourt	01/03/1917	12/03/1917
War Diary	Gezaincourt	13/03/1917	13/03/1917
War Diary	Labroye	15/03/1917	19/03/1917
War Diary	Fillievres	20/03/1917	20/03/1917
War Diary	St Pol	21/03/1917	31/03/1917
War Diary		01/04/1917	30/04/1917
War Diary	Le Cauroy	01/05/1917	02/05/1917
War Diary	St. Nicholas	03/05/1917	21/05/1917
War Diary	B-30.c	22/05/1917	29/05/1917

War Diary	H.1.D.33.	30/05/1917	31/05/1917
War Diary		01/05/1917	31/05/1917
War Diary	Railway Cutting H.7.C.3.G Sheet 51 B	01/06/1917	11/06/1917
War Diary	Wanquetin	12/06/1917	15/06/1917
War Diary	Pommera	16/06/1917	20/06/1917
War Diary	Railway Cutting H.7b.3.a. Sheet 51.C	21/06/1917	31/06/1917
War Diary		19/06/1917	20/06/1917
War Diary	Pommera	21/06/1917	21/06/1917
War Diary	Rly. Cutting. H.7b.3.9.	22/06/1917	30/06/1917
War Diary	Railway Cutting. H.7.b.3.9. Sheet 51B.	01/06/1917	11/06/1917
War Diary	Wanquetin	12/06/1917	15/06/1917
War Diary	Pommera	16/06/1917	18/06/1917
War Diary	Railway Cutting H.7.b.3.9 Sheet 51.B.NW	01/07/1917	07/07/1917
War Diary	Effie Trench	08/07/1917	31/07/1917
War Diary	Railway Cutting H.7.b.3.9 Sheet. 51.B	01/07/1917	07/07/1917
War Diary	Effie Trench	08/07/1917	31/07/1917
War Diary	Coy H.Q. Effie Trench	01/08/1917	01/08/1917
War Diary	Horse Line E G.16.a.9.9 Sheet 51.B.N.W.	02/08/1917	15/08/1917
War Diary	Coy hdqrs Effie Trench	16/08/1917	16/08/1917
War Diary	Horse Lines G.16.a.9.9 Sheet 51 B.N.W.	17/08/1917	31/08/1917
War Diary	Coy HQd Effie Trench	01/08/1917	04/08/1917
War Diary	Horse Lines G.16.a.9.9 Sheet 51 B.N.W.	05/08/1917	31/08/1917
War Diary	Effie Trench Anocam Valley	01/09/1917	01/09/1917
War Diary	Horseline G.S.T. Nicholas G.16.a.9.9. Sheet. 51. B.N.W.	02/09/1917	24/09/1917

War Diary	Lehameau	25/09/1917	25/09/1917
War Diary	Ivergny	26/09/1917	30/09/1917
War Diary	H.Q. Effie Trench	01/09/1917	01/09/1917
War Diary	Horse Lines	02/09/1917	02/09/1917
War Diary	St Nicholas G.16.a.9.5. Sheet 51. B.N.W.	02/09/1917	30/09/1917
War Diary	Ivergny	01/10/1917	04/10/1917
War Diary	Salem Camp	05/10/1917	11/10/1917
War Diary	Canal Bank.	11/10/1917	26/10/1917
War Diary	Proven	27/10/1917	31/10/1917
War Diary		01/10/1917	30/10/1917
War Diary	Patagonia Camp Proven. Sheet 27 E.17.d.5.3	01/11/1917	30/11/1917
War Diary	Patagonia Camp Proven. Sheet 51 E.17.d.5.4	01/11/1917	05/11/1917
War Diary	Sedirmal	06/11/1917	06/11/1917
War Diary	Canal Bank C.19.a.0.2.	07/11/1917	08/11/1917
War Diary	Transport B.24.C.0.2 Sheet 28. N.W.	09/11/1917	30/11/1917
War Diary	Sheet 28. Belgium.	01/12/1917	05/12/1917
War Diary	Billets C.19.a.0.2	05/12/1917	05/12/1917
War Diary	Transport B.24.C.0.2	06/12/1917	07/12/1917
War Diary	Pardo. Camp. Proven.	08/12/1917	09/12/1917
War Diary	Hocquinghem	09/12/1917	10/12/1917
War Diary	Westrove	11/12/1917	12/12/1917
War Diary	Barastra	13/12/1917	16/12/1917
War Diary	Lechelle	17/12/1917	31/12/1917
War Diary	Sheet 28 Belgium	01/12/1917	02/12/1917
War Diary	Billets C.19.a.0.2 Transport B.24.C.0.2	03/12/1917	05/12/1917
War Diary	Pardoe Camp Proven	06/12/1917	07/12/1917
War Diary	Wulverdinghe	08/10/1917	08/10/1917
War Diary	Hocquinchem	09/12/1917	31/12/1917
War Diary	Sport Heap	15/01/1918	31/01/1918
War Diary	Having Court	01/01/1918	07/01/1918
War Diary	Spoil Heap K.20	08/01/1918	14/01/1918

War Diary	Havrincourt Sheet. 57. C. K.28.a.2.4.	01/01/1918	07/01/1918
War Diary	Spoil Bank K 28 Central	08/01/1918	14/01/1918
War Diary	Transport Lines at P.17.d.4.4	15/01/1918	31/01/1918
War Diary	Spoil Heap Sheet 57. C. K.21 Central	01/02/1918	04/02/1918
War Diary	Brohen Houses H.3.6.d.	05/02/1918	16/02/1918
War Diary	Brohen Houses Sheet 57 C. H.3.6.d.	14/02/1918	28/02/1918
War Diary		01/02/1918	28/02/1918
Heading	17th Div. 77th Field Company. R.E. March 1918		
War Diary		01/03/1918	31/03/1918
Heading	17th Divisional Engineers War Diary 77th Field Company R.E. April 1918		
War Diary		01/04/1918	30/04/1918
War Diary		01/04/1918	12/05/1918
War Diary	La Vicogne	13/05/1918	18/05/1918
War Diary	Beauquesne	19/05/1918	26/05/1918
War Diary	P.12.b.9.9	27/05/1918	31/05/1918
War Diary	Clairfaye Farm Coy at Forceville	01/05/1918	07/05/1918
War Diary	La Vicogne	08/05/1918	17/05/1918
War Diary	Beauquesne	18/05/1918	25/05/1918
War Diary	Coy at P.12.b.9.9 Horselines at 6.6. (Central)	25/05/1918	31/05/1918
War Diary	Beaussart	01/06/1918	23/06/1918
War Diary	T.5.A.6.5 57D	24/06/1918	30/06/1918
War Diary	Transport at O.6.c Central Coy at P.12.b.9.9. Coy at P.5.a.5.0	01/06/1918	30/06/1918
War Diary	Herissart	01/07/1918	09/07/1918
War Diary	V.2.d.6.3	10/07/1918	17/07/1918
War Diary	P.36.a.1.9.	20/07/1918	31/07/1918
War Diary	Company at T.5.a.6.5	01/07/1918	08/07/1918
War Diary	Transport Lines at U.11.c.5.7. Coy at V.2.d.6.3	09/07/1918	19/07/1918
War Diary	P.36.a.1.9. Transport at U.11.c.5.7	20/07/1918	25/07/1918
War Diary	No 2 Pln "B" Coy 1st Bn 365th U.S.E. att for work	26/07/1918	31/07/1918
Heading	17th Divl. Engineers 77th Field Co. Royal Engineers. August 1918		
War Diary	Company at P.36.a.1.9 Transport at U.11.C.5.7	01/08/1918	06/08/1918
War Diary	Toutencourt Daours	07/08/1918	13/08/1918
War Diary	Fouilloy	16/08/1918	16/08/1918
War Diary	Vecquemont	17/08/1918	18/08/1918
War Diary	Herrisart	18/08/1918	19/08/1918
War Diary	Toutencourt	20/08/1918	31/08/1918
War Diary	Englebelmer	01/08/1918	06/08/1918
War Diary	Toutencourt	06/08/1918	06/08/1918
War Diary	Daours	08/08/1918	08/08/1918
War Diary	Vaux-Sur-Somme	09/08/1918	12/08/1918
War Diary	Gailly	13/08/1918	16/08/1918
War Diary	Fouilloy	16/08/1918	17/08/1918
War Diary	Herissart	18/08/1918	25/08/1918
War Diary	R.32.b.1.9.	26/08/1918	28/08/1918
War Diary	Courcellette	28/08/1918	30/09/1918
War Diary	M19.d.2.2. O.26.d.7.5.	03/09/1918	06/09/1918
War Diary	V.7.b.7.6. Transport V.1.a.0.4	07/09/1918	16/09/1918
War Diary	V.6.c.5.4. W.9.c.9.3.	17/09/1918	24/09/1918
War Diary	U.6.b.6.7	25/09/1918	30/09/1918
War Diary	V.1.a.0.4 57.C.5.E.	01/10/1918	04/10/1918
War Diary	14.6.C.4.9. 57.C.5.E	05/10/1918	07/10/1918
War Diary	X.3.a.80.15 57.c.5.E N.27.c.8.7. 57.b.5.N	08/10/1918	09/10/1918
War Diary	J.21.c. Central 57.b.	10/10/1918	19/10/1918

War Diary	J.17.c.7.7. (57.b.)	20/10/1918	23/10/1918
War Diary	J.20.d.08.05 (57.b)	24/10/1918	25/10/1918
War Diary	Vendegies	26/10/1918	28/10/1918
War Diary	Neuvilly	29/10/1918	31/10/1918
War Diary	U.6.b.0.7	01/10/1918	04/10/1918
War Diary	W.6.c.4.5.	05/10/1918	06/10/1918
War Diary	X.3.a.80.15	08/10/1918	08/10/1918
War Diary	N27.c.8.7 J.21.c. Cent.	09/10/1918	19/10/1918
War Diary	J.17.c.7.7	20/10/1918	23/10/1918
War Diary	J.20.d.05.05	24/10/1918	25/10/1918
War Diary	F.7.a.5.0.	26/10/1918	27/10/1918
War Diary	J.8.b.6.6	29/10/1918	31/10/1918
War Diary	Neuvilly Englefontaine	01/11/1918	02/11/1918
War Diary	Vendegies	03/11/1918	03/11/1918
War Diary	Poix du Nord	04/11/1918	04/11/1918
War Diary	Lochnignol	05/11/1918	06/11/1918
War Diary	Berlaimont	07/11/1918	14/11/1918
War Diary	Troisvillers	15/11/1918	30/11/1918
War Diary	Vendegies	01/11/1918	02/11/1918
War Diary	Poix Du Nord	04/11/1918	05/11/1918
War Diary	Locquinol	06/11/1918	06/11/1918
War Diary	Berlaimont	07/11/1918	07/11/1918
War Diary	Bachant	08/11/1918	09/11/1918
War Diary	Beaufort	10/11/1918	10/11/1918
War Diary	Berlaimont	11/11/1918	12/11/1918
War Diary	Englefontaine	14/11/1918	14/11/1918
War Diary	Troisvilles	15/11/1918	06/12/1918
War Diary	Picquigny	07/12/1918	07/12/1918
War Diary	Bailleul	08/12/1918	10/12/1918
War Diary	Bray Les Mareuil	11/12/1918	31/12/1918
War Diary	Troisville	01/12/1918	05/12/1918
War Diary	Transport-Pont Noyelles	06/12/1918	07/12/1918
War Diary	Bailleul	08/12/1918	09/12/1918
War Diary	Bray-Les-Mareuil	11/12/1918	31/12/1918
War Diary	Bray	01/01/1919	31/01/1919
War Diary	Bray-Les-Mareuil	02/01/1919	28/02/1919
War Diary	Longpre-le-Corps-Saints	01/05/1919	23/05/1919
War Diary	Bray-Les-Mareuil	01/02/1919	10/03/1919
War Diary	Hangest Sur Somme	11/03/1919	31/03/1919
War Diary	Hangest Sur Somme	01/03/1919	24/04/1919
War Diary	Longpre	25/04/1919	30/04/1919
War Diary	Hangest-Sur-Somme	01/04/1919	23/04/1919
War Diary	Longpre	24/04/1919	01/05/1919
War Diary	Le-Corps-Saints	02/05/1919	17/05/1919
War Diary	Longpre	18/05/1919	18/05/1919
War Diary	Le Havre	19/05/1919	19/05/1919
War Diary	Harfleur	20/05/1919	23/05/1919

WO 95-1993 / 1

17 DIV

1915 July - 1919 May

77 FIELD COY RE

17TH DIVISION

77TH FIELD COY R.E.

JLY 1915-MAY 1919

17th Division

121/6607

77th F.C. R.E.
Vol: I

From 14 July to 31 Aug. 15

[illegible] May 19

Sheet No 1

Army Form C. 2118

WAR DIARY
or
INTELLIGENCE SUMMARY
(Erase heading not required.)

Instructions regarding War Diaries and Intelligence Summaries are contained in F. S. Regs., Part II. and the Staff Manual respectively. Title Pages will be prepared in manuscript.

Place	Date	Hour	Summary of Events and Information	Remarks and references to Appendices
SOUTHAMPTON	14	AM 9.15	Embarked on "CHYEBASSA" No 3 Section on the "VIPER".	
HAVRE	15	PM 12.30	Disembarked. Remained in Rest Camp No 5 until next morning.	
— " —	16		Entrained at HAVRE goods Station. Railway Journey of 20 hours.	
	17		Detrained at WIZERNE and marched to billets at SETQUES.	
	18		marched from SETQUES to EBBLINGHAM Billetted at CHATEAU-la-GAREME	
	19		marched from EBBLINGHAM to EECKE. Billetted at M. DALBECQS FARM.	
	20 21 22		} Resting in Billets	
	23		Major Stockley, Lieuts Lundie & Bent together with four N.C.O's visit trenches near Hill 60. Dismounted men march to MONT DES CATS	
	24		Capt Oakes, Lt Moncrieff, 2nd Lt Haughton & four N.C.O's visit trenches near Hill 60	
	25/26		night march from EECKE to RENINGHELST	
	27	PM 9.30	No 2 Section march to advance Billets at DICKEBUSCH LAKE. Major Stockley visited trenches in front of BOIS CARRE with CRE XVII Divn & CRE III Divn One Horse (Draught) died from Colic	

1875 Wt. W593/826 1,000,000 4/15 J.B.C. & A. A.D.S.S./Forms/C. 2118.

SHEET No 2.

Instructions regarding War Diaries and Intelligence Summaries are contained in F. S. Regs., Part II. and the Staff Manual respectively. Title Pages will be prepared in manuscript.

WAR DIARY
or
INTELLIGENCE SUMMARY
(Erase heading not required.)

Army Form C. 2118.

Place	Date	Hour	Summary of Events and Information	Remarks and references to Appendices
	28		Company move from Rest Camp to WESTOUTRE ROAD FARM	
	29		Major Stockley, IInd Lt Haughton, C.S.M Pearce & four N.C.O.s visit trenches in front of VIERSRAAT. No 1 Section relieve No 2 Section at advanced billets	
	30		Capt Oakes with CRE visits trenches.	
	31		Company moved to new Headquarter Billets near Ouderdom No 1 Section returned to Headquarters.	
	1.8.15		Night march to camp near KRUISSTRAAT with 51st Brigade as Corps Reserve	
	2		Major Stockley & Lt Bent to YPRES to reconnoitre Route No 1 to HOOGE. Lt Moncrieff to ZILLEBEKE to reconnoitre Route No 3 2nd Lt Haughton to " " " No 4.	
	3		Capt Oakes & Lt Moncrieff to YPRES to reconnoitre Route No 1. Lt Lundie to ZILLEBEKE to reconnoitre No 4 IInd Lt Haughton & No 3 Section to advance Billets near DICKEBUSCH LAKE to commence VIERSTRAAT Defences.	
	4		Major Stockley & Lt Bent to SANCTUARY WOOD to reconnoitre HOOGE trenches. Lt Lundie with party to YPRES to collect materials	
	5.		Lt Moncrieff with party to YPRES to collect materials. Lt Lundie to VOORMEZEELE on reconnaissance.	

1875 Wt. W593/826 1,000,000 4/15 J.B.C. & A. A.D.S.S./Forms/C. 2118.

Sheet No 3.

Army Form C. 2118.

WAR DIARY
or
~~INTELLIGENCE SUMMARY~~
(Erase heading not required.)

Instructions regarding War Diaries and Intelligence Summaries are contained in F. S. Regs., Part II. and the Staff Manual respectively. Title Pages will be prepared in manuscript.

Place	Date	Hour	Summary of Events and Information	Remarks and references to Appendices
	6.8.15		Lt Bent with party to YPRES to collect material. Lt Moncrieff reconnoitring at VOORMEZEELE. Major Stockley to VIERSTRAAT defences. Night march to Headquarter Billets near OUDERDOM* less No 4 Section.	* G. 36. a. 6. 4. Sheet 28 Scale 1/40,000
G. 36. a 6. 4.*	7.		No. 4 Section rejoined at Headquarter Billets.	
	8.		Lt Moncrieff to STEENVOORDE to purchase engine for CRE.	
	9.		Lt Lundie with No 2 Section to VLAMERTINGHE to collect material. Capt Oakes with No 1 Section to DICKEBUSCH to collect material. No 4 Section to advance Billets to construct magazines & VIERSTRAAT defences.	
	10.		Lt Lundie to VOORMEZEELE on reconnaissance. Lt Moncrieff to DICKEBUSCH to purchase band saw, for CRE. No 1 Section to DICKEBUSCH to collect material. No 2 Section constructing hut for Signals at Headquarters.	
G 36. a 6. 4	11.		No 1 Section marched out to relieve No 3 at advance Billets N. 8. b. 2. 6.* No. 3 returned to Company Head-Quarters	* Sheet 28 Scale 1/40,000
	12.		CRE allotted definite sector of line held by 17th Divn to each Field Company. Sector allotted to 77th Coy is from ST ELOI exclusive to TRIANGULAR WOOD ⊙ inclusive. This sector together with next to the South, allotted to 78th Company, is held alternately by 50th & 51st Brigades, the Brigade not in occupation being behind in reserve. To the north of our Sector the line is held at present by the 3rd Division.	

1875 Wt. W593/826 1,000,000 4/15 J.B.C. & A. A.D.S.S./Forms/C. 2118.

SHEET No 4.

Instructions regarding War Diaries and Intelligence Summaries are contained in F. S. Regs., Part II. and the Staff Manual respectively. Title Pages will be prepared in manuscript.

WAR DIARY
or
~~INTELLIGENCE SUMMARY~~
(Erase heading not required.)

Army Form C. 2118.

Place	Date	Hour	Summary of Events and Information	No of Casualties & cause	No of arrivals	Remarks and references to Appendices
	13		Major Stockley & 2nd Lt Haughton reconnoitred trenches in our Sector. At night Search Light Section ran a light at the Divl H. Qrs for exhibition to G.O.C. & Staff. These lights do not seem sufficiently powerful to be of much use. They are not being used at all & the men of the Search Light Section are being used sometimes for reinforcements, sometimes for various duties at H. Qrs.			
	14.		Capt Oakes & Lt Lundie reconnoitred trenches in our Sector. No 4. Section march at night from advanced Billet N.3 b 2 5.* to establish advanced Billet at H 35. b 0.5 in SCOTTISH WOOD. Search Light Section march there also to assist putting up Huts etc.			* Sheet 28 Scale 1/20000
	15		No1 Section followed No4 leaving work at VIERSTAAT which is now out of our area & being carried on by the Pioneer Battalion. No 2 marched out also to SCOTTISH WOOD from H.Q. the 3 Sections being quartered there, to start engineer work in our Sector			
	16		No1 Section starts work on Communication Trenches & strong points in neighbourhood of VOORMEZEELE. No2 Section starts sapping to straighten front fire trench SQUARE WOOD (O.3.c.9.9.)* & to improve Communication Trench back to Canal. No.4 Section starts work on Communication Trenches G.H.Q Line & new wagon track between VOORMEZEELE & DICKEBUSCH - YPRES Road.			
	17		No.3 Section goes to YPRES to collect material			
	18		One Draught Horse with mob. Vet. Sections reported evacuated			
	19		No.4 Section was relieved by No3 & returned to H Qrs.			
	20		Much rain last few days. Communication Trenches in very bad state.			

1875 Wt. W593/826 1,000,000 4/15 J.B.C. & A. A.D.S.S./Forms/C. 2118.

Sheet No. 5.

WAR DIARY
or
INTELLIGENCE SUMMARY

(Erase heading not required.)

Army Form C. 2118.

Instructions regarding War Diaries and Intelligence Summaries are contained in F. S. Regs., Part II. and the Staff Manual respectively. Title Pages will be prepared in manuscript.

Place	Date	Hour	Summary of Events and Information	Nos of Casualties & Cause	No of arrivals	Remarks and references to Appendices
	21		Search Light Section return to H.Qrs. The work by the 3 Sections in advance has been much hindered during the past week through lack of material, & by infantry working parties not turning up, or two parties turning up for the same job.			
	22		No 4. Section leave H.Qrs & march to Canal Bank near LANKHOF CHATEAU I 32.C to prepare dug-outs there, for section working in that area (No 2 at present)			
			One driver wounded by rifle bullet in arm after unloading near LANKHOF CHATEAU The first casualty apart from sickness sustained by Company. Interpreter transferred to ST OMER & not yet replaced.	1		
	23		One Sapper joined from base at Rouen.			
	24		No 2 Section return to H.Qrs for rest			
	25		Searchlight Section march out to join ~~assist~~ No 1 Section in support trenches			
	26		1st Batch 12 men No 1 Section return to H.Qrs for two days rest.			
x	27		1 L.D. Horse arrived to make up the establishment for Horses			
	28		1st Batch 12 men No 1 Section return to VOORMEZEELE to carry on their work & 2nd Batch march back to H.Qrs. for two days rest.			
	29		Driver Draper sent to 52nd F.A. suffering from skin disease			
	30		No. 3 Section return to H.Qrs, also 3rd Batch of No 1 Section, 2nd Batch No 1 return to work			

1875 Wt. W593/826 1,000,000 4/15 J.B.C. & A. A.D.S.S./Forms/C. 2118.

SHEET No 6

Army Form C. 2118.

WAR DIARY
or
INTELLIGENCE SUMMARY
(Erase heading not required.)

Instructions regarding War Diaries and Intelligence Summaries are contained in F. S. Regs., Part II. and the Staff Manual respectively. Title Pages will be prepared in manuscript.

Place	Date	Hour	Summary of Events and Information	No. of Casualties & Cause	No. of Arrivals	Remarks and references to Appendices
	27.8.15 to 31.8.15		Canal Bank Section (Lieut Bent). This Section began the following defensive work according to materials available. from dugouts at Canal Bank. Breastwork in front of 'SAP' formed to straighten front line 24 to 23. Communication trench from CANAL BANK to 26 Fortifications & machine Gun emplacements ARUNDEL & UPPER OASTHOEK FARM. Repairs to front line traverses & parados.			
	27.8.15 to 31.8.15		VOORMEZEELE Section (Lieut Moncrieff) This Section began the following defensive work according to materials available. from dugouts at Voormezeele. New support trench behind R1 & T1. Fortifications at V4. Communication trench VOORMEZEELE to R7. Connection between V6, V7 & Convent. Repairs to front line traverses & parados.			
	27.8.15 to 31.8.15		SCOTTISH WOOD Section (2nd Lt Laughton or Lt Lundie) This section began the following defensive work according to materials available from dugouts at Scottish Wood. Communication trench ELZENWALLE to VOORMEZEELE. Wagon track HEMELRY CABARET to ELZENWALLE - KRUISSTRAAT HOEK Road. V.8. Completion of fire trench and connection to V7.			
	27.8.15 to 31.8.15		HEAD Quarters remains at farm G36 a 6.4. and one Section in turn remains at headqrs: the normal roster of relief being three weeks out on the works, and one week at headquarters. All horses and drivers remain at headqrs and carry out work in the collection of material and night convoy service to the outlying sections.			

E M Tickle Major RE
31-8-15. OC 77th Coy RE

1875 Wt. W593/826 1,000,000 4/15 J.B.C. & A. A.D.S.S./Forms/C. 2118.

17th Division

121/6971

77th F. C. R.E.

Vol: II

Sept. 15

Instructions regarding War Diaries and Intelligence Summaries are contained in F. S. Regs., Part II. and the Staff Manual respectively. Title Pages will be prepared in manuscript.

WAR DIARY or INTELLIGENCE SUMMARY

(Erase heading not required.)

Army Form C. 2118

Place	Date	Hour	Summary of Events and Information	Remarks and references to Appendices
			The Company Hd Qrs. remained during the month at Farm G.36.a.6.4. and carried on work in the Section ST. ELOI to CANAL BANK. The work carried out was as under. Section at CANAL BANK. Communication trench Canal BANK to trench 26 with new support trench 25 and communication to 25 - also Communication 25 to 24 - revetted & duck boarded. Fortification at ARUNDEL FARM with Machine Gun Emplacement. Shell Shelter tunnels in CANAL BANK, and machine Gun emplacement in CANAL BANK. Screens were erected in front of trench 7.T.C & a dummy canvas redoubt laid out at I.32.d and succeeded in drawing the enemy's fire. A tunnel was made through the embankment blocking the CANAL near LANKHOF CHATEAU under the LILLE - YPRES to take away flood water. Section at VOORMEZEELE. Communication trench VOORMEZEELE (CONVENT LANE) to R.7 revetting & duck boarding continued - and four drains cut to carry away water to N.E. Fortification at V4. MAP 28 I.31.d. continued. New support trench behind R1. improved & fire step commenced. Section at SCOTTISH WOOD. Communication trench ELZENWALLA to VOORMEZEELE, revetting, draining, & duck boarding continued. Wagon track Corduroy Road HEMELRY - CABARET to PIONEER WOOD continued. Trench tramway PIONEER WOOD to VOORMEZEELE Commenced with steel rails PIONEER WOOD to ELZENWALLA & wooden rails thence to VOORMEZEELE. V8. MAP 28 I.31.a raising of parapets traverses & revetting continued. Clearing out of BOLLAART beek from & including the Culverts under CANAL to VOORMEZEELE Completed. 30.9.15. E M Blockley Major RE OC. 77 (Fd) C.R.E.	

1875 Wt. W593/826 1,000,000 4/15 J.B.C. & A. A.D.S.S./Forms/C. 2118.

Instructions regarding War Diaries and Intelligence Summaries are contained in F. S. Regs., Part II. and the Staff Manual respectively. Title Pages will be prepared in manuscript.

WAR DIARY
or
INTELLIGENCE SUMMARY
(Erase heading not required.)

Army Form C. 2118

with mob'n ver. Sect

Place	Date	Hour	Summary of Events and Information	Arrivals Officers N.C.O.s & men	Arrivals Horses & mules	Officers, N.C.O.s & men K	W	D	H	E	Horses & mules K	W	D	H	E	Remarks and references to Appendices
MAP. 28 O.3.b.	2nd		3 men No. 4 Section wounded by shell burst. (Sapr Smith L, Saps Burdon & Pnr Lenne.				3		1	2						
	3rd		No 1 Section return to Hd Qrs relieved at Voormezeele by No 3 Section.													
	4th		Reinforcement of 3 men arrived (Sapper Pearce, Sapr Gillivir & Driver Ramsay)	3												
MAP 28 I.33	5th		1 Horse slightly wounded (No 40).									1				
	9th		Searchlight Section returned to Hd Qrs													
			1 Horse died. (No 34)										1			
	10th		No. 4 Section returned to Hd Qrs, relieved by No 1 Section (Canal Bank)													
	13th		Searchlight Section moved to VOORMEZEELE.													
	16th		Reinforcement of 3 men arrived (Sappers Hammett, Shiels & McGroggan	3												
MAP 28 I3.c.	17th		1 man No 3 Section wounded (Sapper Gwen).				1		1							
	23rd		No. 2 Section returned to Hd Qrs. relieved at SCOTTISH WOOD by No 4													
			1 Mule severely wounded (No 80)									1				
MAP 28. I.33.a	24th		1 Man No 1 Section wounded (Pnr Henson).				1		1							
			No 3. Section returned to Hd Qrs, relieved at VOORMEZEELE by No 2.													
	25th		1 Mule died of wounds (No 80.)										1			
			1 Horse slightly wounded (No 12)									1				
	28th		1 Horse severely wounded (No 111.).									1				
	29th		1 Horse died of wounds (No 111.).										1			

1875 Wt. W593/826 1,000,000 4/15 J.B.C. & A. A.D.S.S./Forms/C. 2118.

17th Division

121/7593

K

77th F.C. R.E.
Vol 3

Oct 15

Army Form C. 2118.

Instructions regarding War Diaries and Intelligence Summaries are contained in F. S. Regs., Part II. and the Staff Manual respectively. Title Pages will be prepared in manuscript.

WAR DIARY
or
~~INTELLIGENCE SUMMARY~~
(Erase heading not required.)

Place	Date	Hour	Summary of Events and Information	Remarks and references to Appendices
	1st to 6th		The Company carried on work as in September.	
	5th		Major E.N. Stockley Major R.E. handed over Command of the Company to Major J.G. Fleming	
	6th & 7th		The Company marched from billets near OUDERDOM (Map 28. G. 3.6.4) to Rest Billets at EECKE	
	20th & 21st		Company ~~moved~~ marched to Huts at H.19 B (Sheet 28).	
	21st		The Company moved to H.28 a 6.8 where its Headquarters were established	
			For work the Company was allotted to the Sector occupied alternately by the 51st & 52nd Brigades (J. 13. C. 1.6 to I. 30 A.9.0.) but excluding work west of ZILLEBEKE village.	
	23rd		Nos 2 & 3 Sections moved to ZILLEBEKE village where advanced billets were occupied & work commenced.	
	26th		No. 4 Section joined Nos 2 & 3 at ZILLEBEKE.	
			The work taken up consisted of draining, revetting & boarding the main communication trenches, clearing the ZILLE BEKE, the construction of a new defence line (WARRINGTON AVENUE) in SANCTUARY WOOD* & the up keep of the tramway up to SANCTUARY WOOD.	* Map 1/10000 HOOGE Sheet I.24

A.F.Y. Oakes Capt. R.E.
for O.C. 77th Fd. Coy R.E.

1875 Wt. W593/826 1,000,000 4/15 J.B.C. & A. A.D.S.S./Forms/C. 2118.

Instructions regarding War Diaries and Intelligence Summaries are contained in F. S. Regs., Part II. and the Staff Manual respectively. Title Pages will be prepared in manuscript.

WAR DIARY
or
~~INTELLIGENCE SUMMARY~~
(Erase heading not required.)

Army Form C. 2118.

Place	Date	Hour	Summary of Events and Information	Reinforcements: Officers NCOs & men	Reinforcements: Horses & mules	Casualties – Officers, NCOs & men: Killed	Wounded	Died	In Hospital	Evacuated	Casualties – Horses & mules: Killed	Wounded	Died	With Mob. Vet. Sect.	Evacuated	Remarks and references to Appendices
	6-10-15		Accident in Barn, Sappers Day C, Kelley J, Mitchell A, Sewter A, Stovold E, Stevenson J, Tostdevine E, Whitby W & Honour J, sent to Hospital.				9			9						
			Sapr Goundry sent to Hospital (sick).						1	1						
	12-10-15		1 mule died No 79.										1			
	13-10-15		1 mule Cast No 82.												1	
	15-10-15		Sapr Cooper E sent to Hospital through sickness.						1	1						
	18-10-15		Reinforcement of two men arrive, Saprs Rickard & Brandon	2												
	19-10-15		Reinforcement of one man arrives Sapr Reid. 2 Mules arrive to make up establishment.	1	2											
	21-10-15		Lc Cpl. Pryce W. accidently injured. Kicked by mule on the leg, breaking it.						1	1						
			Sergt Wankling rejoined this Company.	1												
	22-10-15		Sergt Morris sent to Hospital (sick)						1							
	30-10-15		Sapr Rowland J.C. accidently drove pick into his foot						1	1						

G. Y. Oakes Capt RE
for OC 77th Coy RE

1875 Wt. W593/826 1,000,000 4/15 J.B.C. & A. A.D.S.S./Forms/C. 2118.

No. of Report 11

FIELD RETURN.

Copy

Army Form B. 213.

(To be furnished by all arms, services, and departments (except A.S.C. units) to the A. G.'s Office at the Base in accordance with Field Service Regulations, Part II.)

RETURN showing numbers RATIONED by, and Transport on charge of, 1/1 Field Co R.E. at In the Field 1-10-15 Date.

Detail	Personnel			Animals. Horses				Mules				Guns, carriages, and limbers and transport vehicles				Horsed		Mechanical					Motor Bicycles	Bicycles	Remarks
	Officers	Other ranks	Natives	Riding	Draught	Heavy Draught	Pack	Large	Small	Camels	Oxen	Guns, carriages and limbers, showing description	Ammunition wagons and limbers	Machine guns	Aircraft, showing description	4 Wheeled	2 Wheeled	Motor Cars	Tractors	Lorries, showing description	Trucks, showing description	Trailers			
Effective Strength of Unit	6	215	–	18	40	–	–	18	–	–	–	–	–	–	–	6	19	–	–	–	–	–	1	33	4 Men in Hospital (Temporary)
Details, *by Arms* attached to unit as in War Establishment:—																									
Total	6	215	–	18	40	–	–	18	–	–	–	–	–	–	–	6	19	–	–	–	–	–	1	33	
War Establishment	6	223	–	18	43	–	–	18	–	–	–	–	–	–	–	6	19	–	–	–	–	–	1	33	
*Wanting to complete (Detail of Personnel and Horses below)	–	8	–	–	3																				
Surplus																									
*Attached (not to include the details shown above) A.S.C.	–	1	–	–	–	2																			
Civilians:— Employed with the Unit																									
Accompanying the Unit																									
Total Rationed	6	215	–	18	40	–	–	18																	

* In the case of field ambulances, hospitals or depots, the number of patients are to be included here, the names being shown in A. F. A. 36.

Signature of Commander.

Date of Despatch.

For information of the A.G.'s Office at the Base.

Officers and men who have become casuals, been transferred or joined since last report.

Place In the Field Date 1-10-15

Regtl. Number	Rank	Name	Corps	Nature of casualty, or name of unit from or to which transferred	Date of being struck off or coming on the ration return	Remarks*
42703	Corpl	Wankling A	R.E.	Sent to FA	2-9-15	Tem
59127	Pnr	Lenne	— " —	— " —	3-9-15	Per
80019	L/Cpl	Jackson J	— " —	— " —	16-9-15	— " —
59203	Sapr	Owen J	— " —	— " —	17-9-15	Tem
44427		Sewter A.	— " —	— " —	20-9-15	— " —
	Corpl	Vecoustre J	Interpreter	Evacuated	21-8-15	Per.
44430	Sapr	Foster J.	R.E.	Sent to FA.	24-9-15	Tem
43324	Pnr	Henson J.	— " —	— " —	25-9-15	Per.
59209	Sapr	Henty P.	— " —	returned to duty	24-9-15	
25253	Pnr	McGrogan P.	— " —		28-9-15	

* State whether absence is of a permanent or temporary nature, adding, in the case of casuals from wounds or disease, any available information for communication to the relatives.

Only additional information regarding "wanting to complete" is to be entered on this side.

4 men Wanted to Complete

Perforated Sheet giving detail of personnel and horses wanting to complete, shown on Army Form B. 213.

Number of Report 11

Detail of Wanting to Complete	Drivers									Farriers				Wheelers						
	R. A.	R. E.	A. S. C.	Car	Lorry	Steam	Gunners	Smith Gunners	Range Takers	Serjeants	Corporals	Shoeing, or Shoeing and Carriage Smiths	Cold Shoers	R. A.	H. T.	M. T.	Saddlers or Harness Makers	Blacksmiths	Bricklayers and Masons	Carpenters and Joiners
CAVALRY																				
R. A.																				
R. E.																				1
INFANTRY																				
R. A. M. C.																				
A. O. C.																				
A. V. C.																				

Detail of Wanting to Complete	Fitters & Turners (R. E.)		Fitters			Electricians			Engine Drivers											
	Wood	Iron	R. A.	Wireless	Plumbers	Ordinary	W. T.	Signalmen	Loco.	Field	Air Line Men	Permanent Line Men	Operators, Telegraph	Cablemen	Brigade Section Pioneers	General-duty Pioneers	Signallers	Instrument Repairers	Motor Cyclists	Motor Cyclist Artificers
CAVALRY																				
R. A.																				
R. E.																				
INFANTRY																				
R. A. M. C.																				
A. O. C.																				
A. V. C.																				

Detail of Wanting to Complete				Armament Artificers					W.O.'s and N.C.O.'s (by ranks) not included in trade columns											TOTAL to agree with wanting to complete		Horses			
	Telephonists	Clerks	Machine Gunners	Fitters	Range Finders	Armourers	Storemen	Privates	Infantry	Pioneer										Officers	Other Ranks	Riding	Draught	Heavy Draught	Pack
CAVALRY																									
R. A.																				-					
R. E.									1	1										-	4	-	3	-	-
INFANTRY																									
R. A. M. C.																									
A. O. C.																									
A. V. C.																									

Remarks :—

__________ Signature of Commander.

__________ Unit.

__________ Formation to which attached.

__________ Date of Despatch.

(82434.) Wt. 4394/2217. 500,000. 6/15. B.M.&S. Forms/B. 213/6.

[P.T.O.

No. of Report 12

FIELD RETURN.

Copy

Army Form B. 213.

(To be furnished by all arms, services, and departments (except A.S.C. units) to the A. G.'s Office at the Base in accordance with Field Service Regulations, Part II.)

RETURN showing numbers RATIONED by, and Transport on charge of, 14th [illegible] Coy at [illegible] 8-10-15 Date.

Detail	Personnel			Animals								Guns, carriages, and limbers and transport vehicles											Motor Bicycles	Bicycles	Remarks
				Horses				Mules								Horsed		Mechanical							
	Officers	Other ranks	Natives	Riding	Draught	Heavy Draught	Pack	Large	Small	Camels	Oxen	Guns, carriages and limbers, showing description	Ammunition wagons and limbers	Machine guns	Aircraft, showing description	4 Wheeled	2 Wheeled	Motor Cars	Tractors	Lorries, showing description	Trucks, showing description	Trailers			
Effective Strength of Unit	6	207	-	18	43	-	-	18	-	-	-	-	-	-	-	6	19		-	-	-	-	-	33	
Details, *by Arms* attached to unit as in War Establishment:—																									
Total	6	207	-	18	43	-	-	18	-	-	-	-	-	-	-	6	19	-	-	-	-	-	-	33	
War Establishment	6	223	-	18	43	-	-	18	-	-	-	-	-	-	-	6	19	-	-	-	-	-	-	3	
Wanting to complete (Detail of Personnel and Horses below)	-	16	-																						
Surplus																									
*Attached (not to include the details shown above) A.S.C.	-	1	-	-	-	2																			
Civilians:— Employed with the Unit																									
Accompanying the Unit																									
TOTAL RATIONED	6	207	-	18	43	-	-	18																	

* In the case of field ambulances, hospitals or depots, the number of patients are to be included here, the names being shown in A. F. A. 36.

Signature of Commander.

Date of Despatch.

For information of the A.G.'s Office at the Base.

Officers and men who have become casuals, been transferred or joined since last report.

Place ______________________ Date ______________________

Regtl. Number	Rank	Name	Corps	Nature of casualty, or name of unit from or to which transferred	Date of being struck off or coming on the ration return	Remarks*
43324	Sapr	Day C	R.E.	Sent to F.A.	6.10.15	
61809		Kelley J	— —	— —	— —	
42886		Mitchell A.	— —	— —	— —	
44474		Hawker A.	— —	— —	— —	
58795		Harold G.	— —	— —	— —	
42434		Stephenson J.	— —	— —	— —	
61706		Southerne E.	— —	— —	— —	
89254		Whatley W.	— —	— —	— —	
42682		Honours J.	— —	— —	— —	
Punishments						
44027	Sapr	Blagdon H	R.E.	1. Having a light in their billet after lights out. 2. Gambling		Deprived 3 days pay.
61845	Pnr	Grundale J	— —			
42816	Sapr	Johnstone C	— —			
42886		Mitchell A	— —			
43320	L/Cpl	Vanverbeke H	— —	1. Drunk. 2. Absent from 9.0 pm till 10.45 pm. (5.10.15)		Deprived Lance Stripe.
60767	L/Cpl	Ruslow W.	— —	1. Drunk 2. Absent from 9 pm until 10.30 pm (5.10.15)		Deprived Lance Stripe
44094	Sapr	Harrison J.	— —	1. Drunk (2) Absent from 9 pm till 10.45 pm 5.10.15. (3) Gambling 4. Having a light in his billet.		Deprived 10 days pay
42687	Sapr	Upton S.	— —	1. Drunk 2. Absent from 9 pm till 10.45 pm 5.10.15		Deprived 7 days pay.

* State whether absence is of a permanent or temporary nature, adding, in the case of casuals from wounds or disease, any available information for communication to the relatives.

42660	Sapr	Gibbons G.	— —	Drunk on the line of march		Deprived 7 days pay.
42851	Pnr	Searle C.	— —	Drunk on line of march		Deprived 7 days pay.

Only additional information regarding "wanting to complete" is to be entered on this side.

3 men wanted to complete in place of undermentioned.

42703 Sergt Wantling A.
59127 Pte Venne P.
43324 " Henson J.

No. of Report 12

FIELD RETURN.

Copy

Army Form B. 213.

(To be furnished by all arms, services, and departments (except A.S.C. units) to the A. G.'s Office at the Base in accordance with Field Service Regulations, Part II.)

RETURN showing numbers RATIONED by, and Transport on charge of, 1/1 (Cty) Cork at In the Field 8.10.15 Date.

Detail	Personnel			Animals. Horses				Mules				Guns, carriages, and limbers and transport vehicles				Horsed		Mechanical							Remarks
	Officers	Other ranks	Natives	Riding	Draught	Heavy Draught	Pack	Large	Small	Camels	Oxen	Guns, carriages and limbers, showing description	Ammunition wagons and limbers	Machine guns	Aircraft, showing description	4 Wheeled	2 Wheeled	Motor Cars	Tractors	Lorries, showing description	Trucks, showing description	Trailers	Motor Bicycles	Bicycles	
Effective Strength of Unit	6	207	-	18	43	-	-	18	-	-	-	-	-	-	-	6	19	-	-	-	-	-	-	33	
Details, *by Arms* attached to unit as in War Establishment:—																									
Total	6	207	-	18	43	-	-	18	-	-	-	-	-	-	-	6	19	-	-	-	-	-	-	33	
War Establishment	6	223	-	18	43	-	-	18	-	-	-	-	-	-	-	6	19	-	-	-	-	-	-	3	
Wanting to complete (Detail of Personnel and Horses below)	-	16	-																						
Surplus																									
*Attached (not to include the details shown above) A.S.C.	-	1	-	-	-	2																			
Civilians:— Employed with the Unit																									
Accompanying the Unit																									
Total Rationed ...	6	207	-	18	43	-	-	18																	

* In the case of field ambulances, hospitals or depots, the number of patients are to be included here, the names being shown in A. F. A. 36.

Signature of Commander.

Date of Despatch.

Perforated Sheet giving detail of personnel and horses wanting to complete, shown on Army Form B. 213.

Number of Report ______________

Detail of Wanting to Complete	Drivers						Gunners	Smith Gunners	Range Takers	Farriers		Shoeing, or Shoeing and Carriage Smiths	Cold Shoers	Wheelers			Saddlers or Harness Makers	Blacksmiths	Bricklayers and Masons	Carpenters and Joiners	Fitters & Turners (R. E.)	
	R. A.	R. E.	A. S. C.	Car	Lorry	Steam				Serjeants	Corporals			R. A.	H. T.	M. T.					Wood	Iron
CAVALRY																						
R. A.																						
R. E.																						
INFANTRY																				1		1
R. A. M. C.																						
A. O. C.																						
A. V. C.																						

Detail of Wanting to Complete	Fitters		Plumbers	Electricians		Signalmen	Engine Drivers		Air Line Men	Permanent Line Men	Operators, Telegraph	Cablemen	Brigade Section Pioneers	General-duty Pioneers	Signallers	Instrument Repairers	Motor Cyclists	Motor Cyclist Artificers	Telephonists	Clerks	Machine Gunners	Armament Artificers		Armourers	Storemen	Privates
	R. A.	Wireless		Ordinary	W. T.		Loco.	Field														Fitters	Range Finders			
CAVALRY																										
R. A.																										
R. E.																										
INFANTRY																										
R. A. M. C.																										
A. O. C.																										
A. V. C.																										

Detail of Wanting to Complete	W.O.'s and N.C.O.'s (by ranks) not included in trade columns											TOTAL to agree with wanting to complete		Horses			
	Interpreter	Pioneers										Officers	Other Ranks	Riding	Draught	Heavy Draught	Pack
CAVALRY																	
R. A.																	
R. E.																	
INFANTRY	1	1										-	4	-	-	-	-
R. A. M. C.																	
A. O. C.																	
A. V. C.																	

Remarks :—

______________________ Signature of Commander.

______________________ Unit.

______________________ Formation to which attached.

______________________ Date of Despatch.

(82434.) Wt. 4394/2217. 500,000. 6/15. B.M.&S. Forms/B. 213/6.

[P.T.O.

No. of Report 13

FIELD RETURN.

Army Form B. 213.

(To be furnished by all arms, services, and departments (except A.S.C. units) to the A. G.'s Office at the Base in accordance with Field Service Regulations, Part II.)

RETURN showing numbers RATIONED by, and Transport on charge of, 77 (Fd) Coy. R.E. at In the Field 15.10.15 Date.

Detail	Personnel			Animals.								Guns, carriages, and limbers and transport vehicles													Remarks
				Horses				Mules								Horsed		Mechanical							
	Officers	Other ranks	Natives	Riding	Draught	Heavy Draught	Pack	Large	Small	Camels	Oxen	Guns, carriages and limbers, showing description	Ammunition wagons and limbers	Machine guns	Aircraft, showing description	4 Wheeled	2 Wheeled	Motor Cars	Tractors	Lorries, showing description	Trucks, showing description	Trailers	Motor Bicycles	Bicycles	
Effective Strength of Unit	6	206	-	18	43	-	-	16	-	-	-	-	-	-	-	5	19	-	-	-	-	-	-	33	
Details, *by Arms* attached to unit as in War Establishment:—																									
Total	6	206	-	18	43	-	-	16	-	-	-	-	-	-	-	5	19	-	-	-	-	-	-	33	
War Establishment	6	223	-	18	43	-	-	18	-	-	-	-	-	-	-	5	19	-	-	-	-	-	-	33	
Wanting to complete (Detail of Personnel and Horses below)	-	17	-	-	-	-	-	2																	
Surplus	Nil																								
*Attached (not to include the details shown above) Acc	-	1	-	-	-	2										1									
Civilians:— Employed with the Unit																									
Accompanying the Unit																									
Total Rationed ...	6	206	-	18	43	-	-	16																	

* In the case of field ambulances, hospitals or depots, the number of patients are to be included here, the names being shown in A. F. A. 36.

Signature of Commander.

Date of Despatch.

For information of the A.G.'s Office at the Base.

Officers and men who have become casuals, been transferred or joined since last report.

Place __________ Date __________

Regtl. Number	Rank	Name	Corps	Nature of casualty, or name of unit from or to which transferred	Date of being struck off or coming on the ration return	Remarks*
42780	Sapr	Martin G.A.	R.E.	Sent to F.A.	8.10.15	
44431		Cooper E.	R.E.	— " —	12.10.15	
44430		Foster W.J.	R.E.	Returned to Duty	13.10.15	

* State whether absence is of a permanent or temporary nature, adding, in the case of casuals from wounds or disease, any available information for communication to the relatives.

Only additional information regarding "wanting to complete" is to be entered on this side.

4 Men Wanted to Complete in place of those who have been evacuated from the Divisional Area.

No. of Report 13

FIELD RETURN.

Army Form B. 213.

(To be furnished by all arms, services, and departments (except A.S.C. units) to the A. G.'s Office at the Base in accordance with Field Service Regulations, Part II.)

RETURN showing numbers RATIONED by, and Transport on charge of, 77th (Fd) Coy. R.E. at In the Field 15.10.15 Date.

Detail	Personnel			Animals.								Guns, carriages, and limbers and transport vehicles													Remarks
				Horses				Mules								Horsed		Mechanical							
	Officers	Other ranks	Natives	Riding	Draught	Heavy Draught	Pack	Large	Small	Camels	Oxen	Guns, carriages and limbers, showing description	Ammunition wagons and limbers	Machine guns	Aircraft, showing description	4 Wheeled	2 Wheeled	Motor Cars	Tractors	Lorries, showing description	Trucks, showing description	Trailers	Motor Bicycles	Bicycles	
Effective Strength of Unit	6	206	-	18	43	-	-	16	-	-	-	-	-	-	-	5	19	-	-	-	-	-	-	33	
Details, *by Arms* attached to unit as in War Establishment:—																									
Total	6	206	-	18	43	-	-	16	-	-	-	-	-	-	-	5	19	-	-	-	-	-	-	33	
War Establishment	6	223	-	18	43	-	-	18	-	-	-	-	-	-	-	5	19	-	-	-	-	-	-	33	
Wanting to complete (Detail of Personnel and Horses below)	-	17	-	-	-	-	-	2																	
Surplus	Nil																								
*Attached (not to include the details shown above) ASC	-	1	-	-	-	2										1									
Civilians:— Employed with the Unit																									
Accompanying the Unit																									
Total Rationed	6	206	-	18	43	-	-	16																	

* In the case of field ambulances, hospitals or depots, the number of patients are to be included here, the names being shown in A. F. A. 36.

Signature of Commander.

Date of Despatch.

Perforated Sheet giving detail of personnel and horses wanting to complete, shown on Army Form B. 213.

Number of Report 13

Detail of Wanting to Complete	Drivers						Gunners	Smith Gunners	Range Takers	Farriers		Shoeing, or Shoeing and Carriage Smiths	Cold Shoers
	R. A.	R. E.	A. S. C.	Car	Lorry	Steam				Serjeants	Corporals		
CAVALRY													
R. A.													
R. E.		1											
INFANTRY													
R. A. M. C.													
A. O. C.													
A. V. C.													

Detail of Wanting to Complete	Wheelers			Saddlers or Harness Makers	Blacksmiths	Bricklayers and Masons	Carpenters and Joiners	Fitters & Turners (R. E.)		Fitters		Plumbers	Electricians		Signalmen
	R. A.	H. T.	M. T.					Wood	Iron	R. A.	Wireless		Ordinary	W. T.	
CAVALRY															
R. A.															
R. E.							1		1						
INFANTRY															
R. A. M. C.															
A. O. C.															
A. V. C.															

Detail of Wanting to Complete	Engine Drivers		Air Line Men	Permanent Line Men	Operators, Telegraph	Cablemen	Brigade Section Pioneers	General-duty Pioneers	Signallers	Instrument Repairers	Motor Cyclists	Motor Cyclist Artificers	Telephonists	Clerks	Machine Gunners	Armament Artificers		Armourers	Storemen	Privates
	Loco.	Field														Fitters	Range Finders			
CAVALRY																				
R. A.																				
R. E.																				
INFANTRY																				
R. A. M. C.																				
A. O. C.																				
A. V. C.																				

Detail of Wanting to Complete	W.O.'s and N.C.O.'s (by ranks) not included in trade columns										TOTAL to agree with wanting to complete		Horses			
	Inspector	[illegible]									Officers	Other Ranks	Riding	Draught	Heavy Draught	Pack
CAVALRY																
R. A.																
R. E.	1										-	4	-	2 mules	-	-
INFANTRY																
R. A. M. C.																
A. O. C.																
A. V. C.																

Remarks :—

______ Signature of Commander.

______ Unit.

______ Formation to which attached.

______ Date of Despatch.

(82434.) Wt. 4394/2217. 500,000. 6/15. B.M.&S. Forms/B. 213/6.

[P.T.O.

No. of Report 14.

FIELD RETURN.

Army Form B. 213.

(To be furnished by all arms, services, and departments (except A.S.C. units) to the A. G.'s Office at the Base in accordance with Field Service Regulations, Part II.)

RETURN showing numbers RATIONED by, and Transport on charge of, 77th Field Coy RE at In the Field 22.10.15. Date.

Detail	Personnel			Animals.								Guns, carriages, and limbers and transport vehicles													Remarks
				Horses				Mules								Horsed		Mechanical							
	Officers	Other ranks	Natives	Riding	Draught	Heavy Draught	Pack	Large	Small	Camels	Oxen	Guns, carriages and limbers, showing description	Ammunition wagons and limbers	Machine guns	Aircraft, showing description	4 Wheeled	2 Wheeled	Motor Cars	Tractors	Lorries, showing description	Trucks, showing description	Trailers	Motor Bicycles	Bicycles	
Effective Strength of Unit	6	210	-	17	43	-	-	18	-	-	-	-	-	-	-	5	19	-	-	-	-	-	-	33	
Details, *by Arms* attached to unit as in War Establishment:—																									
Total	6	210	-	17	43	-	-	18	-	-	-	-	-	-	-	5	19	-	-	-	-	-	-	33	
War Establishment	6	223	-	17	43	-	-	18	-	-	-	-	-	-	-	5	19	-	-	-	-	-	-	33	
Wanting to complete (Detail of Personnel and Horses below)	-	13																							
Surplus	Nil																								
*Attached (not to include the details shown above) A.S.C.	-	1	-	-	-	2	-	-	-	-	-	-	-	-	-	1									
Civilians:— Employed with the Unit																									
Accompanying the Unit																									
Total Rationed ...	6	210	-	17	43	-	-	18																	

* In the case of field ambulances, hospitals or depots, the number of patients are to be included here, the names being shown in A. F. A. 36.

(Sgd) G. Y. Y. Oakes Capt RE. for Major RE 77th Coy RE. Signature of Commander.

22.10.15. Date of Despatch.

Copy

For information of the A.G.'s Office at the Base.

Officers and men who have become casuals, been transferred or joined since last report.

Place In the Field Date 22 10 15

Regtl. Number	Rank	Name	Corps	Nature of casualty, or name of unit from or to which transferred	Date of being struck off or coming on the ration return	Remarks*
Promotions						
46610	Corpl	Livingstone W.	R.E.	Promoted a/Sergt from 2/9/15		
43071	2/Cpl	Glidle G.	R.E.	Promoted a/Cpl from 2/9/15		
59215	L^c Cpl	Mitchell R.	R.E.	Promoted a/Cpl from 2/[illegible]		
42860	L^c Cpl	Law W.J.	R.E.	Appointed paid L^c Cpl. from 6/10/15		
52109	Dr.	Pryce W.	R.E.	Appointed unpaid L^c Cpl on	15.10.15	
Reinforcements						
42703	Sergt	Wankling A	R.E.	Joined on	21.10.15	
36561	Sapr	Branden C	--			
42936	"	Reid J.	--	Joined on	19.10.15	
63832	"	Rickard W	--			
Punishments						
44068	Corpl	Ellis W.	R.E.	Severely Reprimanded	16.10.15	
42886	Sapr	Johnstone J	R.E.	Deprived one day's pay on	17.10.15	
Sent to F.A.						
52109	L^c Cpl	Pryce W.	R.E.	Sent to F.A (accidently Injured)	20.10.15	

* State whether absence is of a permanent or temporary nature, adding, in the case of casuals from wounds or disease, any available information for communication to the relatives.

Only additional information regarding "wanting to complete" is to be entered on this side.

13 men wanted to complete in place of those who have left this unit.

Perforated Sheet giving detail of personnel and horses wanting to complete, shown on Army Form B. 213.

Number of Report 14.

Detail of Wanting to Complete	Drivers R.A.	Drivers R.E.	Drivers A.S.C.	Drivers Car	Drivers Lorry	Drivers Steam	Gunners	Smith Gunners	Range Takers	Farriers Serjeants	Farriers Corporals	Shoeing, or Shoeing and Carriage Smiths	Cold Shoers	Wheelers R.A. (RE)	Wheelers H.T.	Wheelers M.T.	Saddlers or Harness Makers	Blacksmiths	Bricklayers and Masons	Carpenters and Joiners	Fitters & Turners (R.E.) Wood	Fitters & Turners (R.E.) Iron	Fitters R.A.	Fitters Wireless	Plumbers
CAVALRY																									
R.A.																									
R.E.		2										2		1				1	1	2		2			1
INFANTRY																									
R.A.M.C.																									
A.O.C.																									
A.V.C.																									

Detail of Wanting to Complete	Electricians Ordinary	Electricians W.T.	Signalmen	Engine Drivers Loco.	Engine Drivers Field	Air Line Men	Permanent Line Men	Operators, Telegraph	Cablemen	Brigade Section Pioneers	General-duty Pioneers	Signallers	Instrument Repairers	Motor Cyclists	Motor Cyclist Artificers	Telephonists	Clerks	Machine Gunners	Armament Artificers Fitters	Armament Artificers Range Finders	Armourers	Storemen	Privates
CAVALRY																							
R.A.																							
R.E.																							
INFANTRY																							
R.A.M.C.																							
A.O.C.																							
A.V.C.																							

Detail of Wanting to Complete	W.O.'s and N.C.O.'s (by ranks) not included in trade columns: Interpreter										TOTAL to agree with wanting to complete: Officers	TOTAL: Other Ranks	Horses Riding	Horses Draught	Horses Heavy Draught	Horses Pack
CAVALRY																
R.A.																
R.E.	1										-	13	-	-	-	-
INFANTRY																
R.A.M.C.																
A.O.C.																
A.V.C.																

Remarks :—

(Sd) G. F. J. Oakes Capt R.E. for Major R.E. Signature of Commander.

OC 77th Co R.E. Unit.

XVII Divn Formation to which attached.

22 10 15 Date of Despatch.

(82434.) Wt. 4394/2217. 500,000. 6/15. B.M.&S. Forms/B. 213/6.

[P.T.O.

No. of Report 15

FIELD RETURN.

Army Form B. 213.

(To be furnished by all arms, services, and departments (except A.S.C. units) to the A. G.'s Office at the Base in accordance with Field Service Regulations, Part II.)

RETURN showing numbers RATIONED by, and Transport on charge of, 77th Fd Co R.E. at In the Field 29.10.15 Date.

Detail	Personnel			Animals.								Guns, carriages, and limbers and transport vehicles													Remarks
				Horses				Mules								Horsed		Mechanical							
	Officers	Other ranks	Natives	Riding	Draught	Heavy Draught	Pack	Large	Small	Camels	Oxen	Guns, carriages and limbers, showing description	Ammunition wagons and limbers	Machine guns	Aircraft, showing description	4 Wheeled	2 Wheeled	Motor Cars	Tractors	Lorries, showing description	Trucks, showing description	Trailers	Motor Bicycles	Bicycles	
Effective Strength of Unit Details, *by Arms* attached to unit as in War Establishment:—	5	210	-	17	43	-	-	18	-	-	-	-	-	-	-	5	19	-	-	-	-	-	-	33	1 Officer on leave CSM on leave 2 men in Hospital temporary.
Total	5	210	-	17	43	-	-	18	-	-	-	-	-	-	-	5	19	-	-	-	-	-	-	33	
War Establishment	6	222	-	17	43	-	-	18	-	-	-	-	-	-	-	5	19	-	-	-	-	-	-	33	
Wanting to complete (Detail of Personnel and Horses below)		9																							
Surplus	Nil																								
*Attached (not to include the details shown above) A.S.C.	-	1	-	-	-	2	-	-	-	-	-	-	-	-	-	1									
Civilians:— Employed with the Unit Accompanying the Unit																									
Total Rationed ...	5	210	-	17	43	-	-	18																	

* In the case of field ambulances, hospitals or depots, the number of patients are to be included here, the names being shown in A. F. A. 36.

Alan Moncrieff Lieut RE for Major R.E. OC 77th Fd Co R.E. Signature of Commander.

29.10.15 Date of Despatch.

For information of the A.G.'s Office at the Base.

Officers and men who have become casuals, been transferred or joined since last report.

Place In the Field Date 29.10.15

Regtl. Number	Rank	Name	Corps	Nature of casualty, or name of unit from or to which transferred	Date of being struck off or coming on the ration return	Remarks*
Punishments						
60795	Dr	Trainer P.	R.E.	Neglect of Duty		Deprived two days pay on 30.10.15
60801	Corpl	Abbott H	R.E.	Neglecting to obey an order		Reprimanded 25.10.15
52632	Dr.	Williams W.	R.E.	Absent from duty whilst on stable Picquet		Deprived one days pay on 27.10.15
Sent to F.A.						
44396	Serjt	Morris W.L.	R.E.	Sent to F.A.	22.10.15	
51373	Dr.	Brown W.G.	R.E.	— " —	— " —	
3656[illegible]	Sapr	Brander C.	R.E.	— " —	— " —	

* State whether absence is of a permanent or temporary nature, adding, in the case of casuals from wounds or disease, any available information for communication to the relatives.

Only additional information regarding "wanting to complete" is to be entered on this side.

9 men wanted to Complete in Place of those who have been evacuated.

Perforated Sheet giving detail of personnel and horses wanting to complete, shown on Army Form B. 213.

Number of Report 15

Detail of Wanting to Complete	Drivers						Gunners	Smith Gunners	Range Takers	Farriers		Shoeing, or Shoeing and Carriage Smiths	Cold Shoers	Wheelers			Saddlers or Harness Makers	Blacksmiths	Bricklayers and Masons	Carpenters and Joiners	Fitters & Turners (R. E.)		Fitters		Plumbers
	R. A.	R. E.	A. S. C.	Car	Lorry	Steam				Serjeants	Corporals			~~R. A.~~ RE	H. T.	M. T.					Wood	Iron	R. A.	Wireless	
CAVALRY																									
R. A.																									
R. E.		2										2		1					1	2					1
INFANTRY																									
R. A. M. C.																									
A. O. C.																									
A. V. C.																									

Detail of Wanting to Complete	Electricians		Signalmen	Engine Drivers		Air Line Men	Permanent Line Men	Operators, Telegraph	Cablemen	Brigade Section Pioneers	General-duty Pioneers	Signallers	Instrument Repairers	Motor Cyclists	Motor Cyclist Artificers	Telephonists	Clerks	Machine Gunners	Armament Artificers		Armourers	Storemen	Privates
	Ordinary	W. T.		Loco.	Field														Fitters	Range Finders			
CAVALRY																							
R. A.																							
R. E.																							
INFANTRY																							
R. A. M. C.																							
A. O. C.																							
A. V. C.																							

Detail of Wanting to Complete	W.O's. and N.C.O's. (by ranks) not included in trade columns											TOTAL to agree with wanting to complete		Horses			
												Officers	Other Ranks	Riding	Draught	Heavy Draught	Pack
CAVALRY																	
R. A.																	
R. E.												-	9	-	-	-	-
INFANTRY																	
R. A. M. C.																	
A. O. C.																	
A. V. C.																	

Remarks :—

Alan Mmacig[?] for Major R.E. Signature of Commander.
Lieut. R.E.

O.C. 4th (Field) Coy R.E. Unit.

XVII Divn Formation to which attached.

29/10/15 Date of Despatch.

(82434.) Wt. 4394/2217. 500,000. 6/15. B.M.&S. Forms/B. 213/6.

[P.T.O.

17th Division

77th Fd. Co. R.E.

Nov

Vol. 4

121/7678

Nov 15

Army Form C. 2118.

Instructions regarding War Diaries and Intelligence Summaries are contained in F. S. Regs., Part II. and the Staff Manual respectively. Title Pages will be prepared in manuscript.

WAR DIARY
or
~~INTELLIGENCE SUMMARY~~

(Erase heading not required.)

Place	Date	Hour	Summary of Events and Information	Remarks and references to Appendices
	1st to 9th		The Company carried on work as before	
	2nd		No. 1. Section went to ZILLEBEKE relieving No 2 which returned to Coy Hd Qrs at H.28 a 6.8 *	* Sheet 28 1/40.000
	9th		Sections 1, 3 & 4 returned to Coy Head Qrs as the section of line then held by the 52nd Bde was handed over to the 9th Division. The 17th Division extended its sector northwards and the section from HOOGE to the trench north of the ROULERS Railway was taken over by the 51st Bde (without relief by another Bde). This Company was transferred to this section with the 51st Bde. The Company Head Quarters however remained as before at H.28 a 6.8.	
	10th		Sections 1 & 2 proceeded to YPRES & occupied billets there.	
	11th		O.C. Company went to live in the Billets at YPRES	
	12th		No 4. Section joined 1 & 2 at YPRES.	
	19th		No 3 Section joined Nos: 1, 2 & 4 at YPRES, a few Sappers being left at Head Qrs: for building Stables.	
			The work carried on in the new sector consists mostly of revetting & trench boarding. The trenches have suffered badly from the weather, becoming nearly impassable. Another important work in hand is the building of a new breastwork in front of the present front line, which is in too bad a state to repair efficiently.	

G. F. S. Oakes
Capt RE
for O.C. 77th Field Coy RE

Instructions regarding War Diaries and Intelligence Summaries are contained in F. S. Regs., Part II. and the Staff Manual respectively. Title Pages will be prepared in manuscript.

Army Form C. 2118

WAR DIARY

or

~~INTELLIGENCE SUMMARY~~

(Erase heading not required.)

Place	Date	Hour	Summary of Events and Information	Reinforcements: Officers N.C.O's & Men	Reinforcements: Horses & Mules	Casualties — Officers N.C.O's & Men: Killed	Wounded	Died	In Hospital	Evacuated	Casualties — Horses & Mules: Killed	Wounded	Died	In Hospital	Evacuated	Remarks and references to Appendices
	9-11-15		Saps Brandon sent to Hospital. Sergt. Morris returned to Duty						1							
	13-11-15		Lieut. Bent J.C. sent to Hospital. 1 Horse No 11 sent to Mob. Sec.						1					1		
	14-11-15		2 Mules arrive to make up establishment. Saps Butterworth sent to Hospital.		2				1							
	16-11-15		Sapr Scott A reported missing. Believed Killed. Lieut. Bent J.C. returned to Company.			1										
	17-11-15		Saps Collis & Saps Page sent to Hospital						2							
	18-11-15		Saps Butterworth returned to duty. 1 Horse No 11 Evacuated.												1	
			Saps Parker accidently injured sent to Hospital						1							
	19-11-15		Saps Collis returned to duty.													
	20-11-15		Saps Jones sent to Hospital.						1							
	21-11-15		Saps Powell sent to Hospital.						1							
	22-11-15		Capt. Oakes G.T.T. takes over duties of Adjutant R.E. 17th Divn (TEM.)													
	23-11-15		Lc Cpl. Porter R.S. reported (~~missing~~ KILLED). 2 Horses Cast Nos 22 & 108. 1 Horse R arrived		1	1									2	
	24-11-15		Dr Burbridge sent to Hospital. 2/Cpl Butcher sent to Hospital						2							
	26-11-15		Dr Cross sent to Hospital. Saps Russell Killed. Sapper Reid sent to Hospital			1			2							
	30-11-15		Saps Collis sent to Hospital. Saps Gamble wounded with piece of Shell admitted to Hospital.				1		2							
			Reinforcement of 3 men arrived	3												

G. T. T. Oakes Capt R.E. for O.C. 77th Fd Coy R.E.

1875 Wt. W593/826 1,000,000 4/15 J.B.C. & A. A.D.S.S./Forms/C. 2118.

Army Form C. 2118

Instructions regarding War Diaries and Intelligence Summaries are contained in F. S. Regs., Part II. and the Staff Manual respectively. Title Pages will be prepared in manuscript.

WAR DIARY
or
INTELLIGENCE SUMMARY
(Erase heading not required.)

Place	Date	Hour	Summary of Events and Information	Reinforcements: Officers N.C.O's & Men	Reinforcements: Horses & Mules	Casualties – Officers N.C.O's & Men: Killed	Wounded	Died	In Hospital	Evacuated	Casualties – Horses & Mules: Killed	Wounded	Died	In Hospital	Evacuated	Remarks and references to Appendices
	2-12-15		Sapr Anthony wounded in stomach (Bullet)				1									
	3-12-15		Corpl Butcher returned to duty. Sapr Anthony died of wound.					1								
	4-12-15		Dr Barbidge returned to Duty.													
	6-12-15		Sapr Reid returned to Duty, Sapr Spares sent to Hospital (Sick). Sapr Powell returned to Duty.						1							
	10-12-15		Sapr Mackie & Pnr Gold sent to Hospital (Sick)						2							
	11-12-15		Driver Cross returned to Duty.													
	12-12-15		Reinforcement of two men arrived. Sapr Turner J & Mills W.	2												
	13-12-15		Sapr Mackie returned to Duty. Sergt Wankling sent to Hospital (Sick). Reinforcement of two horses arrived.		2				1							
	14-12-15		Sapr Spares returned to duty.													
	16-12-15		Driver Evans slightly wounded G.S.W. Cheek. 1 Horse No 120 wounded.				1					1				
	18-12-15		Driver Hicks W.H. sent to Hospital (Sick). Sergt. Wankling returned to duty. Sapr McMullen sent to Hospital (Sick). Horse No 120 evacuated.						2						1	
	19-12-15		Sapr Jones G.E. Returned to Duty. Corpl Abbott Killed. Sapr Whitfield Killed. Driver Pierce A wounded, died of wounds on same date. Dr Lynch J wounded, Sapr Adams J. Three Horses Killed (Nos. 60, 57, 115)			2	3	1	3		3					
	20-12-15		1 Horse No 70 wounded. Driver Lynch J died of wounds. Driver Hicks W.H. returned to duty.					1				1				
	22-12-15		Corpl Farrow sent to Hospital (Sick). Sapr Powell sent to Hospital (Sick.) 1 Horse No 70 evacuated.						2						1	
	23-12-15		Horse No 70 sent to Mobile VET. Sect. Driver Taylor & Sapr Campbell sent to Hospital. (Sick).						2					1		
	26-12-15		Sapr Mackie & Sapr Roberts W.R. Sent to Hospital. (Sick).						2							
	27-12-15		Sapr Powell returned to Duty.													
	29-12-15		Sapr Campbell returned to Duty. Horse No 66. Cast.													

1875 Wt. W593/826 1,000,000 4/15 J.B.C. & A. A.D.S.S./Forms/C. 2118.

Army Form C. 2118

WAR DIARY
or
~~INTELLIGENCE SUMMARY~~
(Erase heading not required.)

Instructions regarding War Diaries and Intelligence Summaries are contained in F. S. Regs., Part II. and the Staff Manual respectively. Title Pages will be prepared in manuscript.

Place	Date	Hour	Summary of Events and Information	Reinforcements		Casualties: Officers N.C.O.s & Men					Casualties: Horses & Mules					Remarks and references to Appendices
				Officers N.C.O.s & Men	Horses & Mules	Killed	Wounded	Died	In Hospital	Evacuated	Killed	Wounded	Died	In Hospital	Evacuated	
	31-12-15		1 Officer joined this unit.	1												

H. McHaughton
2 Lieut R.E.
for O.C. 77 (Field) Co. R.E.

1875 Wt. W593/826 1,000,000 4/15 J.B.C. & A. A.D.S.S./Forms/C. 2118.

No. of Report 20.

FIELD RETURN.

Army Form B. 213.

(To be furnished by all arms, services, and departments (except A.S.C. units) to the A. G.'s Office at the Base in accordance with Field Service Regulations, Part II.)

RETURN showing numbers RATIONED by, and Transport on charge of, 97th (Field) Co R.E. at In the Field 4-12-15 Date.

Detail	Personnel: Officers	Personnel: Other ranks	Personnel: Natives	Animals: Horses: Riding	Animals: Horses: Draught	Animals: Horses: Heavy Draught	Animals: Horses: Pack	Animals: Mules: Large	Animals: Mules: Small	Animals: Camels	Animals: Oxen	Guns, carriages and limbers, showing description	Ammunition wagons and limbers	Machine guns	Aircraft, showing description	Horsed: 4 Wheeled	Horsed: 2 Wheeled	Mechanical: Motor Cars	Mechanical: Tractors	Mechanical: Lorries, showing description	Mechanical: Trucks, showing description	Mechanical: Trailers	Motor Bicycles	Bicycles	Remarks
Effective Strength of Unit	6	205	-	17	41	-	-	18	-	-	-	-	-	-	-	5	19	-	-	-	-	-	-	33	1 N.C.O & 3 men on leave
Details, *by Arms* attached to unit as in War Establishment:—																									
Total	6	205	-	17	41	-	-	18	-	-	-	-	-	-	-	5	19	-	-	-	-	-	-	33	
War Establishment	6	222	-	17	43	-	-	18	-	-	-	-	-	-	-	5	19	-	-	-	-	-	-	33	
Wanting to complete (Detail of Personnel and Horses below)	-	3	-	-	2																				
Surplus		nil																							
*Attached (not to include the details shown above) A.S.C.	-	1	-	-	-	2	-	-	-	-	-	-	-	-	-	1									
Civilians:— Employed with the Unit																									
Accompanying the Unit																									
Total Rationed ...	6	205	-	17	41	-	-	18																	

* In the case of field ambulances, hospitals or depots, the number of patients are to be included here, the names being shown in A. F. A. 36.

for O.C. Lieut R.E. 97 (Fd) Co R.E. Signature of Commander.

3-12-15. Date of Despatch.

For information of the A.G.'s Office at the Base.

Officers and men who have become casuals, been transferred or joined since last report.

Place In the Field Date 3-12-15.

Regtl. Number	Rank	Name	Corps	Nature of casualty, or name of unit from or to which transferred	Date of being struck off or coming on the ration return	Remarks*
Punishments.						
42886	Sapr	Johnstone J.	R.E.	"as Malingering" on 26-11-15	Deprived 3 days pay on 26-11-15	
43069	Sapr	Anthony C.	-"-	Absent from the works from 8.0 am to 8.45 am on 29-11-15	Awarded deprivation 1 days pay on 29/11/15.	
43079	"	Clements A.	-"-			
43068	"	Gibbons W.H.	-"-			
42891	"	Middleton F.	-"-			
44605	"	Whiteside H.	-"-			
42780	Sapr	Martin G.A.	-"-	Conduct to the prejudice of good order & Military discipline on 29-11-15.		Deprived 14 days pay on 30-11-15
52126	Dr.	Allman A.	-"-			
36478	Dr	Ramsden G.	-"-	Non-Compliance with Standing Orders		Deprived 4 days pay on 1-12-15.
42851	Pnr	Searle C.	-"-	Non-Compliance with Standing orders.		Deprived 1 days pay on 3-12-15
Sent to Hospital						
51360	Dr	Cross T.	-"-	Sent to Hos.	26-11-15	
42936	Sapr	Reid J	-"-	-"-	26-11-15	
43480	"	Parker P.	-"-	-"-	18-11-15	
48103	"	Collis E.	-"-	-"-	30-11-15	
43396	"	Gamble P.	-"-	-"-	30-11-15	
43069	"	Anthony C.	-"-	-"-	2-12-15	
Reinforcements						
69918	L/Cpl	Radford C.	-"-	Joined since last report.	30-11-15.	
58061	Sapr	Matthew J.	-"-			
103563	"	Raistrick T	-"-			
Killed						
33506	Sapr	Russell W	-"-	Killed with shell.	26-11-15	

* State whether absence is of a permanent or temporary nature, adding, in the case of casuals from wounds or disease, any available information for communication to the relatives.

Only additional information regarding "wanting to complete" is to be entered on this side.

3 Men wanted to Complete

Perforated Sheet giving detail of personnel and horses wanting to complete, shown on Army Form B. 213.

Number of Report 20.

Detail of Wanting to Complete	Drivers: R. A.	Drivers: R. E.	Drivers: A. S. C.	Drivers: Car	Drivers: Lorry	Drivers: Steam	Gunners	Smith Gunners	Range Takers	Farriers: Serjeants	Farriers: Corporals	Shoeing, or Shoeing and Carriage Smiths	Cold Shoers
CAVALRY													
R. A.													
R. E.													
INFANTRY													
R. A. M. C.													
A. O. C.													
A. V. C.													

Detail of Wanting to Complete	Wheelers: R. A.	Wheelers: H. T.	Wheelers: M. T.	Saddlers or Harness Makers	Blacksmiths	Bricklayers and Masons	Carpenters and Joiners	Fitters & Turners (R. E.): Wood	Fitters & Turners (R. E.): Iron	Fitters: R. A.	Fitters: Wireless	Plumbers	Electricians: Ordinary	Electricians: W. T.	Signalmen
CAVALRY															
R. A.															
R. E.						1	2								
INFANTRY															
R. A. M. C.															
A. O. C.															
A. V. C.															

Detail of Wanting to Complete	Engine Drivers: Loco.	Engine Drivers: Field	Air Line Men	Permanent Line Men	Operators, Telegraph	Cablemen	Brigade Section Pioneers	General-duty Pioneers	Signallers	Instrument Repairers	Motor Cyclists	Motor Cyclist Artificers	Telephonists	Clerks	Machine Gunners	Armament Artificers: Fitters	Armament Artificers: Range Finders	Armourers	Storemen	Privates
CAVALRY																				
R. A.																				
R. E.																				
INFANTRY																				
R. A. M. C.																				
A. O. C.																				
A. V. C.																				

Detail of Wanting to Complete	W.O.'s and N.C.O.'s (by ranks) not included in trade columns											TOTAL to agree with wanting to complete: Officers	TOTAL: Other Ranks	Horses: Riding	Horses: Draught	Horses: Heavy Draught	Horses: Pack
CAVALRY																	
R. A.																	
R. E.												-	2	-	2	-	-
INFANTRY																	
R. A. M. C.																	
A. O. C.																	
A. V. C.																	

Remarks :—

Lieut RE Signature of Commander.

for O.C. 77th (Field) Co RE. Unit.

17th Divn Formation to which attached.

3.12.15. Date of Despatch.

(82434.) Wt. 4394/2217. 500,000. 6/15. B.M.&S. Forms/B. 213/6.

[P.T.O.

No. of Report 21

FIELD RETURN.

Army Form B. 213.

(To be furnished by all arms, services, and departments (except A.S.C. units) to the A. G.'s Office at the Base in accordance with Field Service Regulations, Part II.)

RETURN showing numbers RATIONED by, and Transport on charge of, 1/1st (Field) Co R.E. at In the Field 10-12-15 Date.

Detail	Personnel			Animals.								Guns, carriages, and limbers and transport vehicles											Motor Bicycles	Bicycles	Remarks
				Horses				Mules								Horsed		Mechanical							
	Officers	Other ranks	Natives	Riding	Draught	Heavy Draught	Pack	Large	Small	Camels	Oxen	Guns, carriages and limbers, showing description	Ammunition wagons and limbers	Machine guns	Aircraft, showing description	4 Wheeled	2 Wheeled	Motor Cars	Tractors	Lorries, showing description	Trucks, showing description	Trailers			
Effective Strength of Unit	5	208	-	17	41	-	-	18	-	-	-	-	-	-	-	5	19	-	-	-	-	-		33	1 Officer 1 N.C.O & 3 men on leave
Details, *by Arms* attached to unit as in War Establishment:—																									
Total	5	208	-	17	41	-	-	18	-	-	-	-	-	-	-	5	19	-	-	-	-	-	-	33	
War Establishment	6	222	-	17	43	-	-	18	-	-	-	-	-	-	-	5	19	-	-	-	-	-	-	33	
Wanting to complete (Detail of Personnel and Horses below)	-	4	-	-	2																				
Surplus	Nil																								
*Attached (not to include the details shown above) ASC	-	1	-	-	-	2	-	-	-	-	-	-	-	-	-	1									
Civilians:— Employed with the Unit																									
Accompanying the Unit																									
Total Rationed ...	5	208	-	17	41	-	-	18																	

* In the case of field ambulances, hospitals or depots, the number of patients are to be included here, the names being shown in A. F. A. 36.

[illegible] Capt R.E. for O.C. 77 [illegible] Signature of Commander.

10-12-15 Date of Despatch.

For information of the A.G.'s Office at the Base.

Officers and men who have become casuals, been transferred or joined since last report.

Place In the Field Date 10-12-15

Regtl. Number	Rank	Name	Corps	Nature of casualty, or name of unit from or to which transferred	Date of being struck off or coming on the ration return	Remarks*
Sent to Hospital.						
46600	Sap.	Spares E.W.	R.E.	Sent to F.A.	6-12-15	
Deaths.						
43069	Sap.	Anthony C.	R.E.	Died of G.S.W. Abdomen	3-12-15	
Punishments.						
80013	Dr	Hicks W.H.	R.E.	1. Absent from parade 7.30 am to 7.40 am (Absent 10 mins) 2. Non-Compliance with Standing Orders.		Deprived 2 days pay on 9-12-15

* State whether absence is of a permanent or temporary nature, adding, in the case of casuals from wounds or disease, any available information for communication to the relatives.

Only additional information regarding "wanting to complete" is to be entered on this side.

4 Men Wanted to Complete

Perforated Sheet giving detail of personnel and horses wanting to complete, shown on Army Form B. 213.

Number of Report 21

Detail of Wanting to Complete	Drivers R.A.	Drivers R.E.	Drivers A.S.C.	Drivers Car	Drivers Lorry	Drivers Steam	Gunners	Smith Gunners	Range Takers	Farriers Serjeants	Farriers Corporals	Shoeing, or Shoeing and Carriage Smiths	Cold Shoers	Wheelers R.A.	Wheelers H.T.	Wheelers M.T.	Saddlers or Harness Makers	Blacksmiths	Bricklayers and Masons	Carpenters and Joiners	Fitters & Turners (R.E.) Wood	Fitters & Turners (R.E.) Iron	Fitters R.A.	Fitters Wireless	Plumbers	Electricians Ordinary	Electricians W.T.	Signalmen	Engine Drivers Loco.	Engine Drivers Field	Air Line Men	Permanent Line Men	Operators, Telegraph	Cablemen	Brigade Section Pioneers	General-duty Pioneers	Signallers	Instrument Repairers	Motor Cyclists	Motor Cyclist Artificers	Telephonists	Clerks	Machine Gunners	Armament Artificers Fitters	Armament Artificers Range Finders	Armourers	Storemen	Privates	W.O.'s and N.C.O.'s (by ranks) not included in trade columns											TOTAL to agree with wanting to complete Officers	TOTAL to agree with wanting to complete Other Ranks	Horses Riding	Horses Draught	Horses Heavy Draught	Horses Pack
CAVALRY																																																																		
R.A.																																																																		
R.E.																		1	1	2																																								-	4	-	2	-	-
INFANTRY																																																																		
R.A.M.C.																																																																		
A.O.C.																																																																		
A.V.C.																																																																		

Remarks :—

Capt R.E. Signature of Commander.

for O.C. 2/1st (Field) Co R.E. Unit.

17th Divn Formation to which attached.

10-12-15 Date of Despatch.

(82434.) Wt. 4394/2217. 500,000. 6/15. B.M.&S. Forms/B. 213/6.

[P.T.O.

No. of Report 22

FIELD RETURN.

Army Form B. 213.

(To be furnished by all arms, services, and departments (except A.S.C. units) to the A. G.'s Office at the Base in accordance with Field Service Regulations, Part II.)

RETURN showing numbers RATIONED by, and Transport on charge of, 4/1st Field CoRE at In the Field 17-12-15 Date.

Detail	Personnel			Animals.								Guns, carriages, and limbers and transport vehicles													Remarks
				Horses				Mules								Horsed		Mechanical							
	Officers	Other ranks	Natives	Riding	Draught	Heavy Draught	Pack	Large	Small	Camels	Oxen	Guns, carriages and limbers, showing description	Ammunition wagons and limbers	Machine guns	Aircraft, showing description	4 Wheeled	2 Wheeled	Motor Cars	Tractors	Lorries, showing description	Trucks, showing description	Trailers	Motor Bicycles	Bicycles	
Effective Strength of Unit	6	220	-	18	43	-	-	18	-	-	-	-	-	-	-	5	19	-	-	-	-	-	-	33	2 N.C.O's & 4 men on leave 7 men in Hospital temporarily 1 Horse attached to CRE 17th Divn
Details, *by Arms* attached to unit as in War Establishment:—																									
Total	6	220	-	18	43	-	-	18	-	-	-	-	-	-	-	5	19	-	-	-	-	-	-	33	
War Establishment	6	222	-	18	43	-	-	18	-	-	-	-	-	-	-	5	19	-	-	-	-	-	-	33	
Wanting to complete (Detail of Personnel and Horses below)	-	2																							
Surplus	nil																								
*Attached (not to include the details shown above) A.S.A.	-	1	-	-	-	2	-	-	-	-	-	-	-	-	-	1									
Civilians:— Employed with the Unit Accompanying the Unit																									
Total Rationed ..	6	207	-	17	43	-	-	18																	

* In the case of field ambulances, hospitals or depots, the number of patients are to be included here, the names being shown in A. F. A. 36.

for O.C. 4/1st (Field) CoRE Capt R.E. Signature of Commander.

17-12-15 Date of Despatch.

For information of the A.G.'s Office at the Base.

Officers and men who have become casuals, been transferred or joined since last report.

Place In the Field Date 17-12-15

Regtl. Number	Rank	Name	Corps	Nature of casualty, or name of unit from or to which transferred	Date of being struck off or coming on the ration return	Remarks*
Punishments.						
80020	Dr	Burbridge J.	R.E.	Absent when Stableman from the Stable on 11/12/15		Deprived 4 days pay on 12-12-15
25669	"	Cowell S	-"-			
36478	Dr	Ramsden G	-"-	Insolence to a N.C.O. on 9-12-15		Deprived 14 days pay on 9-12-15
Sent to F.A.						
61769	Pnr	Gold A.	R.E.	Sent to F.A.	10-12-15	
42703	Sergt	Wankling A	-"-	" " "	13-12-15	
Joined since last report.						
65716	Sap.	Mills W.	R.E.	12-12-15		
61639	"	Turner T.	-"-	12-12-15		

* State whether absence is of a permanent or temporary nature, adding, in the case of casuals from wounds or disease, any available information for communication to the relatives.

Only additional information regarding "wanting to complete" is to be entered on this side.

2 Men wanted to Complete

Perforated Sheet giving detail of personnel and horses wanting to complete, shown on Army Form B. 213.

Number of Report 22

Detail of Wanting to Complete	Drivers R.A.	Drivers R.E.	Drivers A.S.C.	Drivers Car	Drivers Lorry	Drivers Steam	Gunners	Smith Gunners	Range Takers	Farriers Serjeants	Farriers Corporals	Shoeing, or Shoeing and Carriage Smiths	Cold Shoers	Wheelers R.A.	Wheelers H.T.	Wheelers M.T.	Saddlers or Harness Makers	Blacksmiths	Bricklayers and Masons	Carpenters and Joiners
CAVALRY																				
R.A.																				
R.E.																		1		1
INFANTRY																				
R.A.M.C.																				
A.O.C.																				
A.V.C.																				

Detail of Wanting to Complete	Fitters & Turners (R.E.) Wood	Fitters & Turners (R.E.) Iron	Fitters R.A.	Fitters Wireless	Plumbers	Electricians Ordinary	Electricians W.T.	Signalmen	Engine Drivers Loco.	Engine Drivers Field	Air Line Men	Permanent Line Men	Operators, Telegraph	Cablemen	Brigade Section Pioneers	General-duty Pioneers	Signallers	Instrument Repairers	Motor Cyclists	Motor Cyclist Artificers	Telephonists	Clerks	Machine Gunners	Armament Artificers Fitters	Armament Artificers Range Finders	Armourers	Storemen	Privates
CAVALRY																												
R.A.																												
R.E.																												
INFANTRY																												
R.A.M.C.																												
A.O.C.																												
A.V.C.																												

Detail of Wanting to Complete	W.O.'s and N.C.O.'s. (by ranks) not included in trade columns									TOTAL to agree with wanting to complete Officers	TOTAL Other Ranks	Horses Riding	Horses Draught	Horses Heavy Draught	Horses Pack
CAVALRY															
R.A.															
R.E.										-	2	-	-	-	-
INFANTRY															
R.A.M.C.															
A.O.C.															
A.V.C.															

Remarks :—

Capt R.E. Signature of Commander.

for O.C. 74th (Field) Co R.E. Unit.

14th Division Formation to which attached.

14-12-15 Date of Despatch.

(82434.) Wt. 4394/2217. 500,000. 6/15. B.M.&S. Forms/B. 213/6.

[P.T.O.

No. of Report 23

FIELD RETURN.

Army Form B. 213.

(To be furnished by all arms, services and departments (except A.S.C. units) to the A. G.'s Office at the Base in accordance with Field Service Regulations, Part II.)

RETURN showing numbers RATIONED by, and Transport on charge of, 77th (Field) CoRE at In the field 24-12-15 Date.

DETAIL	Personnel			Animals								Guns, carriages, and limbers, and transport vehicles.													REMARKS
				Horses				Mules								Horsed		Mechanical							
	Officers	Other ranks	Natives	Riding	Draught	Heavy Draught	Pack	Large	Small	Camels	Oxen	Guns, carriages and limbers, showing description	Ammunition wagons and limbers	Machine guns	Aircraft, showing description	4 Wheeled	2 Wheeled	Motor Cars	Tractors	Lorries, showing description	Trucks, showing description	Trailers	Motor Bicycles	Bicycles.	
Effective Strength of Unit	6	216	-	17 *	39	-	-	18	-	-	-	-	-	-	-	5	19	-	-	-	-	-	-	33	7 O.R's on leave 11 O.R's in Hospital
Details, *by Arms* attached to unit as in War Establishment:—				* 1 attached to CRE 17 Divn.																					
Total	6	216	-	17	39	-	-	18	-	-	-	-	-	-	-	5	19	-	-	-	-	-	-	33	
War Establishment	6	222	-	18	43	-	-	18	-	-	-	-	-	-	-	5	19	-	-	-	-	-	-	33	
Wanting to complete (Detail of Personnel and Horses below)	-	6	-	* 1	4	-	-	-																	1 officers Charger Height of Officer 6ft. weight " " 14 stone
Surplus	Nil																								
*Attached (not to include the details shown above) acc	-	1	-	-	-	2	-	-	-	-	-	-	-	-	-	1									
Civilians:— Employed with the Unit / Accompanying the Unit																									
TOTAL RATIONED ...	6	198	-	15	39	-	-	18																	

* In the case of field ambulances, hospitals or depots, the number of patients are to be included here, the names being shown in A. F. A. 36.

[illegible] Capt R.E. for OC 77th (Fd) CoRE Signature of Commander.

24-12-15 Date of Despatch.

For information of the A.G.'s Office at the Base.

Officers and men who have become casuals, been transferred or joined since last report.

Place In the Field Date 24-12-15

Regtl. Number	Rank	Name	Corps	Nature of casualty, or name of unit from or to which transferred	Date of being struck off or coming on the ration return	Remarks*
Casualties.						
60801	Corpl	Abbott H.	R.E.	Killed	19-12-15	
42672	Sapr	Whitfield W.	"	Killed	19-12-15	
52092	Driver	Lynch J.	"	Wounded	19-12-15	
52092	"	" "	"	(Died of wounds)	20-12-15	
42686	Driver	Pierce A.	"	Wounded	19-12-15	
42686	"	"	"	Died of wounds	19-12-15	
41997	Sapr	Adams J.	"	Wounded (Slightly)	19-12-15	Sent to Hos:
Sent to Hospital (Sick.)						
42419	Sapr	Mc Mullen R.	"	Sent to F.A.	18-12-15	
60802	Dr	Taylor A	"	"	23-12-15	
43452	Sapr	Campbell J	"	"	23-12-15	
48566	2/Cpl	Farrow E.	"	"	22-12-15	
42408	Sapr	Powell W.	"	"	22-12-15	
Returned to Duty.						
42408	Sapr	Powell W	"	Returned to Duty	8-12-15	
80020	Driver	Burbridge	"	"	4-12-15	
42445	2/Cpl	Butcher P.	"	"	3-12-15	
51360	Dr	Cross T	"	"	11-12-15	
42936	Sapr	Reid J.	"	"	6-12-15	
46600	"	Spares E. W.	"	"	14-12-15	
44397	"	Mackie W.	"	"	13-12-15	
46602	"	Jones G.E.	"	"	19-12-15	
42703	Sergt	Wankling A.	"	"	18-12-15	
Promotions.						
44488	Pnr	Roe H.	"	Appointed unpaid L/c Cpl on 15-12-15 Supernumerary to Establishment		

* State whether absence is of a permanent or temporary nature, adding, in the case of casuals from wounds or disease, any available information for communication to the relatives.

Only additional information regarding "wanting to complete" is to be entered on this side.

6 Men wanted to Complete.

Perforated Sheet giving detail of personnel and horses wanting to complete, shown on Army Form B. 213.

Number of Report 23

Detail of Wanting to Complete.	Drivers.						Gunners	Smith Gunners	Range Takers	Farriers		Shoeing, or Shoeing and Carriage Smiths	Cold Shoers	Wheelers			Saddlers or Harness Makers	Blacksmiths	Bricklayers and Masons	Carpenters and Joiners	Fitters & Turners (R. E.)		Fitters		Plumbers	Electricians		Signalmen	Engine Drivers		Air Line Men	Permanent Line Men	Operators, Telegraph	Cablemen	Brigade Section Pioneers	General-duty Pioneers	Signallers	Instrument Repairers	Motor Cyclis's	Motor Cyclist Artificers	Telephonists	Clerks	Machine Gunners	Armament Artificers		Armourers	Storemen	Privates	W.O.'s and N.C.O.'s (by ranks) not included in trade columns.											TOTAL to agree with wanting to complete		Horses			
	R. A.	R. E.	A. S. C.	Car	Lorry	Steam				Serjeants	Corporals			R. A.	H. T.	M. T.					Wood	Iron	R. A.	Wireless		Ordinary	W. T.		Loco.	Field														Fitters	Range Finders																Officers	Other Ranks	Riding	Draught	Heavy Draught	Pack
CAVALRY																																																																	
R. A.																																																																	
R. E.		3																1		1									1																																-	6	1	4	-	-
INFANTRY																																																																	
R. A. M. C.																																																																	
A. O. C.																																																																	
A. V. C.																																																																	

Remarks:— 1 Officers Charger
Height of Officer 6 ft.
Weight " " 14 stone

[signature] Capt R.E. Signature of Commander.

for O.C. 77th (Field) Co R.E. Unit.

17th Divn Formation to which attached.

24-12-15 Date of Despatch.

(26149.) Wt. W. 10698/4046. 500,000. 10/15. M.R.Co.,Ltd. Forms/B. 213/6.

[P.T.O.

No. of Report 24

FIELD RETURN.

Army Form B. 213.

(To be furnished by all arms, services and departments (except A.S.C. units) to the A. G.'s Office at the Base in accordance with Field Service Regulations, Part II.)

RETURN showing numbers RATIONED by, and Transport on charge of, 1/1st (Field) Co R.E. at In the field 31-12-15 Date.

DETAIL	Personnel: Officers	Personnel: Other ranks	Personnel: Natives	Animals: Horses: Riding	Animals: Horses: Draught	Animals: Horses: Heavy Draught	Animals: Horses: Pack	Animals: Mules: Large	Animals: Mules: Small	Animals: Camels	Animals: Oxen	Guns, carriages and limbers, showing description	Ammunition wagons and limbers	Machine guns	Aircraft, showing description	Horsed: 4 Wheeled	Horsed: 2 Wheeled	Mechanical: Motor Cars	Mechanical: Tractors	Mechanical: Lorries, showing description	Mechanical: Trucks, showing description	Mechanical: Trailers	Motor Bicycles	Bicycles.	REMARKS
Effective Strength of Unit	6	214	-	17	38	-	-	18	-	-	-	-	-	-	-	5	19	-	-	-	-	-	-	33	1 Officer on leave 7 O.R. on leave 10 O.R. in Hospital.
Details, *by Arms* attached to unit as in War Establishment:—																									
Total	6	214	-	17	38	-	-	18	-	-	-	-	-	-	-	5	19	-	-	-	-	-	-	33	
War Establishment	6	222	-	18	43	-	-	18	-	-	-	-	-	-	-	5	19	-	-	-	-	-	-	33	
Wanting to complete (Detail of Personnel and Horses below)	-	8	-	1	5																				[illegible]
Surplus	Nil																								
*Attached (not to include the details shown above) A.S.C.	-	1	-	-	-	2	-	-	-	-	-	-	-	-	-	1									
Civilians:— Employed with the Unit																									
Accompanying the Unit																									
TOTAL RATIONED ...	5	197		15	38	-	-	18																	

* In the case of field ambulances, hospitals or depots, the number of patients are to be included here, the names being shown in A. F. A. 36.

[illegible] Capt R.E. Signature of Commander.

O.C. 1/1st Fd Co R.E.

31-12-15 Date of Despatch.

For information of the A. G.'s Office at the Base.

Officers and men who have become casuals, been transferred or joined since last report.

Place In the Field   Date 31-12-15

Regtl. Number	Rank	Name	Corps	Nature of casualty, or name of unit from or to which transferred	Date of being struck off or coming on the ration return	Remarks*
Sent to Hospital.						
44307	Spr	Mackie W.	R.E.	Sent to F.A.	26-12-15	
42858	"	Roberts W.R.	--	--	26-12-15	
43041	"	Roberts T.	--	--	28-12-15	
Returned to Duty.						
42408	Spr	Powell W.	--	Returned to Duty	27-12-15	
43452	"	Campbell J.	--	--	29-12-15	
Punishments						
42454	L/Cpl	Scott J.R.	--	Not Complying with an order on 24/12/15		Severely Reprimanded

* State whether absence is of a permanent or temporary nature, adding, in the case of casuals from wounds or disease, any available information for communication to the relatives.

Only additional information regarding "wanting to complete" is to be entered on this side.

8 Men Wanted to Complete.

Perforated Sheet giving detail of personnel and horses wanting to complete, shown on Army Form B. 213.

Number of Report 24

Detail of Wanting to Complete.	Drivers. R. A.	Drivers. R. E.	Drivers. A. S. C.	Drivers. Car	Drivers. Lorry	Drivers. Steam	Gunners	Smith Gunners	Range Takers	Farriers Serjeants	Farriers Corporals	Shoeing, or Shoeing and Carriage Smiths	Cold Shoers	Wheelers R. A.	Wheelers H. T.	Wheelers M. T.	Saddlers or Harness Makers	Blacksmiths	Bricklayers and Masons	Carpenters and Joiners	Fitters & Turners (R. E.) Wood	Fitters & Turners (R. E.) Iron	Fitters R. A.	Fitters Wireless	Plumbers	Electricians Ordinary	Electricians W. T.	Signalmen	Engine Drivers Loco.	Engine Drivers Field	Air Line Men	Permanent Line Men	Operators, Telegraph	Cablemen	Brigade Section Pioneers	General-duty Pioneers	Signallers	Instrument Repairers	Motor Cyclis's	Motor Cyclist Artificers	Telephonists	Clerks	Machine Gunners	Armament Artificers Fitters	Armament Artificers Range Finders	Armourers	Storemen	Privates	W.O's. and N.C.O's (by ranks) not included in trade columns.											TOTAL to agree with wanting to complete Officers	TOTAL to agree with wanting to complete Other Ranks	Horses Riding	Horses Draught	Horses Heavy Draught	Horses Pack
CAVALRY																																																																	
R. A.																																																																	
R. E.		2																1		1	1	1							1																															-	8	1	5	-	-
INFANTRY																																																																		
R. A. M. C.																																																																		
A. O. C.																																																																		
A. V. C.																																																																	

Remarks :—

A. Y. Oakes Capt. R.E. Signature of Commander.

for O.C. 77 (Field) Co. R.E. Unit.

11th Div. Formation to which attached.

31-12-15 Date of Despatch.

(26149.) Wt. W. 10698/4046. 500,000. 10/15. M.R.Co.,Ltd. Forms/B. 213/6.

[P.T.O.

77th F.C.R.E.
Vol: 6

17

Jan '16

Army Form C. 2118

Instructions regarding War Diaries and Intelligence Summaries are contained in F. S. Regs., Part II. and the Staff Manual respectively. Title Pages will be prepared in manuscript.

WAR DIARY
or
INTELLIGENCE SUMMARY
(Erase heading not required.)

Place	Date	Hour	Summary of Events and Information	Reinforcements		Casualties: Officers N.C.O's & Men					Casualties: Horses & Mules					Remarks and references to Appendices
				Officer N.C.O's & Men	Horses & Mules	Killed	Wounded	Died	In Hospital	Evacuated	Killed	Wounded	Died	In Hospital	Evacuated	
	1-1-16		1 Horse No. 23 Cast. Dr Burbridge sent to Hospital (Sick).						1						1	
			Sap: Birch wounded G.S.W. Leg. Lc Cpl Low sent to Hospital. (Sick)				1		1							
	2-1-16		Reinforcement of three men (mounted) arrived.	3												
	4-1-16		11 Horses arrive to make up establishment. Lc Cpl Low returned to duty.		11											
	8-1-16		Sap: Upton sent to Hospital.						1							
	12-1-16		Sappers Mills & Campbell sent to Hospital						2							
	13-1-16		Driver Burbridge & Sap: Upton returned to duty.													
	14-1-16		1 Mule sent to 29th Mob: Vet: Section, (No 84)											1		
	15-1-16		Sap: Abbott attached temporarily to 93rd (Field) Co RE for shoeing													
			1 mule evacuated (No. 84.)												1	
	16-1-16		Saps Mills & Sap: Campbell returned to Duty.													
	17-1-16		Two Horses No 44 & No 53 sent to Mob: Vet: Sect:											2		
	18-1-16		Two Horses No 44 & No 53 Evacuated. Reinforcement of five men arrived	5											2	
	19-1-16		Pnr Jewell sent to Hospital (Evacuated)						1	1						
	20-1-16		Corpl Ellis & Sap: Reid sent to Hospital (Sick)						2							
	23-1-16		Pnr Duncan sent to Hospital (Sick)						1							
	24-1-16		Corpl Ellis returned to duty.													
	25-1-16		Pnr Duncan returned to duty. Sap: Roberts T & Sap: Batchelor W sent to Hospital (Sick).						2							
	28-1-16		1 Horse No. 56 died.										1			
	31-1-16		Capt Oakes proceeded to take over command of 130th (Fd) Co RE													
			Reinforcement of 5 men arrive. 1 Horse No 50 sent to Mob. Vet Sect.	5										1		
			Pnr Edwards & Dr Williams accompany Capt Oakes.													

R C Lundie Lt RE for O.C. 77th (Fd) Coy RE.

1875 Wt. W593/826 1,000,000 4/15 J.B.C. & A. A.D.S.S./Forms/C. 2118.

17

77th FCRE.

Vol: 7

Instructions regarding War Diaries and Intelligence Summaries are contained in F. S. Regs., Part II. and the Staff Manual respectively. Title Pages will be prepared in manuscript.

WAR DIARY
or
~~INTELLIGENCE SUMMARY~~
(Erase heading not required.)

Army Form C. 2118

Place	Date	Hour	Summary of Events and Information	Reinforcements: Officers N.C.O.s Men	Reinforcements: Horses & Mules	Casualties, Officers N.C.O.s & Men: Killed	Wounded	Died	In Hospital	Evacuated	Casualties, Horses & Mules: Killed	Wounded	Died	In Hospital	Evacuated	Remarks and references to Appendices
1-2-16	1-2-16		Reinforcement of two men arrive. One Mounted & One Dismounted	2												
	2-2-16		Driver Gregory sent to Hospital (Sick). Sapr Roberts W.R. sent to Hospital (Sick)						2							
	4-2-16		Sapr Mackie sent to Hospital (Sick).						1							
	5-2-16		Sapr Roberts W.R. returned to duty.													
	8-2-16		Driver Sutton sent to Hospital. (Sick).						1							
	9-2-16		Sapr Middleton sent to Hospital. (Sick).						1							
	11-2-16		Sapr Griffiths sent to Hospital. (Sick)						1							
	14-2-16		Sapr Middleton returned to Duty. Lieut R.C. Lundie, wounded. Sergt. Livingstone H, L/Cpl. Low W.J., Saprs Upton, Powell, Barlow T, Sefford, Harrison J, Walker W.E, Turner J, Foster H & Miles, wounded. Sapr Miles died of wounds. Sapr Rickard killed, L/Cpl Dawell reported missing.			1	12	1	10							
	15-2-16		Lieut J.C. Bent wounded, 2/Cpl Smith H, Saprs Beaston, Plant, Church, Turner W.E., Hill, Lowe E, Lymm, Hurrell & Wood wounded sent to Hospital. Lieut. A. Moncrieff, 2/Lieut C.B. Dunlop, wounded, at Duty. L/Cpl Harrison, Saprs Littlewood & Hudson wounded, still at Duty. Saprs Hancock G, Pearce P, & Braisher W.R. Killed.			3	16		11							
	19-2-16		Sapr Roberts T sent to Hospital. (Sick).						1							
	20-2-16		Sapr Hurrell J.W. died of wounds.					1								
	21-2-16		Sapr Hill M.G. died of wounds. Sapr Wood G.J. Died of Wounds					2								
	22-2-16		Corpl Prior R. & Sapr Whiteside H. Sent to Hospital. (Sick).						2							
	23-2-16		Sapr Griffiths returned to duty.													
	25-2-16		Sapr Lewis A sent to Hospital (Sick)						1							
	26-2-16		Reinforcement of two Officers joined. 2/Lieut H.C. Butler & 2/Lieut G. De la P. Beresford	2												
	27-2-16		Sapr Birch H sent to Hospital. (Sick).						1							
	28-2-16		Sapr Martin G.A. Wounded.				1									
	29-2-16		Pnr Collings B sent to Hospital (Sick).						1							
	29-2-16		Reinforcements of 28 men arrived.	28												J. [illegible] Major R.E. O.C. 77 (Fd) Coy R.E.

1875 Wt. W593/826 1,000,000 4/15 J.B.C. & A. A.D.S.S./Forms/C. 2118.

Army Form C. 2118

Instructions regarding War Diaries and Intelligence Summaries are contained in F. S. Regs., Part II. and the Staff Manual respectively. Title Pages will be prepared in manuscript.

WAR DIARY
or
INTELLIGENCE SUMMARY
(Erase heading not required.)

Place	Date	Hour	Summary of Events and Information	Remarks and references to Appendices
	19/2/16		The following order was received from G.O.C 17th Divn. C.R.E 17th Division. I am directed by the Major General, Commanding the Division, to ask you to convey to the 77th Field Company R.E. his appreciation of the gallantry displayed by the Officers and men of the Company under Lieutenant Lundie, on the nights of 14th/15th and 15th/16th February 1916; which was especially brought to his notice by the Brigadier, Commanding 51st Infantry Brigade. (Sd) J. Muspratt. Colonel, A.A. & Q.M.G 17th Divn. 19-2-16. O.C 77th (Fd) Co.R.E. Forwarded. Please convey this to your Officers & men. I hope to visit your Company shortly, to express to you all my appreciation also. (Sd) C M Carpenter Lieut. Col. C.R.E. 17th Divn. 20-2-16 certified true copy [signature] Major R.E. O.C. 77th Co. R.E.	

1875 Wt. W593/826 1,000,000 4/15 J.B.C. & A. A.D.S.S./Forms/C. 2118.

77th FCRE

VOL 8

17 Div

Instructions regarding War Diaries and Intelligence Summaries are contained in F. S. Regs., Part II. and the Staff Manual respectively. Title Pages will be prepared in manuscript.

WAR DIARY
or
~~INTELLIGENCE SUMMARY~~
(Erase heading not required.)

Army Form C. 2118

Place	Date	Hour	Summary of Events and Information	Remarks and references to Appendices
	3-3-16		Nos 1 & 3 Sections march out to CANAL BANK under LIEUT MONCRIEFF & 2nd LIEUT BUTLER	
	4-3-16		Nos 1 & 3 SECTIONS return to Company Head Quarters.	
	6-3-16		Company move to rest billet near STEENWERCK.	
	9-3-16		ii LIEUT H.C. BUTLER attached to 78th FIELD Company RE.	
	17-3-16		SERGT. STRATTON A. & SAPPER CLEMENTS A. awarded Distinguished Conduct Medals.	
	18-3-16		Company move out of rest area to ARMENTIERES. Billets in RUE NATIONALE & RUE ST CHARLES.	
	31-3-16		Company move into Billets previously occupied by 98th FIELD Company RE. No RUE DE FLANDRES.	

[signature]
Major RE.
O.C. 1/1st (Lon) Co RE.

1875 Wt. W593/826 1,000,000 4/15 J.B.C. & A. A.D.S.S./Forms/C. 2118.

Instructions regarding War Diaries and Intelligence Summaries are contained in F. S. Regs., Part II. and the Staff Manual respectively. Title Pages will be prepared in manuscript.

WAR DIARY
or
~~INTELLIGENCE SUMMARY~~
(Erase heading not required.)

Army Form C. 2118

Place	Date	Hour	Summary of Events and Information	Reinforcements: Officers N.C.O's & Men	Reinforcements: Horses & Mules	Casualties – Officers N.C.O's & Men: K	W	A	In Hospital	Evac'd	Casualties – Horses & Mules: K	W	A	In Hospital	Evac'd	Remarks and references to Appendices
	MARCH 1916															
	2-3-16		Sapr Cockerton wounded.				1									
	4-3-16		Reinforcement of 1 N.C.O arrived Sergt. Livingston W. Sap. MARTIN G.A. returned to duty from Hospital. Pnr Field sent to Hospital (Sick).	1					1							
	5-3-16		Pnr Winters sent to Hospital (Sick). One Horse No 54 Killed.						1		1					
	6-3-16		Sapper Livesey & Driver Benbow sent to Hospital (Sick).						2							
	8-3-16		Pionr Field, Pionr Winters & Driver Benbow, returned to duty from Hospital.													
	9-3-16		II Lieut. Butler attached to 78th (Fd) Coy RE.													
	11-3-16		Sapr Raistrick & Driver Trainer sent to Hospital (Sick.) Reinforcement of one N.C.O arrived. Corpl Prior R.													
	13-3-16		Sapper Batchelor G, Sapr Hart W.R. sent to Hospital (Sick). Corpl Prior sent to Hospital (Sick).	1					1 2 1							
	15-3-16		Reinforcement of four men arrived.	4												
	16-3-16		Sapper Worsley, Sapr Gibson, Pnr. Meaney & Driver Lowe sent to Hospital (Sick)						4							
	17-3-16		Pioneer Woodruff sent to Hospital (Sick).						1							
	18-3-16		Sapper Proctor returned to Duty.													
	21-3-16		Sapper Harrison J. sent to Hospital (Sick). Sapr Littlewood returned to duty.						1							
	22-3-16		Sapper Batchelor returned to Duty.													
	23-3-16		Sapr Harrison J returned to Duty.													
	24-3-16		Sapr Slade A.C wounded sent to Hospital.													
	25-3-16		2/Cpl Mitchell R, & Sapr Kirby wounded sent to Hospital. Pnr Meaney & Driver Lowe returned to duty from Hospital.				1 2		1 2							
	26-3-16		1 Horse No. 131 sent Mobile Vet. Section.											1		
	28-3-16		Driver Williams T.P sent to Hospital (Sick)						1							

[signature] Major R.E.
O.C. 77 (Fd) Co R.E.

1875 Wt. W593/826 1,000,000 4/15 J.B.C. & A. A.D.S.S./Forms/C. 2118.

XVII

Army Form C. 2118

77 FERE Vol 9

WAR DIARY
or
~~INTELLIGENCE SUMMARY~~
(Erase heading not required.)

Instructions regarding War Diaries and Intelligence Summaries are contained in F. S. Regs., Part II. and the Staff Manual respectively. Title Pages will be prepared in manuscript.

Place	Date	Hour	Summary of Events and Information	Reinforcements: Officers N.C.O.s & Men	Reinforcements: Horses & Mules	Casualties Officers N.C.O.s & Men: K	W	D	In Hos	Evac	Casualties Horses & Mules: K	W	D	In Hos	Evac	Remarks and references to Appendices
	1-4-16		Pte Griffin wounded.				1									
	2-4-16		Sap: Cole wounded at duty.				1									
	3-4-16		Sap: Clements wounded. Lieut Lundie transferred to Head Quarters RE 17 Divn as Adjt. Pte Allman transferred with Lieut Lundie				1									
	4-4-16		Driver Williams T.P. returned to duty.													
	5-4-16		Driver Caney sent to Hospital (Sick).						1							
	7-4-16		L/Cpl Perks W. wounded. Reinforcement of two men (mounted) arrived from 103rd CoRE	2			1									
	8-4-16		L/Cpl Maxim C.W. wounded. Driver Ramsden transferred to Head Quarters RE 17 Division to accompany Lieut Lundie.				1									
	11-4-16		Lieut H.C. Butler rejoined from 78 (Fd) CoRE													
	13-4-16		Reinforcement of 7 OR. arrived. (2 mounted) (5 dismounted)	7												
	15-4-16		Two men sent to Hospital Saps Littlewood R. & Johnstone J.						2							
	17-4-16		1 Officer & 1 O.R. attached to this unit.													
			Pte Winters J & Sap: Jackson R. wounded				2									
	19-4-16		Reinforcement of 2 Sappers arrived	2												
	20-4-16		Sap: Henty sent to Hospital (Sick).						1							
	25-4-16		Sap: Batchelor W sent to Hospital (Sick)						1							
	26-4-16		Driver Benbow sent to Hospital (Sick)						1							
	26-4-16		" Benbow returned to Duty. Lieut Holbrow 2/Cpl Carmichael & Driver Trainer sent to Hos						3							
	28-4-16		Sapper Johnstone J & Sapper Henty returned to Duty													
	29-4-16		Sapper O'Brien J wounded.				1		1							

[signature] MAJOR, R.E.
COMMDG. 77th (FIELD) COY. R.E.

1875 Wt. W593/826 1,000,000 4/15 J.B.C. & A. A.D.S.S./Forms/C. 2118.

Instructions regarding War Diaries and Intelligence Summaries are contained in F. S. Regs., Part II. and the Staff Manual respectively. Title Pages will be prepared in manuscript.

WAR DIARY
or
INTELLIGENCE SUMMARY

(Erase heading not required.)

Army Form C. 2118.

Place	Date	Hour	Summary of Events and Information	Remarks and references to Appendices
LILLE POST	April 1916	–	1 Machine Gun Tub in position with dug-out, Communication Trench completed except sandbagging – Machine Gun Emplacement, work being carried on – Breastwork in progress ditto front fire trench – Communication Trench Stop in progress.	–
LEITH WALK	----		Reclaiming Communication Trench	
SUPPORT LINE 68.S	----		Revetting & making Support Line – Trench nearly completed – Parados & Dugouts still to be done	
CHARDS FARM	----		Making Locality – work being done by Infantry with R.E. assistance	
SUPPORT 69S & 70S	----		Making & reclaiming Support Line	
HEAD QUARTER WALK	----		Building up Parapet.	
TRENCH TRAMWAY	----		Repairing Trench Tramway – Maintenance.	
MUSHROOM & F. TRENCH	----		Reclaiming Trench	
73.S	----		Remaking & Reclaiming Trench.	
PORT EGAL AVENUE.			Remaking Trench.	
PORT EGAL AVENUE STOP			Making Stop.	

J. [illegible] Fleming
MAJOR, R.E.
COMMDG. 77th (FIELD) COY. R.E.

2449 Wt. W14957/M90 750,000 1/16 J.B.C. & A. Forms/C.2118/12.

17

77 F.C. RE
Vol 10

Army Form C. 2118.

Instructions regarding War Diaries and Intelligence Summaries are contained in F. S. Regs., Part II. and the Staff Manual respectively. Title Pages will be prepared in manuscript.

WAR DIARY
or
INTELLIGENCE SUMMARY
(Erase heading not required.)

Place	Date	Hour	Summary of Events and Information	Reinforcements: Officers N.C.O. & Men	Reinforcements: Horses & Mules	Casualties, Officers N.C.O. & Men: Killed	Wounded	Died	In Hospital	Evacuated	Casualties, Horses & Mules: Killed	Wounded	Died	In Hospital	Evacuated	Remarks and references to Appendices
	1-5-16		Interpreter M HOLTHIUS joined	1												
	3-5-16		Sapr Yarrington accidently injured, Reinforcement of 6 O.R. joined & 1 Officer 2/Lieut Morris E.G. joined the Company.	7					1							
	5-5-16		Driver Starkie accidently injured. Sapr Hall slightly wounded sent to Hospital.				1		2							
	6-5-16		Sapr Hall returned to Duty.													
	8-5-16		Corpl A. Neale & ii Corpl Gardner F. transferred to No 4 General Base Depot.													
	11-5-16		Sapper Woodcock sent to Hospital (Sick).						1							
	12-5-16		Driver Starkie returned to Duty.													
	14-5-16		Sapr Henty (Sick) Sapr Hall (wounded) sent to Hospital				1		2							
	18-5-16		Sapr Henty & Sapr Woodcock return to Duty. Sapr Carter & Pionr Bennett sent to Hospital.						2							
	20-5-16		Sapr Smith J.E. sent to Hospital (Sick.) ii Corpl Jones sent to Hospital (Sick).						2							
	25-5-16		ii Cpl Jones Returned to Duty. Reinforcement of 1 O.R. (mounted) arrived.	1												
	26-5-16		1 Riding horse & 4 Light Draught horses evacuated												5	
	27-5-16		Sapr McGuinness sent to Hospital (Sick).						1							
	28-5-16		Sapr Robertson sent to Hospital (Sick).						1							
	30/5-16		Sapr Brown C.L. sent to Hospital (Sick)						1							
	30-5-16		Reinforcement of 1 O.R. (mounted) arrived.	1												

[signature] Major R.E.
O.C. 77 (Fd) Coy R.E.

Instructions regarding War Diaries and Intelligence Summaries are contained in F. S. Regs., Part II. and the Staff Manual respectively. Title Pages will be prepared in manuscript.

WAR DIARY
or
INTELLIGENCE SUMMARY

(Erase heading not required.)

Army Form C. 2118.

Place	Date	Hour	Summary of Events and Information	Remarks and references to Appendices
	1-5-16 to 14-5-16		Work carried on as in April	
	15-5-16		Company move from ARMENTIERES to RACQUINGHEM	
	16-5-16		" " RACQUINGHEM to MORBECQUE.	
	17-5-16		" " MORBECQUE. to MORINGHEM	
	19-5-16		" " MORINGHEM to SALPERWICK	
			DESPATCHES	
			The Major General Commanding is proud to be able to congratulate the following unit of the Division on the [illegible] praise bestowed upon them by SIR. DOUGLAS HAIG the Commander in Chief of the British Expeditionary Force in his last Despatch	
			77th (Field) Company RE	
			[illegible signature] Major RE	
			O.C. 77 (Field) Co RE	

2449 Wt. W14957/M90 750,000 1/16 J.B.C. & A. Forms/C.2118/12.

XVI   June

Army Form C. 2118

77 F. C. R.E

WAR DIARY
or
INTELLIGENCE SUMMARY
(Erase heading not required.)

Instructions regarding War Diaries and Intelligence Summaries are contained in F. S. Regs., Part II. and the Staff Manual respectively. Title Pages will be prepared in manuscript.

Vol 11

Place	Date	Hour	Summary of Events and Information	Remarks and references to Appendices
	1-6-16 to 8-6-16		Intensive training for attack	
	8-6-16		Company march to ST OMER and Entrain	
	9-6-16		" detrain at LONGUEAU and March to VILLE-SOUS-CORBIE	
	19-6-16		" March from VILLE-SOUS CORBIE to HEILLY	
	30-6-16		" " " HEILLY to MORLANCOURT	
	8-6-16 to 30-6-16		Work in connection with preparations for attack Attached to XXI ST DIVISION	

Alan Emery Lieut RE
for Major RE
O.C 77th Field Co RE

1875 Wt. W593/826 1,000,000 4/15 J.B.C. & A. A.D.S.S./Forms/C. 2118.

Instructions regarding War Diaries and Intelligence Summaries are contained in F. S. Regs., Part II. and the Staff Manual respectively. Title Pages will be prepared in manuscript.

WAR DIARY
or
INTELLIGENCE SUMMARY
(Erase heading not required.)

Army Form C. 2118

Place	Date	Hour	Summary of Events and Information	Reinforcements: Officers NCOs & Men	Reinforcements: Horses & Mules	Casualties: Officers NCOs & Men: Killed	Wounded	Died	In Hospital	Evacuated	Casualties: Horses & Mules: Killed	Wounded	Died	In Hospital	Evacuated	Remarks and references to Appendices
		1-6-16	Sapr Robertson returned to Duty													
		7-6-16	Reinforcement of 1 OR (Dismounted) arrived	1												
		9-6-16	Corpl Butcher Sent to Hospital (Sick)						1							
		11-6-16	Corpl Butcher returned to Duty													
		14-6-16	Driver Starkie Sent to Hospital (Sick)						1							
		15-6-16	Sapr Jones F.E. Sent to Hospital (Sick)						1							
		17-6-16	Sapr Reading Sent to Hospital . wounded.						1							
		17-6-16	Sapr Lee Slightly wounded returned to Duty													
		19-6-16	Sapr Woseley Sent to Hospital (Wounded)						1							
		19-6-16	Sapr McGuinness returned to Duty													
		19-6-16	Lieut. R.B. Dunlop Sent to Hospital (Sick)				2		1							
		25-6-16	Reinforcement of 1 OR (Dismounted) arrived	1												
		25-6-16	Lieut W.E. Pike joined this Company	1												
		28-6-16	Corpl Ellis Sent to Hospital (Sick)						1							
		29-6-16	Reinforcements of 4 OR (1 Mounted 3 Dismounted) arrived	4												
		29-6-16	Sapr Jackson - Sent to Hospital (Sick)						1							
		30-6-16	2 Riding Horses evacuated												2	
		30-6-16	Sapr Laurie Sent to Hospital (Sick)						1							

Alan Moncreiff Lieut RE
for Major RE
OC 77th (Fd) Co RE

Instructions regarding War Diaries and Intelligence Summaries are contained in F. S. Regs., Part II. and the Staff Manual respectively. Title Pages will be prepared in manuscript.

WAR DIARY
or
INTELLIGENCE SUMMARY
(Erase heading not required.)

17

Army Form C. 2118

77 F Co RE

Vol 12

Place	Date	Hour	Summary of Events and Information	Remarks and references to Appendices
	1-7-16 to 31-7-16		Work in Connection with advance AM Lt. RE	
	2-7-16		Company march from MORLANCOURT to MEAULTE AM Lt RE	
	11-7-16		" Transport move by road from MEAULTE to SAISSEVAL AM Lt RE Dismounted men march to DERNANCOURT & Entrain. Detrain at SALEUX & March to SAISSEVAL	AM Lt RE
	15-7-16		Company march from SAISSEVAL to AILLY LE HAUT CLOCHER AM Lt RE	
	22-7-16		" Transport move by road from AILLY LE HAUT CLOCHER AM Lt RE	
	23-7-16		" arrive at BUIRE. AM Lt RE	
	23-7-16		Dismounted men march from AILLY to HANGEST and Entrain AM Lt RE	
	24-7-16		" " detrain at MERICOURT and march to BUIRE AM Lt RE	

Alan Moncrieff Lieut RE for Major RE O.C 77th Field Co RE

1875 Wt. W593/826 1,000,000 4/15 J.B.C. & A. A.D.S.S./Forms/C. 2118.

Army Form C. 2118

Instructions regarding War Diaries and Intelligence Summaries are contained in F. S. Regs., Part II. and the Staff Manual respectively. Title Pages will be prepared in manuscript.

WAR DIARY
or
INTELLIGENCE SUMMARY
(Erase heading not required.)

Place	Date	Hour	Summary of Events and Information	Reinforcements: Officers NCOs & Men	Reinforcements: Horses & Mules	Casualties, Officers NCOs & Men: Killed	Wounded	Died	In Hospital	Evacuated	Casualties, Horses & Mules: Killed	Wounded	Died	In Hospital	Evacuated	Remarks and references to Appendices
	3-7-16		Sapr Bodman T Sent to Hospital (Wounded)				1									
	4-7-16		Reinforcement of 2 OR (Dismounted)	2												
	7-7-16		Lieut T.L.S Hobson returned to Duty													
	8-7-16		Reinforcement of 1 OR (Mounted) 1 LD Horse sent to MVC	1											1	
	10-7-16		Sapr Ray Sent to Hospital (Sick)						1							
	13-7-16		" Ames " " " "						1							
	13-7-16		Dr Coles " " " "						1							
	14-7-16		Sapr McGuiness Transferred to Home Establishment							1						
	16-7-16		Reinforcement of 1 OR (Dismounted)	1												
	17-7-16		Pnr Duncan Sent to Hospital (Sick)						1							
	18-7-16		Sapr Cole " " " "						1							
	19-7-16		II Cpl Simillie " " " "						1							
	19-7-16		Reinforcement of 2 OR (Mounted)	2												
	21-7-16		Saprs Bridges & Hoyce Sent to Hospital (Sick)						2							
	22-7-16		Sapr Cot Sent to Hospital (Sick)						1							
	24-7-16		Lieut R.B Dunlop returned to Duty. II Cpl Jones to Hos (Sick)						1							
	27-7-16		Corpl Sime J. awarded Military Medal													
	28-7-16		Reinforcement of 2 OR (Dismounted)	2												
	28-7-16		Lieut T.L.S Hobson Taken on Strength													
	29-7-16		II Cpl Jones returned to Duty. 1 LD sent to M.V.C.												1	
	30-7-16		Sapr Wesley Sent to Hospital (Sick)						1							
	31-7-16		Saprs Vanwersbeke & Willson Sent to Hos (Sick)						2							
	31-7-16		LCpl Platt accidently injured (Sent to Hos)						1							

Alan [signature]
Lieut RE for Major RE O.C. 77th Fd Co RE

1875 Wt. W593/826 1,000,000 4/15 J.B.C. & A. A.D.S.S./Forms/C. 2118.

17th Divisional Engineers

77th FIELD COMPANY R. E.

AUGUST 1 9 1 6 ::

Vol 18

Army Form C. 2118

Instructions regarding War Diaries and Intelligence Summaries are contained in F. S. Regs., Part II. and the Staff Manual respectively. Title Pages will be prepared in manuscript.

WAR DIARY
or
INTELLIGENCE SUMMARY

(Erase heading not required.)

77th [illegible] FIELD Coy RE

Place	Date	Hour	Summary of Events and Information	Remarks and references to Appendices
BECORDEL	Aug: 1st	7.0pm	Dismounted portion of company moved from DERNANCOURT to MAMETZ Mounted " " " " " to BECORDEL. At both places the company was in bivouacs.	[initials]
	2nd		Work carried on in completion of dugouts etc: commenced by 5th Div: RE. who the company had relieved. Forward billets shelled. Water cart badly damaged	[initials]
	3rd		Work commenced on communication trench & support line	[initials]
	4th		Work of yesterday carried on. Waggons carting forward materials from back dumps to FRICOURT Dump.	[initials]
	5th		Work of yesterday carried on	[initials]
	6th		All work as yesterday.	[initials]
	7th		do:-	[initials]
	8th		do:-	[initials]
	9th		Work carried on as yesterday	[initials]
	10th		Work as yesterday. Night work with Pioneers & Border Regt: on C.T.	[initials]
	11th		Work on C T & Support trenches carried on. The following message was received from the G.O.C. 17th Div:- "Divisional Commander is very pleased to hear of good work done last night & this morning on C.T. from YORK Trench to DELVILLE WOOD"	[initials]

1875 Wt. W593/826 1,000,000 4/15 J.B.C. & A. A.D.S.S./Forms/C. 2118.

Army Form C. 2118.

Instructions regarding War Diaries and Intelligence Summaries are contained in F. S. Regs., Part II. and the Staff Manual respectively. Title Pages will be prepared in manuscript.

WAR DIARY
or
INTELLIGENCE SUMMARY

(Erase heading not required.)

Place	Date	Hour	Summary of Events and Information	Remarks and references to Appendices
DERNANCOURT.	12th		The dismounted portion of the Coy: moved back from camp near MAMETZ & the mounted portion from the camp at BECORDEL to the camp where they were bivouaced on 1st Aug near DERNANCOURT. [initials]	
do:-	13th		Coy: rested in camp today. Bathing parades etc! [initials]	
do:-	14th		As yesterday. [initials]	
GEZAINCOURT.	15th		Dismounted men entrained at MERICOURT at 4.0 a.m and detrained at CANDAS at 10.30 a.m and marched to GEZAINCOURT. (near DOULLENS) Mounted portion of company accompanied by C.R.E's transport moved off at 4.0 a.m. & marched to GEZAINCOURT. 24 miles. The company was bivouaced in a field for the night. [initials]	
NEUVILLETTE.	16th		The company moved at 2.45 p.m to billets in LE. CLOSERIE. Fm near NEUVILLETTE arriving 5.0 p.m. The men were all billeted in the farm buildings [initials]	
do:-	17th		Drill parades in the morning. Recreation in the afternoon [initials]	
do:-	18th		As yesterday. Major Fleming Lieut Dunlop & details proceeded to SOUASTRE to see the new line about to be taken over [initials]	
St AMAND	19th		The company marched from NEUVILLETTE at midday to relieve 2/2nd London Field Coy:- 56th Division No 1 Section at SOUASTRE. No 2 & No 3 Sections at FONQUEVILLERS with Lieut Holbrow. No 4 Section with Major Fleming at BIENVILLERS. Horse lines at St AMAND [initials]	
do:-	20th		Work commenced by forward sections Nos 2.3.4. on dugouts & revetting communication trenches. No 4 section also commenced work on a new dugout at BIENVILLERS to accomodate No 1 Section. [initials]	

1875 Wt. W593/826 1,000,000 4/15 J.B.C. & A. A.D.S.S./Forms/C. 2118.

Instructions regarding War Diaries and Intelligence Summaries are contained in F. S. Regs., Part II. and the Staff Manual respectively. Title Pages will be prepared in manuscript.

WAR DIARY
or
INTELLIGENCE SUMMARY
(Erase heading not required.)

Army Form C. 2118.

Place	Date	Hour	Summary of Events and Information	Remarks and references to Appendices
ST AMAND.	21st		Work as yesterday. No 1 Section sent men up also for trench work. Others working on making inverse A frames. [initials]	
do:-	22nd		Work as yesterday. [initials]	
SOUASTRE	23rd		Work as yesterday. Mounted section and Hd'. Qr Section moved to camp at SOUASTRE [initials]	
do:	24th		As yesterday [initials]	
do:	25th		No 1 Section moved up to billets with No 4 Section in BIENVILLERS. Party of 13 men under Sergt. Martin proceeded to HENU for work in workshops. Work as yesterday [initials]	
do:	26		As yesterday [initials]	
do:	27		as yesterday [initials]	
do:	28		as yesterday [initials]	
do	29		as yesterday [initials]	
do	30		as yesterday [initials]	
do	31		as yesterday [initials]	

Alan [signature] Lieut. RE
for O.C. 77th Coy RE
1-9-16

2449 Wt. W14957/M90 750,000 1/16 J.B.C. & A. Forms/C.2118/12.

Army Form C. 2118

Instructions regarding War Diaries and Intelligence Summaries are contained in F. S. Regs., Part II. and the Staff Manual respectively. Title Pages will be prepared in manuscript.

WAR DIARY
or
INTELLIGENCE SUMMARY
(Erase heading not required.)

Place	Date	Hour	Summary of Events and Information	Reinforcements: Officers N.C.Os & Men	Reinforcements: Horses & Mules	Casualties – Officers N.C.Os & Men: Killed	Wounded	Died	In Hospital	Evacuated	Casualties – Horses & Mules: Killed	Wounded	Died	In Hospital	Evacuated	Remarks and references to Appendices
	2-8-16		Sapr Wilson M returned to duty													
	2-8-16		Sergt McTaggart Sent to Hos wounded. Pnr Davidson J slightly wounded (at duty)				2									
	3-8-16		Sapr Coulins slightly wounded (at duty)				1									
	5-8-16		Reinforcement of 1 OR (Dismounted) II CpL	1												
	6-8-16		Sapr Wood Sent To Hos Sick Sapr Foster W J Sent to Hos (wounded)				1									
	6-8-16		" Harrison L slightly wounded (at duty)				1									
	7-8-16		Reinforcement of 5 OR (dismounted)	5												
	8-8-16		Sapr Pigott J accidently injured						1							
	8-8-16		Sapr Carden W Sent to hospital wounded				1									
	8-8-16		Sapr Walker and II Cpl Kermode Slightly Wounded at duty				2									
	10-8-16		" Woodcock H Sent to Hospital (Sick)						1							
	11-8-16		1 Riding and 1 Ld Sent to M.V.C												2	
	11-8-16		2 Mules received.		2											
	12-8-16		Sapr Skevington T Sent to Hospital (Sick)		~~2~~				1							
	14-8-16		Sapr Walker T Sent to Hospital (Sick)						1							
	15-8-16		Reinforcement of 7 OR 5 dismounted 2 mounted	7												
	17-8-16		LCpl Radford C Sent to Hospital (Sick)						1							
	19-8-16		Sapr Cook C " " " "						1							
	20-8-16		LCpl Radford C and Sapr Walker T returned to duty													
	21-8-16		One Officers Charger and one Ld received		2											
	25-8-16		Sapr White J and Sapr Langworth J Sent to Hos (Sick)						2	1						
	28-8-16		Sapr White J returned to duty													
	31-8-16		Sapr Tomlinson F Sent to Hos (Sick)													

Alan Mromcreiff Lieut RE
for O.C 77th Coy RE
1-9-16

1875 Wt. W593/826 1,000,000 4/15 J.B.C. & A. A.D.S.S./Forms/C. 2118.

Instructions regarding War Diaries and Intelligence Summaries are contained in F. S. Regs., Part II. and the Staff Manual respectively. Title Pages will be prepared in manuscript.

WAR DIARY
or
INTELLIGENCE SUMMARY

(Erase heading not required.)

Army Form C. 2118.

77 Fd Coy RE vol 14

Place	Date	Hour	Summary of Events and Information	Remarks and references to Appendices
SOUASTRE	Sept. 1st	-	Nos 1 & 4 Sections with Major Fleming in billets at BIENVILLERS } engaged on work duck-boarding & revetting Communication Trenches & deep dugout work. working with 51st Inft. Bgde. Nos 2 & 3 " " Lieut. Holbrow " " " FONQUEVILLERS } Mounted Section & Coy. Hd. Qr. Section at SOUASTRE. work continuing on winter horse-lines	
"	2nd		As yesterday	
"	3rd		As yesterday	
"	4th		As yesterday	
"	5th		As yesterday	
"	6th		Work as yesterday. II Lieut E.G. MORRIS RE took over Horselines and Hd. Qr. Sect at SOUASTRE. LIEUT. A. MONCRIEFF RE took over No 1 Section at BIENVILLERS	
"	7th		Work as yesterday	
"	8th		as yesterday.	
"	9th		As yesterday.	
"	10th		Work by Nos 2 & 4 Section as yesterday. No 1 Section under Lt Moncrieff returned to SOUASTRE in the morning and in the evening No 3 Section under 2nd Lt Butler returned to SOUASTRE	

3449 Wt. W14957/M90 750,000 1/16 J.B.C. & A. Forms/C.2118/12.

Army Form C. 2118.

Instructions regarding War Diaries and Intelligence Summaries are contained in F. S. Regs., Part II. and the Staff Manual respectively. Title Pages will be prepared in manuscript.

WAR DIARY
or
INTELLIGENCE SUMMARY

(Erase heading not required.)

Place	Date	Hour	Summary of Events and Information	Remarks and references to Appendices
SOUASTRE	11th		Work as yesterday by No 2 & 4 Sections. No 1 Section employed making billets for 2 & 4 Section and No 3 Section employed on making new Horse Standing at SOUASTRE. – E. Glen	
"	12th		Work as yesterday by Nos 1, 2, & 3 Sections. No 4 Section returned to SOUASTRE in morning. No 2 Section returned to SOUASTRE in evening. Major Fleming & Lt Holbrow returned to SOUASTRE. E. Glen	
	13th		Nos 1, 2 & 3 Sections under Lt Moncrieff moved to SAILLY; No 4 Section & Lt Holbrow moved to HEBUTERNE. } Nos 1, 2 & 3 Sections making drainage & duckwalking Communication trenches. No 4 Section deep dug out work. E. Glen	
"	14		Work as yesterday. E. Glen	
"	15		As yesterday. E. Glen	
"	16		As yesterday. E. Glen	
"	17		As yesterday. E. Glen	
"	18		As yesterday. E. Glen	
"	19		As yesterday. No 4 Section and Lt Holbrow returned to SOUASTRE. E. Glen	
"	20		No 4 Section employed in billets. No 1, 2 & 3 Sections returned to SOUASTRE. Major Fleming [illegible] of C.R.E. E. Glen	
"	21		Company all back at SOUASTRE. Packing waggons etc. & preparing for move. Decamp handed over to 33rd Div. Major Fleming took over C.R.E.'s duties. Lieut T. L. S. Holbrow, RE temporarily in command of the Company. [initials] The following note was received from VII Corps G.S. 1082 d/20-9-16. Although 17th Div: has only been in VII Corps area a short time the Corps Commander has been much struck by the work done during that period on the trenches in front of HEBUTERNE. He hopes you will inform the units concerned how much he appreciates their hard work. (Sd) F. Lyon, Brig-Gen Gen Staff VII Corps.	

Instructions regarding War Diaries and Intelligence Summaries are contained in F. S. Regs., Part II. and the Staff Manual respectively. Title Pages will be prepared in manuscript.

WAR DIARY
or
INTELLIGENCE SUMMARY
(Erase heading not required.)

Army Form C. 2118

Place	Date	Hour	Summary of Events and Information	Remarks and references to Appendices
GRENAS	22nd	-	Coy moved with 51st Bgd:- from SOUASTRE to GRENAS [initials]	
REMAISNIL	23rd	-	Coy moved with 51st Infy. Bgd:- from GRENAS to REMAISNIL [initials]	
NEUILLY-LE-DIEN	24.		Coy moved from REMAISNIL to training billets at NEUILLY-LE-DIEN [initials]	
do:-	25		Coy in rest [initials]	
do:-	26		Coy in training. Marched to YVRENCHEUX to see tanks. Route march Kit inspection etc:- [initials]	
do:-	27	-	Coy: training II Lieut. E. J. Morris went to Div: Gas school for a course of instruction [initials]	
do:-	28th		Coy training [initials]	
do:-	29th		Coy training [initials]	
do	30th		Coy training [initials]	

Alan [signature] Lieut. RE
for O.C. 77th Coy RE

Instructions regarding War Diaries and Intelligence Summaries are contained in F. S. Regs., Part II. and the Staff Manual respectively. Title Pages will be prepared in manuscript.

WAR DIARY
or
INTELLIGENCE SUMMARY
(Erase heading not required.)

Army Form C. 2118

Place	Date	Hour	Summary of Events and Information	Reinforcements: Officers N.C.O's & Men	Reinforcements: Horses & Mules	Casualties, Officers N.C.O's & Men: Killed	Wounded	Died	In Hospital	Evacuated	Casualties, Horses & Mules: Killed	Wounded	Died	In Hospital	Evacuated	Remarks and references to Appendices
	1-9-16		Sergt Livingstone W, Sapr Gibbs L and Sapr Dunkley W sent to Hos (sick)						3							
	2-9-16		One L.D. Horse sent to M.V.C. Reinforcement of 1 OR (Dismounted)	1											1	
	3-9-16		Sapr Bott T sent to Hospital (sick)						1							
	4-9-16		Sergt Livingstone W returned to Duty. Reinforcement 2 OR (Dismounted)	2												
	5-9-16		Saprs Brown T, Cooke R and Poole F sent to Hos (sick)						3	1						
	6-9-16		Dr Williams sent to Hos (sick) one L D Horse received		1				1							
	7-9-16		Sapr Lee L wounded by shell. sent to (Hos)						1							
	8-9-16		Sapr Jackson S. sent to Hospital (sick)							1						
	9-9-16		Sapr McQuiston W sent to Hos (sick) Sapr Tomlinson F returned to duty						1							
	11-9-16		Dr Williams returned to duty													
	12-9-16		Sappers Cooke R, Gibbs L and Lee L returned to duty													
	14-9-16		Sergt Stratton A and Sapr McLaren sent to Hos (sick)						2							
	"		Sapr Poole F returned to duty													
	15-9-16		Pion Field S sent to Hospital (sick)						1						1	
	16-9-16		Sapr Wilson W wounded (rifle grenade)												1	
	17-9-16		Sergt Wells H and Sapr Hudson W wounded (shell)												2	
	17-9-16		Sapr Dunkley returned to Duty													
	18-9-16		Dr Mercer A sent to Hospital (sick)						1							
	19-9-16		Sapr Ford sent to Hos (sick) Dr Mercer returned to duty						1							
	20-9-16		Sergt Stratton and Sapr Ford returned to duty													
	21-9-16		Sapr McLaren returned to duty													
	25-9-16		" Sims sent to hospital sick						1							
	26-9-16		Corpl Bird T, Sapr Paston E and Pion Cushing E						3							
	27-9-16		Sapr Brown C L and Sapr Owen J sent to Hos (sick) Reinforcement 2 OR (Dis)	2					2							
	29-9-16		II Cpl Loveday J and Sapr Henty P sent to Hospital sick						2							
	30-9-16		Cpl Bird T and Sapr Paston E returned to duty Dr Colbourne F sent to Hos (SICK)						1							

1875 Wt. W593/826 1,000,000 4/15 J.B.C. & A. A.D.S.S./Forms/C. 2118.

Alan Mennell [signature] Lieut R.E.
for O.C 77th Fd Co R.E.

Instructions regarding War Diaries and Intelligence Summaries are contained in F. S. Regs., Part II. and the Staff Manual respectively. Title Pages will be prepared in manuscript.

WAR DIARY
or
INTELLIGENCE SUMMARY
(Erase heading not required.)

Army Form C. 2118

77 Fd Coy R.E.
Vol 15

Place	Date	Hour	Summary of Events and Information	Remarks and references to Appendices
NEUILLY-LE-DIEN	Oct:- 1st	–	Coy in training	
BARLY	2nd		Coy moving up to the trenches moved from NEUILLY-LE-DIEN to BARLY	
HALLOY	3rd		Coy: moved to HALLOY.	
SOUASTRE	4th		Coy moved into the line No 1.2.4 Sections at HEBUTERNE No 3 Sect:- & H.Q. at SAILLY. Waggon lines at SOUASTRE	
do:-	5th		Work commenced in the trenches duckboarding & opening up trenches & C.Ts.	
SAILLY	6th		Work as yesterday. Waggon lines moved from SOUASTRE to Dump behind SAILLY	
do:-	7th		Work continued on duckboarding trenches dugouts & Bgd:- HQ at. HEBUTERNE	
do:-	8th		As yesterday	
do:-	9th		As yesterday	
do:-	10th		Work as yesterday. No3 Section went from SAILLY & relieved No4 at HEBUTERNE No 4 returned to ~~HEB~~ SAILLY	
do:-	11th		Work as yesterday	

(Each entry initialled.)

1875 Wt. W593/826 1,000,000 4/15 J.B.C. & A. A.D.S.S./Forms/C. 2118.

Army Form C. 2118

Instructions regarding War Diaries and Intelligence Summaries are contained in F. S. Regs., Part II. and the Staff Manual respectively. Title Pages will be prepared in manuscript.

WAR DIARY
or
INTELLIGENCE SUMMARY
(Erase heading not required.)

Place	Date	Hour	Summary of Events and Information	Remarks and references to Appendices
SAILLY	12th		Work as yesterday	
do:	13th		No 4 Section went from SAILLY to HEBUTERNE. No 2 & 1 from HEBUTERNE to SAILLY	
do:	14th		No 1 Section proceeded to SOUASTRE to arrange billets for Coy. moving tomorrow No 3 Section came in to SAILLY	
SOUASTRE	15		No 2 & 4 Sections & Hd: Qrs & waggon lines moved to SOUASTRE No 3 Section went out to HEBUTERNE	
do:	16th		No 3 Section carried on work on advanced Bgde: HQ at HEBUTERNE Remainder of Coy: resting at SOUASTRE	
do:	17th		No 3 Section work as yesterday. Coy resting at SOUASTRE also making road at c. Dump	
do	18th		No 3 Section return to SOUASTRE	
MILLY	19th		Coy marched from SOUASTRE to MILLY with 51st Inf. Bgde: group. Lieut. R.B. Dunlop RE took over C.R.E.'s adj: in the absence of adj:	
MILLY	20th		Coy resting at MILLY	
TALMAS.	21st		Transport of coy & Hd: Qrs moved from MILLY to TALMAS. Dismounted men remained at MILLY with Lieut. Holloway RE	

1875 Wt. W593/826 1,000,000 4/15 J.B.C. & A. A.D.S.S./Forms/C. 2118.

Army Form C. 2118

Instructions regarding War Diaries and Intelligence Summaries are contained in F. S. Regs., Part II. and the Staff Manual respectively. Title Pages will be prepared in manuscript.

WAR DIARY
or
INTELLIGENCE SUMMARY
(Erase heading not required.)

Place	Date	Hour	Summary of Events and Information	Remarks and references to Appendices
VILLE.	22nd		Transport marched from TALMAS to VILLE. Dismounted portion of Coy:- moved by motor bus from MILLY to MERICOURT & marched to VILLE. [signature]	
do:-	23.		Coy resting at VILLE [signature]	
do:-	24		do:- [signature]	
do:-	25.		do:- [signature]	
do:-	26		do:- [signature]	
CITEDAL	27th		Coy moved to camp at CITEDAL Major Fleming handed over the company to Lieut. Holloway [signature]	
do:-	28		Coy employed on camp improvements. II Lieut. Whitehead RE joined the company [signature]	
do:-	29th		Coy employed on camp improvements also making duck walks [signature]	
CARNOY.	30th		Dismounted portion of company moved to billets in cellars at LONGEVAL. Mounted portion moved to camp at CARNOY. [signature]	
do:-	31st		Coy commenced work on Deep Dugouts. Steel shelters & duckwalk tracks to the trenches. The last 3 miles being impassable to waggons & the transport of rations etc.:- being carried out by pack. [signature]	

Alan [signature] Lieut RE
for O.C. 77th Coy RE

Army Form C. 2118

Instructions regarding War Diaries and Intelligence Summaries are contained in F. S. Regs., Part II. and the Staff Manual respectively. Title Pages will be prepared in manuscript.

WAR DIARY
or
INTELLIGENCE SUMMARY
(Erase heading not required.)

Place	Date	Hour	Summary of Events and Information	Reinforcements: Officers N.C.O's & Men	Reinforcements: Horses & Mules	Casualties — Officers N.C.O's & Men: Killed	Wounded	In Hospital	Evacuated	Died	Casualties — Horses & Mules: Killed	Wounded	In Hospital	Died	Evacuated	Remarks and references to Appendices
	3-10-16		Sergt Wankling A, Sapr's Dempsey R, Harris J, Hoare S.													
			Upton S, and Woods W.J. Sent to Hospital (Sick)					6								
	-"-		one L.D. Horse sent to M.V.C.												1	
	4-10-16		Sapper Sayers F sent to Hospital (Sick)					1								
	7-10-16		Reinforcement of 3 OR arrive Sapr Dunkley W.R (Slightly Wounded)	3			1									
	8-10-16		Sapr Dempsey R returned to duty Sapr McLaren sent to Hos (Sick)					1								
	10-10-16		Sapr Outram R Killed in action			1										
	-"-		II Cpl McPherson D, Sapr Cowley E and Sapr Stantial J (wounded)				3									
	-"-		Corpl King C slightly wounded. Dr Lowe T sent to Hos (Sick)				1	1								
	12-10-16		1 LD Horse received		1											
	13-10-16		Sapr Gibbs L (Killed in action) Sapr Adlem R (wounded)			1	1									
	16-10-16		Dr Whybrow E G sent to Hospital (Sick)					1								
	-"-		Sergt Martin H " "					1								
	17-10-16		II Cpl McPherson D returned to duty													
	19-10-16		II Lieut W.C Butler admitted to Hospital (Sick)													
	-"-		one officers charger sent to M.V.C Reinforcement 13 OR arrive	13											1	
	22-10-16		Sapr Fisk E sent to Hospital (Sick)					1								
	23-10-16		Sapr Hammett C, Pion Abbott W & Pion Howe sent to Hos (Sick)					3								
	24-10-16		Dr Brown W sent to Hos (Sick) Two LD Horses sent to M.V.C												2	
			Reinforcement of 2 OR arrive	2												
	25-10-16		" of 6 OR arrive Pion Howe W returned	6												
			to duty Sapr Hammett C returned to duty													
	26-10-16		Sapr Perkins C and Dr Burbridge J sent to Hos (Sick)					2								
	28-10-16		II Lieut J.G.O Whitehead joined	1												
	27-10-16		Sapr Henty P sent to Hospital (Sick)					1								
	29-10-16		one officers charger received		1											

Alan Moncrieff Lieut R E
for O.C 77th Field Co R E

1875 Wt. W593/826 1,000,000 4/15 J.B.C. & A. A.D.S.S./Forms/C. 2118.

Instructions regarding War Diaries and Intelligence Summaries are contained in F. S. Regs., Part II. and the Staff Manual respectively. Title Pages will be prepared in manuscript.

WAR DIARY
or
INTELLIGENCE SUMMARY
(Erase heading not required.)

Army Form C. 2118

77 Fd Coy R.E.

Vol 16

Place	Date	Hour	Summary of Events and Information	Remarks and references to Appendices
CARNOY, + LONGEVAL	1st	—	Waggon lines at CARNOY. Sappers billeted in old cellars & deep dugouts at LONGEVAL. Work on deep dugouts in trenches also Bgde. HQrs with assistance of Sapping platoons opening up trenches & cutting support line & C.T.s [signature]	
do:-	2		do:- [signature]	
do:-	3		do:- [signature]	
do:	4		do:- [signature]	
do:	5		do:- [signature]	
do:-	6		do:- [signature]	
do:-	7		do:- [signature]	
do:	8th		do:- [signature]	
do:-	9th		do:- [signature]	
do:-	10		do: [signature]	
do:-	11th		do [signature]	
do			[signature]	

1875 Wt. W593/826 1,000,000 4/15 J.B.C. & A. A.D.S.S./Forms/C. 2118.

Army Form C. 2118

Instructions regarding War Diaries and Intelligence Summaries are contained in F. S. Regs., Part II. and the Staff Manual respectively. Title Pages will be prepared in manuscript.

WAR DIARY
or
INTELLIGENCE SUMMARY
(Erase heading not required.)

Place	Date	Hour	Summary of Events and Information	Remarks and references to Appendices
MEAULTE	12.		Dismounted portion of company moved from LONGEVAL & mounted portion from CARNOY, to MEAULTE on completion of relief by the Field Coys: of the Guards' Divn. [signature]	
do:-	13		Coy in billets at MEAULTE [signature]	
do:-	14		Coy moved billets in MEAULTE [signature]	
do:-	15		Mounted portion of company & Hd:-Qrs moved with C group of the divisional transport to DAOURS. Dismounted portion of company remained in billets at MEAULTE [signature]	
ARGOEUVES.	16		Mounted portion of company moved from DAOURS to ARGOEUVES. Dismounted " " " entrained at EDGE HILL & moved to HANGEST. [signature]	
St PIERRE	17		Mounted portion of company moved from ARGOEUVES to St PIERRE Dismounted " " " " HANGEST to " to rest billets [signature]	
do:-	18th		Coy resting at St PIERRE [signature]	

1875 Wt. W593/826 1,000,000 4/15 J.B.C. & A. A.D.S.S./Forms/C. 2118.

Instructions regarding War Diaries and Intelligence Summaries are contained in F. S. Regs., Part II. and the Staff Manual respectively. Title Pages will be prepared in manuscript.

WAR DIARY
or
INTELLIGENCE SUMMARY
(Erase heading not required.)

Army Form C. 2118

Place	Date	Hour	Summary of Events and Information	Remarks and references to Appendices
St. PIERRE	19th		No 1 Section moved for work on baths etc:- to MOLLIENS VIDAME. Remainder of Coy: resting at St PIERRE [initials]	
FOURDRINOY	20th		Coy moved to FOURDRINOY [initials]	
do:	21st		Coy resting at FOURDRINOY [initials]	
do:	22nd		do: [initials]	
do:	23rd		do: [initials]	
do:	24th		do: [initials]	
do:	25		do [initials]	
do:	26		do: [initials]	
do:	27		do: [initials]	
do:	28th		do: [initials]	
do:	29		do: [initials]	
do:	30		do: [initials]	

Alan Moncrieff Lieut-RE for O C 77th Coy RE

1875 Wt. W593/826 1,000,000 4/15 J.B.C. & A. A.D.S.S./Forms/C. 2118.

Army Form C. 2118

Instructions regarding War Diaries and Intelligence Summaries are contained in F. S. Regs., Part II. and the Staff Manual respectively. Title Pages will be prepared in manuscript.

WAR DIARY
or
INTELLIGENCE SUMMARY
(Erase heading not required.)

Place	Date	Hour	Summary of Events and Information	REINFORCEMENTS		CASUALTIES. Officers NCOs + MEN					Horses + Mules					Remarks and references to Appendices
				Officers NCOs + MEN	Horses + Mules	Killed	Wounded	In Hospital	Evacuated	Died	Killed	Wounded	In Hospital	Died	Evacuated	
	1-11-16		Pion Howe W. Sent to Hospital					1								
	2-11-16		Sapr Griffiths J. " " "					1								
	4-11-16		" Harris W.B. " " " wounded (Shell). Sapr G. Batchelor Sent to Hos (sick)				1	2								
	4-11-16		Reinforcement of 2 O.R. arrive. Corpl Glidle G. Sapr Lewis W. Johns H.,	2												
			Knight W., Holeman A., Meader L.J., Davies R., Bayley J.,													
			wounded (Shell) Sapr Tomlinson F. wounded-shell (remained on duty)				9									
	5-11-16		Sapr Cocke R. wounded (remains at duty)				1									
	6-11-16		" Langworth J. Sent to Hospital (Sick)					1	1							
	9-11-16		L/Corpl Doyle J reverts to rank of Sapper at own request.													
	-do-		Reinforcement of 1 O.R. (mounted) arrives	1												
	11-11-16		Saprs Prest, S.E. + Mills W. sent to R.E. Base Depot, being under age.						2							
	11-11-16		Corpl Butcher P. Sent to Hospital (sick)					1								
	12-11-16		Dr Burbridge J. returned to duty (from Hospital)													
	13-11-16		Corpl Farrow C. sent to Hospital (Sick). Two Officers' Chargers sent to M.V.S.					1	1				2			
	14-11-16		Sapr Griffiths J. returns to duty.													
	15-11-16		Corpl Butcher P. " " " . 2/Lieut J.G.O. Whitehead, R.E. Sent to Hospital (Sick)					1								
	16-11-16		Reinforcements of 8 O.R. arrive.	8												
	18-11-16		Corpl Butcher P. Sent to Hospital (Sick). Sapr Morris W.L. Sent to Hospital (sick)					2								
	20-11-16		Drs Burbridge J. Cowell J., sent to Hospital (sick-evac) " Balmforth " " " "					3	2							
	21-11-16		Reinforcements of 6 O.R. arrives	6												
	26-11-16		Sapr Butler sent to Hospital (Sick)					1								
	27-11-16		Corpl Butcher P. + Sapr Morris W.L. return to duty. Two officers' chargers arrive		2											
	28-11-16		Sapr Cocke R. Sent to Hospital (Sick)					1								
	29-11-16		Reinforcement of 2 O.R. arrive	2												
	30-11-16		Dr Salmon sent to Hospital (Sick)					1								

Alan [signature] Lieut R.E.
for O.C. 77th Field Co, R.E.

1875 Wt. W593/826 1,000,000 4/15 J.B.C. & A. A.D.S.S./Forms/C. 2118.

Army Form C. 2118

77 Fd Coy RE

Vol 17

Instructions regarding War Diaries and Intelligence Summaries are contained in F. S. Regs., Part II. and the Staff Manual respectively. Title Pages will be prepared in manuscript.

WAR DIARY
or
INTELLIGENCE SUMMARY
(Erase heading not required.)

Place	Date	Hour	Summary of Events and Information	Remarks and references to Appendices
MEAULTE	16th		As for previous day. No 4 Section moved to MORLANCOURT.	
"	17th		- do - No 2 Section joined No 4 Section at MORLANCOURT for work Erecting hangars for R.F.C.	
"	18		- do:-	
"	19		- do -	
"	20		- do	
"	21		- do	
"	22nd		Nos 2. 3 & 4 Section rejoined Coy:- at MEAULTE	
BERNAFAY WOOD	23rd		Company moved to BERNAFAY WOOD & relieved 96th (Field) Coy of 20th Div:- and took over work as reserve (field) Company.	
"	24th		Work commenced on wiring & draining intermediate line. Mule Track repairs of duckwalk track. GUILLEMONT Stn Camp. Repairs of Dugouts at Div:- H.Q and Camp improvements.	
"	25		do:-	
"	26		do:-	
"	27		do	

1875 Wt. W593/826 1,000,000 4/15 J.B.C. & A. A.D.S.S./Forms/C. 2118.

Instructions regarding War Diaries and Intelligence Summaries are contained in F. S. Regs., Part II. and the Staff Manual respectively. Title Pages will be prepared in manuscript.

WAR DIARY
or
INTELLIGENCE SUMMARY
(Erase heading not required.)

Army Form C. 2118

Place	1916 Date DECEMBER	Hour	Summary of Events and Information	REINFORCEMENTS: Officers	REINFORCEMENTS: N.C.O's Men	REINFORCEMENTS: Horses & Mules	CASUALTIES Officers N.CO's & Men: Killed	Wounded	In Hospital	Evacuated	Died	CASUALTIES Horses & Mules: Killed	Wounded	In Hospital	Evacuated	Died	Remarks and references to Appendices
	3 –		Sapr Tinneny. F. sent to Hospital						1								
	6th		" White J.E. " " " Reinforcement of 4 O.R. arrive	4					1								
	7th		Saprs Johnstone J & Boxer. T. sent to Hospital. 1 Mule sent to M.V.S. (Sick)						2						1		
	5th		II Cpl Jones. W.G. & Lc Cpl Hicks. F. revert to permanent grade of driver.														
	6th		Corpl G. Gibbons promoted to a/Sergt. II Cpl Murphy. C. to a/Cpl. Dr Lunn. F. to a/Lc Cpl.														
	8th		Sapr Balmforth returned to duty from Hospital														
	– 9 –		Dr Jones W.G. sent to Hospital. Corpl Farrow C. returned from Hospital.						1								
	– 9 –		II Lieut. J.G.O. Whitehead. R.E. evacuated. II Lieut. E. Lonnon R.E. joined unit	1						1							
	– 11 –		Sapr Butler. A.W. returned from Hospital. Sapr Banner J sent to Hospital	[illegible]					1								
			Sapr Johnstone J evacuated							1							
	– 13 –		Reinforcement of 4 O.R. arrive	4													
	– 14 –		Sapr White. J.E. & Drs Jones. W.G. & Salmon returned from Hospital														
	– 18 –		Dr Jones. W.G. evacuated to Rouen for Dental treatment. Sapr Balmforth. S. sent to Hospital						1	1							
	– 20 –		Sapr Hammett. C & Pion. Meaney. M. sent to Hospital						2								
	– 21 –		Pion Chapman. F sent to Hospital; Dr Atwill F. sent to Hospital						2								
	– 22 –		Sapr Malcolm sent to Hospital						1								
	– 26 –		Saprs Blagdon H., Evans. W., & Brown. L.F. sent to Hospital						3								
	– 27 –		Sapr Butler. A.W. sent to Hospital						1								
	– 28 –		Sapr Deeks. slightly wounded by shell fire. Returned to duty.					1									
	– 26 –		Pion. Chapman. F evacuated to C.C.S							1							
	3-11-16		Sapr Savage. W. transferred to (Left half) 109th Railway Co. R.E.														

Alan Moncrieff Lieut. R.E.
for O.C. 77th Field Co. R.E.

1875 Wt. W593/826 1,000,000 4/15 J.B.C. & A. A.D.S.S./Forms/C. 2118.

Army Form C. 2118

WAR DIARY
or
INTELLIGENCE SUMMARY
(Erase heading not required.)

Instructions regarding War Diaries and Intelligence Summaries are contained in F. S. Regs., Part II. and the Staff Manual respectively. Title Pages will be prepared in manuscript.

Place	Date Dec '16	Hour	Summary of Events and Information	Remarks and references to Appendices
FOURDRINOY	1st		Company resting at FOURDRINOY. No 1 Section at MOLLIENS VIDAME	[illegible]
"	2nd		— do — — do —	[illegible]
"	3rd		— do — No 1 Section rejoined from ~~MOLL~~ MOLLIENS VIDAME	[illegible]
"	4th		— do	[illegible]
"	5th		— do —	[illegible]
"	6th		— do —	[illegible]
"	7th		— do —	[illegible]
"	8th		— do —	[illegible]
"	9th		— do —	[illegible]
"	10th		— do —	[illegible]
"	11th		— do —	[illegible]
CORBIE	12th		Company moved from FOURDRINOY to CORBIE	[illegible]
"	13th		" at CORBIE resting	[illegible]
MEAULTE	14th		" moved from CORBIE to MEAULTE	[illegible]
"	15th		Company at MEAULTE employed under C.E. XIV Corps. No 3 Section moved to GROVETOWN.	
"			Erecting Hospital Huts. No 4 Section erecting hangars for R.F.C. at MORLANCOURT	[illegible]
			Nos 1 & 2 Sections employed improving billets and Bathhouse in MEAULTE	

1875 Wt. W593/826 1,000,000 4/15 J.B.C. & A. A.D.S.S./Forms/C. 2118.

Instructions regarding War Diaries and Intelligence Summaries are contained in F. S. Regs., Part II. and the Staff Manual respectively. Title Pages will be prepared in manuscript.

WAR DIARY
or
INTELLIGENCE SUMMARY
(Erase heading not required.)

Army Form C. 2118

Place	Date	Hour	Summary of Events and Information	Remarks and references to Appendices
BERNAFAY WOOD.	28th		Work as yesterday. AM	
do	29		" do " AM	
do:-	30		" do " AM	
do:-	31		" do ! AM	

Alan Moncrieff Lieut RE
for O.C.
77th (Field) Coy RE

1875 Wt. W593/826 1,000,000 4/15 J.B.C. & A. A.D.S.S./Forms/C. 2118.

WAR DIARY
or
INTELLIGENCE SUMMARY
(Erase heading not required.)

Army Form C. 2118

Instructions regarding War Diaries and Intelligence Summaries are contained in F. S. Regs., Part II. and the Staff Manual respectively. Title Pages will be prepared in manuscript.

Place	1917 Date January	Hour	Summary of Events and Information	Reinforce: Off. N.C.O. & Men	Reinforce: Horses & Mules	Casualties – Officers N.C.O's & Men: Killed	Wounded	In Hosp	Evac	Died	Casualties – Horses & Mules: Killed	Wounded	In Hosp	Evacuated	Died	Remarks and references to Appendices
	2		Sapper. Hammett C. returned to duty from Hosp.													
	2		Sapper Griffiths J + Sapper Mosely J. Killed by Shell fire			2										
	3		Reinforcements of 2 O.R. arrived	2												
	4		Sapper. W. Evans returned to duty from Hosp.													
	5		Dr. Cross. T. wounded gun shot; returned to duty				1									
	7		Sapper. Balmforth returned from F.A.													
	9		Sapper Stantial J. sent to F.A. Sapper Harrop sent to F.A. + evac to C.C.S.					1	1							
	14		Sapper Maskell and Driver Broom. Evacuated						2							
	17		Reinforcements 2 O.R. arrived.	2												
	25		4 O.R. sent to England for commission.						4							
	24		Sapper France J. sent to F.A.					1								
	28		Sapper Gilkes H. sent to F.A.					1								
	29		Sapper Evans W. sent to F.A.					1								
	30		Sapper Stantial J evac to C.C.S.						1							
	30		Sapper. Schofield E. sent to F.A.					1								
	31		II Lieut. Pike W. E. killed in action. Machine Gun ~~fire~~			1										

G Connon II Lieut R.E.
for O.C. 77th Field Co. R.E.

1875 Wt. W593/826 1,000,000 4/15 J.B.C. & A. A.D.S.S./Forms/C. 2118.

? 1917

Instructions regarding War Diaries and Intelligence Summaries are contained in F. S. Regs., Part II. and the Staff Manual respectively. Title Pages will be prepared in manuscript.

WAR DIARY
or
INTELLIGENCE SUMMARY
(Erase heading not required.)

~~7th Field~~ 77 Fd Coy RE
Vol 18

Army Form C. 2118

Place	Date	Hour	Summary of Events and Information	Remarks and references to Appendices
BERNAFAY WOOD	1st Jan 1916	-	Coy:- working as Div:- reserve company. Wiring intermediate line: Erecting Guillemont Camp. Erecting Div:- Bomb store. Work at Div:- H.Q. [signature]	
"	2		do: [signature]	
"	3		do: [signature]	
"	4		do: [signature]	
"	5		do: [signature]	
"	6		do: [signature]	
"	7		do: [signature]	
"	8		do: [signature]	
"	9		No 1 Section proceeded to CARNOY camps to work under D.O.R.E [signature]	
"	~~10~~ 10th		Div: wood cutting party joined Coy at BERNAFAY to cut wood in TRONES WOOD. [signature]	
"	11th		Work as previous days. [signature]	
"	12th		do: [signature]	
"	13th		do: [signature]	
"	14th		do: [signature]	
"	15th		do:- [signature]	

1875 Wt. W593/826 1,000,000 4/15 J.B.C. & A. A.D.S.S./Forms/C. 2118.

Instructions regarding War Diaries and Intelligence Summaries are contained in F. S. Regs., Part II. and the Staff Manual respectively. Title Pages will be prepared in manuscript.

WAR DIARY
or
INTELLIGENCE SUMMARY
(Erase heading not required.)

Army Form C. 2118

Place	Date	Hour	Summary of Events and Information	Remarks and references to Appendices
MEAULTE	16th		Coy: moved to MEAULTE	
do:	17th		No 2 & 4 Sections went to No 9 Squadron R.F.C to carry on erection of Hangars No 3 " " " XIV Corps rest station to erect huts. No1 Work in MEAULTE & district	
do.	18th		As yesterday.	
do:-	19		do:	
do	20		do:	
do:-	21		do:	
do	22		do:	
do	23		do:	
do	24		do:	
do:	25		No 2. 3 & 4 Sections returned to MEAULTE	
~~WEDGE~~ COMBLES	26th		Coy moved to Forward area. No 1 2 & 4 at COMBLES. No 3. H.Q & [illegible] at WEDGE WOOD	
do.	27		Duckwalk continued past end of DURHAM TRENCH to hedges at west side of SAILLY SAILLISEL at U8a4.1 Duckwalks laid = 120. Wiring thickened and extended in front of strongpoint U7.a.6.6.	

Instructions regarding War Diaries and Intelligence Summaries are contained in F. S. Regs., Part II. and the Staff Manual respectively. Title Pages will be prepared in manuscript.

WAR DIARY
or
INTELLIGENCE SUMMARY
(Erase heading not required.)

Army Form C. 2118

Place	Date	Hour	Summary of Events and Information	Remarks and references to Appendices
COMBLES.	28.1.17		Duckwalk continued U8a 4.1. to U8a 6.1. to roadway. Work complete. Wiring continued & thickened in front of Strongpoint U.7a.6.6.	
— do —	29.1.17		Wiring continued at Strong Point U7a66. Work started on Trench and Dugout for Coy Hdqts DURHAM TRENCH. Work started on Dugouts in COPSE RESERVE Strong Point.	
— do —	30.1.17		Thickening wire at Strong Point U7a66. Dugout in DURHAM TRENCH progressing favourably, and also Dugouts in COPSE RESERVE.	
— do —	31.1.17		Wire finished round strongpoints U7a66. Dugouts in DURHAM TRENCH — CAMEL COPSE — COPSE RESERVE making good progress.	

E Lonnon
2 Lt R.E.
for OC 77th Field Coy R.E.

1875 Wt. W593/826 1,000,000 4/15 J.B.C. & A. A.D.S.S./Forms/C. 2118.

Instructions regarding War Diaries and Intelligence Summaries are contained in F. S. Regs., Part II. and the Staff Manual respectively. Title Pages will be prepared in manuscript.

WAR DIARY
or
INTELLIGENCE SUMMARY
(Erase heading not required.)

1/1 Fd Coy RE

Army Form C. 2118

Vol 19

Place	Date	Hour	Summary of Events and Information	Remarks and references to Appendices
	FEBRUARY			
COMBLES.	1		Working on new Support line on left and right of CHEESE SUPPORT — Dugouts at CAMEL COPSE DURHAM TRENCH — COPSE RESERVE. NEW STRONG POINT U7665. — CHEESE SUPPORT.	[illegible]
do —	2		do -	[illegible]
— do —	3.		do.	[illegible]
do	4th		do.	[illegible]
— do —	5th		"	[illegible]
— do —	6th		"	[illegible]
— do —	7th		"	[illegible]
— do —	8th		"	[illegible]
— do —	9th		"	[illegible]
— do —	10th		"	HDS
— do —	11		"	HDS
— do —	12		"	HDS
— do —	13		"	HDS
— do —	14		"	HDS
— do —	15		"	HDS
— do —	16		"	HDS
— do —	17		"	HDS
— do —	18		"	HDS
— do —	19		"	HDS
MANSEL CAMP	20		Resting	HDS
FRANVILLERS	21		Coy in Billets training	HDS
— do —	22		— do —	HDS
— do —	23		— do —	HDS
	24		— do — Nos 2 & 4 Sections proceeded to Heilly on detachment — for work on 36 C.C.S.	HDS

1875 Wt. W593/826 1,000,000 4/15 J.B.C. & A. A.D.S.S./Forms/C. 2118.

Instructions regarding War Diaries and Intelligence Summaries are contained in F. S. Regs., Part II. and the Staff Manual respectively. Title Pages will be prepared in manuscript.

WAR DIARY
or
INTELLIGENCE SUMMARY
(Erase heading not required.)

7th Fd Coy RE

Army Form C. 2118

Place	Date	Hour	Summary of Events and Information	Remarks and references to Appendices
	FEBRUARY.			
FRANVILLERS	25th		Company fitted + tested with small box respirator	HDS
	26th		No 1 Section proceeded on detachment to Contay working under Town Major	HDS
	27th			HDS
	28.		No. 2 + 4 Section returned from Heilly	

1875 Wt. W593/826 1,000,000 4/15 J.B.C. & A. A.D.S.S./Forms/C. 2118.

Instructions regarding War Diaries and Intelligence Summaries are contained in F. S. Regs., Part II. and the Staff Manual respectively. Title Pages will be prepared in manuscript.

WAR DIARY
or
INTELLIGENCE SUMMARY
(Erase heading not required.)

Army Form C. 2118

Place	1917 Date FEBRUARY	Hour	Summary of Events and Information	REINFORCEMENTS Off	REINFORCEMENTS H+M	CASUALTIES Officers N.C.Os + Men: Killed	Wounded	In Hosp	Evac	Died	CASUALTIES Horses + Mules: Killed	Wounded	In Hosp	Evac	Died	Remarks and references to Appendices
	4th		Sapper Boxer T. J. sent to F.A					1								
	6		Major Holbrow to No. New Zealand Stat. Hosp. Amien. Cpl Sime sent to F.A					2								
	7th		Dr Hargreaves A. sent to F.A. Sap Gilkes returned from F.A.					1								
	9th		C.Q.M.S. Dickensen H. evacuated to C.C.S. Sapr Boxer evacuated to C.C.S.						2							
	9th		A/Cpl Belmont W. promoted to a/Cpl.													
	12th		Cpl Murphy C. slightly wounded by shell fire returned to duty				1									
	13th		Sapr Schofield returned from F.A. Reinforcements 3 officers + 56 R arrived	8												
	13th		Sapr Evans evacuated to C.C.S.						1							
	14th		Dr Young sent to F.A					1								
	15th		Cpl Murphy + Sapper Davis sent to F.A					2								
	16th		Pion Searle sent to F.A. Cpl Murphy + Pion Searle evacuated to C.C.S.						2							
	16th		Sap Griffin to be L/Cpl. Dr Hargreaves returned from F.A. Dr Young returned from F.A.													
	17th/16th		L/Cpl Cooper to be a/2 Cpl.													
	17th		a/2 Cpl Cooper to be a/Cpl.													
	18th		Sapr Barry sent to F.A. Pion Chapman returned from F.A. Sap Davis + Blogg? evac to C.C.S.					1	2							
	19th		Sergt Livingstone to be a/C.S.M. Sapr France evac to C.C.S.						1							
	21st		Cpl Sime returned from F.A. Reinforcements 1 O. R arrived	1												
	22nd		Sapper Storey sent to F.A					1								
	23rd		L/Cpl Shields sent to F.A. 1 L.D. Horse sent to M.V.S					1	*				1			
	24th		Saprs. Morris + Jackson sent to F.A					2								
	25th		-do. Day + Anderson sent to F.A					2								
	27th		L/Cpl Shields returned from F.A.													
	28th		Sapper Jackson returned from F.A. Cpl Belmont granted 3rd rate of E Pay													
	28th		Sapper William granted 3rd rate of E Pay													

H. D. Stanier Lt. R.E.
for O.C. 77th Field Coy R.E.

1875 Wt. W593/826 1,000,000 4/15 J.B.C. & A. A.D.S.S./Forms/C. 2118.

Instructions regarding War Diaries and Intelligence Summaries are contained in F. S. Regs., Part II. and the Staff Manual respectively. Title Pages will be prepared in manuscript.

77th Field Coy RE

WAR DIARY
or
INTELLIGENCE SUMMARY
(Erase heading not required.)

Army Form C. 2118

vol 20

Place March 1st 1917	Date	Hour	Summary of Events and Information	Remarks and references to Appendices
VADENCOURT	1st		Company moved to VADENCOURT, in billets	HDS
– do –	2nd		" " "	HDS
– do –	3rd		– do – do –	HDS
– do –	4th		– do " " do " "	HDS
– do –	5th		" do " " do " "	HDS
– do –	6th		" do " " do " "	HDS
– do –	7th		"	HDS
– do –	8th			HDS
– do –	9th			HDS
– do –	10th			HDS
– do –	11th			HDS
– do –	12			HDS
GEZAINCOURT	13		Company moved to GEZAINCOURT, in huts	HDS
BERNATRE	14.3.17		" " " BERNATRE, in billets	HDS
LABROYE	15.3.17		" " " LABROYE, in billets	HDS
– do –	16.3.17		" " " " "	HDS
– do –	17.3.17		" " " " "	HDS
– do –	18.3.17			

March 1917

Instructions regarding War Diaries and Intelligence Summaries are contained in F. S. Regs., Part II. and the Staff Manual respectively. Title pages will be prepared in manuscript.

77th Field Coy R.E.

WAR DIARY
or
INTELLIGENCE SUMMARY.
(Erase heading not required.)

Army Form C. 2118.

Place	Date	Hour	Summary of Events and Information	Remarks and references to Appendices
LABROYE	18.3.17		Company in billets.	HDS
-do-	19.3.17		" " "	HDS
FILLIEVRES	20.3.17		" " "	HDS
ST. POL	21.3.17		Company under canvas. Erecting 18th Corps Reinforcement Depôt Camp.	HDS
-do-	22.3.17		" " " " " "	HDS
-do	23.3.17		" " " " " "	HDS
-do-	24.3.17		" " " " " "	HDS
-do-	25.3.17		" " " " " "	HDS
-do	26.3.17		" " " " " "	HDS
-do	27.3.17		" " " " " "	HDS
-do-	28.3.17		" " " " " "	HDS
-do-	29.3.17		" " " " " "	HDS
-do-	30.3.17		" " " " " "	HDS
-do-	31.3.17		" " " " " "	HDS
-do-			"	

A5834 Wt. W4973/M687 750,000 8/16 D. D. & L. Ltd. Forms/C.2118/13.

March 1917

77th Field Coy R.E.

Instructions regarding War Diaries and Intelligence Summaries are contained in F. S. Regs., Part II. and the Staff Manual respectively. Title pages will be prepared in manuscript.

WAR DIARY
or
INTELLIGENCE SUMMARY.
(Erase heading not required.)

Army Form C. 2118.

Place	Date March 1917	Hour	Summary of Events and Information	Reinforcements: Officers + O.R.	Reinforcements: Horses + Mules	Casualties Officers, N.C.Os and Men: Killed	Wounded	In Hosp	Evacuated	Died	Casualties Horses and Mules: Killed	Wounded	In Hosp	Evac	Died	Remarks and references to Appendices
VADENCOURT	1.3.17.		1 L.D. Horse Vet. Evac. Sapr Storey A. Evacuated						1					1		
"	2.3.17		Cpl Sime J. to F.A. Cpl Sime J. Evacuated, Saprs Barry, Anderson, and Pnr Day from F.A.					1	1							
"	5.3.17		L/Cpl Griffin C. raised to Std rate of E. Pay.													
"	6.3.17.		Sapr Hoare sent to F.A. 11 O.R. Reinforcements joined from Base	11												
"	8.3.17		L/Cpl Carter A. appd 2/Cpl, Sapr Parton appd 2/L/Cpl. Sapr Hoare Evacuated						1							
"	10.3.17		2/Cpl Carter A. to be A/Cpl.													
"	11.3.17		Sergt Stephenson, Cpl Gibbons, Saprs Black + Barrett raised to Std rate of E. Pay													
"	12.3.17		Sapr Harrison transferred to 149th Army Troops Coy, 3 Riding, 1 L.D. Reinforcements		4											
GEZAINCOURT	13.3.17		Sapr Robertson to Base for dentures, Sapr Cadwallader to F.A. Sapr Cadwallader Evac.					1	1							
LABROYE	15.3.17		Sapr Campbell to F.A. Cpl Farrow to Special Works Park Boulogne					1								
"	16.3.17		Sergt Bird, Spr Brealey + Dr Round sent to F.A. sick					3								
"	18.3.17		Sergt King awarded Italian Decoration, Bronze Medal for Military Valour													
"	19.3.17		1 O.R. joined from Base, Sergt Brindly left on leave to U.K.													
FILLIEVRES	20.3.17		2 Lt Lemon E. left on leave to U.K.													
ST POL	21.3.17.		Sapr Morris from Hosp., Sapr Bartlett returned from leave.													
"	23.3.17.		L/Cpl Roberts to be 2/L/Cpl. Saprs Upton, Massey, Scott raised to Std rate of E.P.													
"			Pnr Holroyd remustered "Shoemaker" Pnr													
"	24.3.17		Capt. C. J. W. Vasey joined vice Major Holbrow evac.	1												
"	25.3.17		2 Lt Morris E. to C.C.S. Sapr Kent to F.A.					1								
"	27.3.17		Sapr Middleton to F.A.					1								
"	28.3.17		Dr Woodman to F.A. 1 O.R. joined from Base	1				1								
"	31.3.17		Saprs Dempsey, Doyle, Fisk raised to Std rate of E. Pay.													
			A/Cpl Carter to be A/Sergt, 2 Cpl Thain to be A/Cpl, 2nd Cpl Sheils to be A/Cpl													

H D S Tamier Lt R.E.
for O.C. 77th Field Coy R.E.

A5834 Wt. W4973/M687 750,000 8/16 D. D. & L. Ltd. Forms/C.2118/13.

April 1917 : 77th Field Coy RE

17

Vol 21

Army Form C. 2118.

Instructions regarding War Diaries and Intelligence Summaries are contained in F. S. Regs., Part II. and the Staff Manual respectively. Title pages will be prepared in manuscript.

WAR DIARY
or
INTELLIGENCE SUMMARY.
(Erase heading not required.)

Place	Date	Hour	Summary of Events and Information	Remarks and references to Appendices
	1.4.17		Company at ST POL working on 18th Corps Reinforcement Camp.	[illegible]
	2.4.17		as for previous day	[illegible]
	3.4.17		as for previous day	[illegible]
	4.4.17		as for previous day	[illegible]
	5.4.17		Company left ST POL at 10.0 am. Arrived MONTS-EN-TERNOIS 2.30 pm.	[illegible]
	6.4.17		Company at MONTS-EN-TERNOIS.	[illegible]
	7.4.17		Company left MONTS-EN-TERNOIS 11.0 am Arrived LIGNEREUIL 2.30 pm.	[illegible]
	8.4.17		Company left LIGNEREUIL 9.0 am. Arrived LATTRE ST QUENTIN 1.30 pm.	[illegible]
	9.4.17		Company at LATTRE ST. QUENTIN	[illegible]
	10.4.17		Company left LATTRE ST. QUENTIN 5.0 pm. in 3 Echelons (A. B & C)	[illegible]
	11.4.17		'A' Echelon arrived ARRAS 11.0 am. 'B' Echelon on Route to ARRAS. C Echelon at BERNEVILLE	[illegible]
	12.4.17		A Echelon at ARRAS. 'B' Echelon arrived ARRAS at 7.0 am. 'C' Echelon at BERNEVILLE. Nos 1 & 4 Sections sent to SCARPE CANAL BANK repairing same. LT STANIER in Command.	[illegible]
	13.4.17		Company HdQrs & 2 Sections ARRAS. 2 Sections SCARPE CANAL repairing same. 'C' Echelon rejoined at 12.0 noon.	[illegible]
	14.4.17		As for 13th. All sappers working on SCARPE CANAL	[illegible]
	15.4.17		As for 13th. 1 & 4 Sections working on SCARPE CANAL 2 & 3 Sections MINING dugouts at QUARRY FEUCHY CHAPEL	[illegible]
	16.4.17		As for 15th. Ammunition taken down canal to ATHIES	[illegible]
	17.4.17		As for 16th " " " " "	[illegible]
	18.4.17		Nos 2 & 3 Sections ceased work on FEUCHY CHAPEL dugouts and returned to billets. Nos 1 & 4 still on canal	[illegible]

A5834 Wt. W4973/M687 750,000 8/16 D. D. & L. Ltd. Forms/C.2118/13.

April 1917. 77th Field Coy R.E. (2)

Instructions regarding War Diaries and Intelligence Summaries are contained in F. S. Regs., Part II. and the Staff Manual respectively. Title pages will be prepared in manuscript.

WAR DIARY
or
INTELLIGENCE SUMMARY.

(Erase heading not required.)

Army Form C. 2118.

Place	Date	Hour	Summary of Events and Information	Remarks and references to Appendices
	19.4.17		Company moved to billets at ATHIES approx H 21. a. 3. 6. No 3 Section digging assembly trench at MONCHY. Site for new assembly trench from LONE COPSE to river SCARPE was reconnoitred by O.C.	[illegible]
	20.4.17		No 2 Section worked on M.G. emplacements in front line near MONCHY.	[illegible]
	21.4.17		Nos 1-3 & 4 Sections working on roads in FEUCHY. ~~No 2 Sect. with working party of 2 Coys of Pioneers digging assembly trench from LONE COPSE to river SCARPE.~~ No 2 Section prepared site for Assembly Trench but owing to non delivery of orders Pioneer working party did not arrive.	[illegible]
	22.4.17		Moved from Billets at ATHIES to Support line in H 29 a. No 2 Sect with 3 Coys Pioneers digging Assembly Trench from LONE COPSE to River SCARPE	[illegible]
	23.4.17		During night company with 3 Coys Pioneers dug ~~trench~~ front line fire trench from LONE COPSE southwards to near BAYONET TRENCH. Orders for work not issued by Bde till 10.30 pm & owing to failure of guide provided by infantry work did not commence till 2 am	
	24.4.17		Wiring & consolidating points in front line trench between LONE COPSE & RIVER SCARPE.	
	25.4.17		Company returned to Billets in ARRAS.	
	26.4.17		Company proceeded by train to SAULTY; thence to billets in LE CAUROY	
	27.4.17		Company resting in LE CAUROY	
	28.4.17		" " "	
	29.4.17		" " " Orders received to move on 2.5.17.	
	30.4.17		" " " Previous order cancelled. Company ordered to move on 1.5.17	
	~~31.4.17~~			

[signature] Capt. R.E.
for O.C. 77th Field Coy R.E.

A5834 Wt. W4973/M687 750,000 8/16 D. D. & L. Ltd. Forms/C.2118/13.

April 1917 77th Field Company RE

Instructions regarding War Diaries and Intelligence Summaries are contained in F. S. Regs., Part II. and the Staff Manual respectively. Title pages will be prepared in manuscript.

WAR DIARY
or
INTELLIGENCE SUMMARY.
(Erase heading not required.)

Army Form C. 2118.

Place	Date	Hour	Summary of Events and Information	Reinforcements: Officers N.C.O.s + Men	Reinforcements: Horses + Mules	Casualties Officers N.C.O.s + Men: Killed	Wounded	In Hospital	Evacuated	Died	Casualties Horses + Mules: Killed	Wounded	In Hospital	Evacuated	Died	Remarks and references to Appendices
	1.4.17		Pion Starbuck + Rainford joined from Base, Sap Bowman + Greenwood joined from Hos. Reinf. Sergt Bryndley appd A/C.S.M.	4												
	2.4.17		Sap Hobbs to Hd. 3 O.Rs joined from No 2 Reinforcement Coy, Sap Prescott transferred to Troops Trans Boulogne	3				1	1							
	3.4.17		Dr Burbridge to F.A. Capt Vasey to be Temp Major.					1								
	4.4.17		Sap Gilkes forfeits 21 days pay, Cpl Glennie to be A/Sergt.													
	5.4.17		L/Cpl Lunn to A/Cpl. Sap Tressier + White to be Pd. L/Cpls.													
	6.4.17		A/Cpl Lunn to be 2/Cpl.													
	7.4.17		Dr Whitaker to F.A.													
	11.4.17		Sap Batchelor transferred to Troops Transportation Depot						1							
	12.4.17		Sap Garforth joined	1												
	10.4.17		Sap Barrett appd Pd L/Cpl													
	~~9.4.17~~	9.4.17	Sap Duncan + Dr Taylor 60802 left on leave, Major Holloway evac to England Dr Owens 14 days F.P. No 1, Dr Saunders 7 days pay						1							
	11.4.17		3 Bicycles received from D.A.D.O.S.													
	16.4.17		L/Cpl Barlin + Sap Hewett slightly wounded remained at duty 2 Lt Morris to 17th Div Hd Qrs				2									
	18.4.17		Sergt Stephenson wounded, Sap Scott killed by shell fire, Sp Smith W J joined. Sap Hobbs transferred	1		1	1									
	19.4.17		Dr Saunders to C.R.S. 2/Cpl Belmont to be A/Sergt.					1								
	20.4.17		Dr Wells killed, Dr Miller died, shell fire			1				1						
	21.4.17		Dr Whitaker evac, L/Cpl Saunders joined, 2/Cpl Clarke to F.A.	1				1	1							
	22.4.17		Dr Taylor rejoined from leave, Saps Francis, Green + Parker joined	3												
	23.4.17		Dr Williams to F.A. evac to C.C.S.					1	1							
	24.4.17		Sergt King F.P. No 1 14 from 1.9.14 Sappers Leaper + Smith joined Sap Owen wounded Pion Abbott to F.A.	2			1	1								
			Sap Brealey to R.E.T.C. Newark 9.4.17						1							
	25.4.17		2 Lt Lemon + 5 O.R wounded by shell fire. Sap Duncan rejoined from leave				6									
	26.4.17		Sap Middleton transferred 12.4.17 L/Cpl Carter, Gibbon G, Gibbon W, Cooper M to be 2/Cpls R.E. Records													
	27.4.17		Sergt Bird granted F.P. No 1 vide art 637 of R.W.													
	28.4.17		Dr Millum to be L/Cpl Pd 2/Cpl Barlow to be 2/Cpl. L/Cpl Crumpler to be A/Cpl													
	30.4.17		Sap Tomlinson 3 days F.P. No 1.													

G W Vasey
Major RE
O.C. 77th Field Coy RE

A5834 Wt. W4973/M687 750,000 8/16 D. D. & L. Ltd. Forms/C.2118/13.

MAY 1917

Instructions regarding War Diaries and Intelligence Summaries are contained in F. S. Regs., Part II. and the Staff Manual respectively. Title pages will be prepared in manuscript.

WAR DIARY
or
INTELLIGENCE SUMMARY.
(Erase heading not required.)

77th Field Coy RE

Army Form C. 2118.

Place	Date	Hour	Summary of Events and Information	Remarks and references to Appendices
LE CAUROY.	1-5-17	3.30pm	Company left LE CAUROY – marched to GRAND RULLECOURT thence by bus to Y huts (Map 51c)	[illegible]
	2-5-17	—	At Y huts.	[illegible]
ST NICHOLAS	3-5-17	8 am.	Marched from above camp to bivouacs E. of ST NICHOLAS.	[illegible]
	4-5-17	—	Bivouacs near ST NICHOLAS. Company employed on fatigues & training.	[illegible]
	5-5-17		—— do ——	[illegible]
	6-5-17		do	[illegible]
	7-5-17		do	[illegible]
	8-5-17		Coy in tents near ST NICHOLAS, G10d 8.2 training & fatigues.	[illegible]
	9-5-17		1 off. and 1 Sect moved up to take over from 64th Coy RE	[illegible]
	10-5-17		Company less one Sect moved to Rly Cutting at H7b4.8 relieve 64th Coy	[illegible]
	11-5-17		Work – making deep dugouts for R.F.A. at gun positions —— 3 Sections	[illegible]
	12-5-17		" Making mining cases etc and working Sawmill for RE – 1 Section.	[illegible]
	13-5-17		do	[illegible]
	14-5-17		do	[illegible]
	15-5-17		do	[illegible]
	16-5-17		do	[illegible]
	17-5-17		do	[illegible]
	18-5-17		do	[illegible]
	19-5-17		do	[illegible]
	20-5-17		do	[illegible]

A5834 Wt. W4973/M687 750,000 8/16 D. D. & L. Ltd. Forms/C.2118/13.

(2)

May 1917

Instructions regarding War Diaries and Intelligence Summaries are contained in F. S. Regs., Part II. and the Staff Manual respectively. Title pages will be prepared in manuscript.

WAR DIARY
or
INTELLIGENCE SUMMARY.
(Erase heading not required.)

77th Field Coy RE

Army Form C. 2118.

Vol 22

Place	Date	Hour	Summary of Events and Information	Remarks and references to Appendices
St Nicholas	21-5-17	–	3 Sections on Deep Dugouts 1 Section on mining cases. Relieved 93rd Coy.	[illegible]
B-30c.	22-5-17		2 Sections on Dugouts. 1 Section wiring front line 1 section Trench work	[illegible]
"	23 –		do: –	[illegible]
"	24 –		do: –	[illegible]
"	25 –		do: –	[illegible]
"	26 –		do: –	[illegible]
"	27 –		do: –	[illegible]
"	28 –		do: –	[illegible]
"	29 –		do: –	[illegible]
H.1.D.3.3.	30.		Moved to railway cutting. Div: moved out to rest. The company was left in to carry on 17th Corps work on Corps line.	[illegible]
"	31		do: – :	

Alan Moncrieff Capt RE
O.C. 77th Coy RE

A5834 Wt. W4973/M687 750,000 8/16 D. D. & L. Ltd. Forms/C.2118/13.

Army Form C. 2118.

WAR DIARY
or
INTELLIGENCE SUMMARY.
(Erase heading not required.)

May 1917 — 77th Field Coy RE

Instructions regarding War Diaries and Intelligence Summaries are contained in F. S. Regs., Part II. and the Staff Manual respectively. Title pages will be prepared in manuscript.

Place	Date	Hour	Summary of Events and Information	Reinforcements: Officers & Men	Reinforcements: Horses & Mules	Casualties Officers & Men: Killed	Wounded	In Hospital	Evacuated	Died	Casualties Horses & Mules: Killed	Wounded	In Hospital	Evacuated	Died	Remarks and references to Appendices
	1.5.17															
	2.5.17		Sapper Laycock & Cook to C.R.S. Sapper Bell transferred to R.E.T.C. Newark					2								
	3.5.17		L/Cpl Tresise G to F.A. Sapper Anderson to R.E.T.C. Aldershot. Dr Worthington to C R S					1								
	4.5.17		Sappers Evans, Unwin & Goodwin joined from No 5 RE Sappers Benstead, Thorne & Marsland from No 2, 2/Cpl Sheils	6				2								
	5.5.17															
	6.5.17		II Lt Phillips to F.A.					1								
	7.5.17		Dr Hall to F.A. Cpl Shelton & Dr Worthington from C.R.S. II Lt Bargeman joined, Dr Lowe from command.	1				1								
	8.5.17		Sap Tomlinson to C.R.S					1								
	9.5.17		Saps Shepherd, Whiston, White & Wright joined, L/Cpl Tresise G evacuated	4					1							
	10.5.17		Sap Rowland to C.R.S, Sapper Laycock from C.R.S, 1 Officers Charger Vet Evac					1						1		
	11.5.17		Sap Cook from C.R.S, Dr Hall evacuated to C.C.S, Sap Rowland Evac						2							
	12.5.17		Sap Morgan joined	1												
	13.5.17		2nd Cpl Clarke from Hosp.													
	14.5.17		8 O.R joined from RE Base Depot	8												
	15.5.17		Sapper Tomlinson evacuated. 2nd Cpl Gibbons W to R.E.T.C Newark						1							
	16.5.17		Sap Rooke to F.A					1								
	17.5.17		Sap Marsland to F.A, 2/Cpl Barlow & Murphy revert to 2nd Cpl, 2nd Cpl Roberts reverts to L/Cpl.					1								
	18.5.17		Pnr Rainford to 210 Field Coy Sap Lloyd to 84th Field Coy 2nd Cpl Edwards & Crumpler to be 2/Cpl L/Cpl Barton to be 2nd Cpl.													
	19.5.17		1 L.D. Mule shot by A.D.V.S, Sap Milne wounded by shell fire to F.A.				1	1			1					
	20.5.17															
	21.5.17		1 Riding Horse condemned, S.Hoe Smith Mosey joined from No 2	1												
	22.5.17		L/Cpl Radford on Leave													
	23.5.17		L/Cpl McPherson on Leave, Cpl Cooper & Sapper Slade to Rest Camp Boulogne, Sapper Milnes from C.C.S.													
	24.5.17		Sapper Marsland from F.A													
	25.5.17		Sap Ketteridge, Drs Baylis & Burbridge & Capt Dunlop on Leave to U.K. 1 L.D Horse died from wounds												1	
	26.5.17		Sapper Skinner to F.A. Sap Kenward joined from Base	1				1								
	27.5.17		Capt Moncrieff & Pnr Grisdale rejoined Unit from Base. Sapper Midland killed, Sap Litchfield wounded by shell fire.			1	1									
	28.5.17		Dr Jarvis to F.A, Pnr Eaton to F.A. Spr Hood wounded shell fire Spr Morris W to F.A				1	1#								
	29.5.17															
	30.5.17															
	31.5.17		Dr Tayler C.W. to C.R.S.					1								

Alan Harwood Capt RE
O.C. 77th Field Coy RE

A5834 Wt. W4973/M687 750,000 8/16 D. D. & L. Ltd. Forms/C.2118/13.

JUNE 1917 77TH FIELD COY R.E.

WAR DIARY

or

INTELLIGENCE SUMMARY

(Erase heading not required.)

Army Form C. 2118

Instructions regarding War Diaries and Intelligence Summaries are contained in F. S. Regs., Part II. and the Staff Manual respectively. Title Pages will be prepared in manuscript.

Sheet No (67)

Place	Date	Hour	Summary of Events and Information	Reinforcements All Ranks	Reinforcements Horses and Mules	Casualties Officers N.C.Os and Men Killed	Wounded	In Hospital	Evacuated	Died	Casualties Horses and Mules Killed	Wounded	In Hospital	Evacuated	Died	Remarks and references to Appendices
RAILWAY CUTTING H.7 b 3.9 SHEET 51B	1.6.17		Sapper Hood A from C.O.R.S to duty. Pion Eaton Evacuated 31.5.17						1							
	2.6.17		Major Vasey, Sergt King + Pion Chapman leave to U.K. Sapper Perry joined from 149 A.T. Coy R.E.	1												
	3.6.17		Dr Jarvis from F.A. Sapper Holroyd to F.A.					1								
	4.6.17		Spr Kerr, Robertson, Pion Abbott W, Dr Woodman + Saunders evacuated. Sapr Halstead to U.P.L.C.						5							
	5.6.17															
	6.6.17		Driver Taylor C.W. from C.R.S. Sapper Halstead to be 9 U.P.L.C. Sapper Stekfield + Skinner to R.E.T.C. Newark													
	7.6.17		x Capt Dunlop. L/Cpl Radford, Spr Kittenidge, Barbridge from leave													
	8.6.17		L/Cpl Longe + Spr Littlewood to 3rd Army Rest C. Boulogne. Cpl Cooper Spr Slade from Rest Camp BOULOGNE. Spr Holroyd from F.A.													
	9.6.17		Lt Slaman, C.S.M. Livingston, Spr Marland + Cook leave to U.K. Lt Jenkins W. joined from 17th Div Depot Batt	1												
	10.6.17															
	11.6.17															
WANQUETIN	12.6.17		1 Riding 1 L.D. 1 MULE drawn from 29 M.V.S. Sapper Garforth evac sick		3				1							
	13.6.17		Lt Dunlop awarded M.C. 10.O.R on detachment to D.O. RE													
	14.6.17		Drs Lowe, Taylor, Sapr Lloyd M. + Ingram to F.A.					4								
	15.6.17		1.O.R on detachment to XVII Corps School. Dr Jones to F.A. Sap Morris from F.A. 1 O.R. Charger drawn		1			1								
POMMERA	16.6.17		2nd Lt Slim, L/Cpl White + Spr McGroggan leave to U.K. C.S.M. Livingston, Spr Cook + Marland from leave.													
	17.6.17		Spr Ingram R.A. evac sick to No 6 Stat. Hospital					1								
	18.6.17		Sapper Sawtell to F.A. Spr Spears to F.A. 10.O.R rejoined from D.O. RE					2								
	19.6.17		Dr Taylor C.W. from F.A. Spr Spears + Sawtell evac sick						2							
	20.6.17															
RAILWAY CUTTING H.7 b 3.9 SHEET 51.B.	21.6.17		2nd Cpl Parlin L/Cpl Treise 1 Dr Evans joined from Base. 2nd Cpl Parlin to be Cpl	3												
	22.6.17		Cpl Parlin to be A/Sergt. L/Cpl Longe + Spr Littlewood from 3rd Army Rest Camp. Drs Lowe + Jones H evac sick						2							
	23.6.17		Cpl Moncrieff, Cpl Smith, Spr Matthews + Pion Meaney leave to U.K.													
	24.6.17		2nd Cpl Carmichael to F.A. Sapper Lloyd M. evac					1	1							
	25.6.17		Spr Harrison to 3rd Army Rest Camp. 2nd Cpl Carmichael from F.A. 1 L.D. Horse to 29th M.V.S.					[illegible]						1		
	26.6.17		Lt Slaman H.D. + Dr Lane to 17th Div Depot Batt. 6 O.R. reinforcements from No 9 R.E. Coy R.E.	6												
	27.6.17		2nd Lt Slim + L/Cpl White rejoined from leave. Spr R. Campbell to XVII Corps School. Spr Dempsey from XVII Corps School													
	28.6.17		A/Sergt Bird to S.M.E. Chatham for commission													
	29.6.17		A/Cpl Sheils + 2nd Cpl Barlow to 51st Brigade School as Instructors. Spr McGroggan from leave. Spr Unwin to C.R.S					x	1							
	30.6.17		A/Sergt Parlin, Spr Dempsey, Drs Taylor W., Cowell + Mercer leave to U.K.													
	31.6.17															

C. W. Vasey
Major RE
O.C. 77th Field Coy R.E.

1875 Wt. W593/826 1,000,000 4/15 J.B.C. & A. A.D.S.S./Forms/C. 2118.

JUNE 1917 77TH FIELD COY RE

WAR DIARY
or
INTELLIGENCE SUMMARY

Army Form C. 2118

Instructions regarding War Diaries and Intelligence Summaries are contained in F. S. Regs., Part II. and the Staff Manual respectively. Title Pages will be prepared in manuscript.

Sheet No (68)

(Erase heading not required.)

Place	Date	Hour	Summary of Events and Information	Remarks and references to Appendices
	19.6.17 } 20.6.17 }		at POMMERA. Drill & training.	[illegible]
POMMERA	21.6.17		Embussed at POMMERA at 8.30 am & proceeded to ST NICHOLAS - Left St NICHOLAS at 8.30 pm for RAILWAY CUTTING.	[illegible]
RLY. CUTTING H7b3.9.	22.6.17		Taking over work on mined dugouts for R.F.A. from 208 Fd Coy (34th Divn).	[illegible]
"	23.6.17		Continued work on dugouts.	[illegible]
"	24.6.17		—— " —— CRA. 17th Divn asked for new dugouts for A78 Bty in lieu of continuing with D160	[illegible]
"	25.6.17		—— " ——	[illegible]
"	26.6.17		—— " ——	[illegible]
"	27.6.17		—— " ——	[illegible]
"	28.6.17		—— do ——	[illegible]
"	29.6.17		—— do ——	[illegible]
"	30.6.17		—— do ——	[illegible]
"				

[illegible signature] Maj. RE

June 1917

Instructions regarding War Diaries and Intelligence Summaries are contained in F. S. Regs., Part II. and the Staff Manual respectively. Title pages will be prepared in manuscript.

Sheet No (69)

WAR DIARY
or
INTELLIGENCE SUMMARY.

(Erase heading not required.)

77th Field Coy. RE.

Army Form C. 2118.

Vol 23

Place	Date	Hour	Summary of Events and Information	Remarks and references to Appendices
RAILWAY CUTTING. H.7.b.3.9. Sheet 51B.	1.6.17		Company employed under C.E 17th Corps working on Corps Line. Constructing	
	2.6.17		M.G.E & deep dugouts. Each section working one dugout with 4. 6hour shifts	
	3.6.17		do:-	
	4.6.17		do:-	
	5.6.17		do:-	
	6.6.17		do:-	
	7.6.17		do:-	
	8.6.17		do:-	
	9.6.17		do:-	
	10.6.17		do:-	
	11.6.17		do:	
WANQUETIN	12.6.17		Coy: relieved at railway cutting by 93rd Coy RE. Coy marched in evening to WANQUETIN.	
	13.6.17		Short drill parades & rest. Work of rebuilding parts of village blown up by ammunition dumps taken in hand	
	14.6.17		Work commenced on rebuilding houses	
	15.6.17		do:. Lieut: R.B Dunlop RE awarded the M.C	
POMMERA	16.6.17		Coy: moved to POMMERA (12 miles) Rejoin 51st Inft Bde:	
	17.6.17		Church Parade & rest. Weather very hot.	
	18.6.17		Drill & practicing for sports etc:	

A5834 Wt. W4973/M687 750,000 8/16 D. D. & L. Ltd. Forms/C.2118/13.

7th Field Coy RE   SHEET No (69)

Instructions regarding War Diaries and Intelligence Summaries are contained in F. S. Regs., Part II. and the Staff Manual respectively. Title pages will be prepared in manuscript.

WAR DIARY
or
~~INTELLIGENCE SUMMARY.~~
(Erase heading not required.)

July 1917

Army Form C. 2118.

77 Fd Coy RE

Place	Date	Hour	Summary of Events and Information	Remarks and references to Appendices
RAILWAY CUTTING H.7.c.3.9	1.7.17		Dugouts for 78th and 79th Brigades R.F.A. continued	[initials]
	2.7.17		— do — do — do — do 2 3 + 4 Sections) No 1 Section clearing dugouts in Rest — Building bomb	[initials]
SHEET 51 B NW	3.7.17		— do — do — do — do — do — do	[initials]
	4.7.17		— do — do — do — do — do — do — do	[initials]
	5.7.17		— do — do — do — do — do — do — do	[initials]
	6.7.17		— do — do — do — do — do — do — do	[initials]
	7.7.17		— do — do — do — do — do Company relieved	[initials]
			78th Field Coy RE No 1 Section dugouts in CORK TRENCH and CIVIL C.T. improvements	[initials]
EFFIE TRENCH	8.7.17		Coy H.d Qrs EFFIE TRENCH Sections 1. 2 & 3 Front line + Support line dugouts + CALEDONIAN and	[initials]
			CHILI C.T. improvements No 4 Section returned to HORSE LINES	[initials]
	9.7.17		SECTIONS 1 2 + 3 as for 8th + Brigade H.d Qrs improvements No 4 as	[initials]
	10.7.17		— do — do — do — do — do	[initials]
	11.7.17		No 2 SECTION relieved No 1 at Tank Dump No 4 relieved No 2 No 1 returned to Horse Lines	[initials]
	12.7.17		— do — do — do — do	[initials]
	13.7.17		— do — do — do — do N.C.O + Cor of No 1 returned to EFFIE	[initials]
			TRENCH for work on Brigade H.d Qrs	[initials]
	14.7.17		— do — do — do — do — do — do — do — do	[initials]
			and 8 Sappers No 1 took part in bombing raid	[initials]
	15.7.17		— do — do — do — do — do — do — do	[initials]

(A7092). Wt. W12839/M1293. 750,000. 1/17. D. D. & L., Ltd. Forms/C.2118/14.

JULY 1917

Instructions regarding War Diaries and Intelligence Summaries are contained in F. S. Regs., Part II. and the Staff Manual respectively. Title pages will be prepared in manuscript.

SHEET NO (70)

WAR DIARY
or
~~INTELLIGENCE SUMMARY.~~ 77TH FIELD COY RE

(*Erase heading not required.*)

Army Form C. 2118.

Place	Date	Hour	Summary of Events and Information	Remarks and references to Appendices
EFFIE TRENCH (Continued)	16.7.17		Remainder No1. Section relieved No 3. No 3 relieved No 2. No 2 returned to Horse Lines. No 4 as 15th	[illegible]
	17.7.17		No1. Dugout CORK. CHILI CT improvement. No 3 carrying on with work taken over from No 2. No 4 – do –	[illegible]
	18.7.17		— do — Joined by 1 NCO & OR from No 2 — do — — do —	[illegible]
	19.7.17		— do — — do — — do —	[illegible]
	20.7.17		— do — — do — — do —	[illegible]
	21.7.17		Major Vasey went as acting CRE. do — do — — do —	[illegible]
	22.7.17		— do — — do — — do —	[illegible]
	23.7.17		No 4 Section relieved No 3. No 2 Section relieved No 4. No 1 Carried on as 22nd. No 3 returned to Horse Lines.	[illegible]
	24.7.17.		No 4. Section CIVIL C.T. + dugout in CORK. No 2. CALEDONIAN CT + dugout in CHARLIE. No1. CHILI CT and dugout in CUBA. No 3 · at horse lines	awk
	25.7.17		do — do — Joined by 1 N.CO + 8 men from No 3. Remainder — do	awk
	26.7.17		do — do — do — do	awk
	27.7.17		do — do — do — do	awk.
	28.7.17		Major Vasey rejoined the Company do — do — Dugout finished + new one started in CUBA — do	awk
	29.7.17		do — do — do — do	awk
	30.7.17		No 3 section came forward and No 4 section returned to Horse Lines. No 1 section replaced No 4 at forward billet.	awk
	31.7.17.		No1 section · CHILI CT + dugout in CUBA. No 2. CALEDONIAN CT. + dugout in CHARLIE. No 3. CIVIL CT and dugout in CORK.	awk.

A5834 Wt. W4973/M687 750,000 8/16 D. D. & L. Ltd. Forms/C.2118/13.

JUNE (struck through) JULY 1917 — 77TH. FIELD. COY. R.E.

Instructions regarding War Diaries and Intelligence Summaries are contained in F. S. Regs., Part II. and the Staff Manual respectively. Title Pages will be prepared in manuscript.

WAR DIARY
or
~~INTELLIGENCE SUMMARY~~
(Erase heading not required.)

Army Form C. 2118

SHEET NO (71)

Place	Date	Hour	Summary of Events and Information	Reinforcements All Ranks	Reinforcements Horses	Reinforcements Mules	Casualties Officers, N.C.Os and Men: Killed	Wounded	In Hospital	Evacuated	Died	Horses and Mules: Killed	Wounded	In Hospital	Evac	Died	Remarks and references to Appendices
RAILWAY CUTTING H.?6.3.9 SHEET 57.B	1.7.17		9 O.R. on detachment to W.S. O XVII Corps St Nicholas. Cpl Thain to be 2/Sergt. 2nd Cpl Parlon to be 2/Cpl. L/Cpl Griffen to be 2nd Cpl. Sapper Longe to be L/Cpl. Spr Spears transferred to R.E.T.C. Newark														Horse Lines at St Nicholas from 1st to 31st
	2.7.17																
	3.7.17		Driver 7 Evans evac							1							
	4.7.17		Capt A Moncrieff from leave														
	5.7.17		Cpl Smith Spr Matthews from leave. Pion Gibson to F.A. Pion Meaney 19th C.C.S. Helmning from leave)						2								
	6.7.17		Pion Gibson evac valid							1							
	7.7.17		Sergt Glennie Sprs Decks + Young Dr Hick leave to U.K.														
EFFIE TRENCH.	8.7.17		2nd Cpl Barlow from 51st Brigade School. 2/Cpl Parlon to 51st Brigade School. Capt Moncrieff Pion Grisdale + Dr Guild to C.E. 3rd Army. Spr Harrison from 3rd Army Rest Camp. Spr Perkin to 3rd Army Rest Camp.														
	9.7.17		Dr Saunders C joined from Base. L/Cpl Millem to F.A. Spr Allbon to F.A. L/Cpl Millem evac.	1					2	1							
	10.7.17		Spr Ingram joined from No 6 Stat Hosp. Spr Lucas wounded. Sergt Carter Dr Taylor Mercer Spr Dempsey from leave	1						1							
	11.7.17																
	12.7.17		Dr Cowell from leave														
	13.7.17																
	14.7.17		Lt. A.W. Holbrook joined from 13th Field Coy Aust. Engineers.	1													
	15.7.17		Cpl Crumpler Spr Massey Harris Woodman Pion Davidson Drs Laffing + Escott leave to U.K.														
	16.7.17		Spr Allbon evac to C.C.S.							1							
	17.7.17																
	18.7.17		Pion Day to F.A. Sergt Carter wounded. 4 O.R. reinforcements. Sergt Glennie Spr Decks from leave.	4				1	1								
	19.7.17		Pion Stewart to F.A. 2/Cpl Steel to be 2/Sergt. 2nd Cpl Murphy to be 2/Cpl. 40220 Jones to be 2nd Cpl. Cpl Shaw from 51st Brigade School						1								
	20/7/17		L/Cpl Longe to 51st Brigade School. Spr Roscoe to F.A. Spr Foley from leave.						1								
	21/7/17		4 O.R. leave to U. Kingdom. (Dr Saunders evac on 22) (1 O.R. from 3rd Army Rest Camp														
	22/7/17		Dr Saunders C to F.A. Dr Shacklock + Garrod wounded Spr Germer + Godwin wounded shell fire					4	1	4							
	23/7/17		Dr Garrod from F.A. Spr Gogie leave to U.K. Pion Day from F.A. 2 O.R. joined (2 O.R. to 3rd Army Rest Camp	2													
	24/7/17		Pion Eales joined. 2nd Cpl Goff to 17th Div Dump.	1													
	25/7/17		Sapr Ball + Lindsay joined from No 2 on 23rd. Spr Allbon joined from 42 C.C.S.	3													
	26/7/17		1 L.D. Horse drawn from 20th M.V.S. L/Cpl White + Spr Wood wounded		1			2									
	27/7/17		Spr Gee, Newman + Parker killed in action. Spr Holmes + Smith wounded				3	2									
	28/7/17		10 O.R. leave to U.K. Dr Harrison to F.A.						1								
	29/7/17		9 O.R. rejoined from XVII Corps W.S.O.														
	30/7/17		Spr Dunn wounded					1									
	31/7/17		Sapr Barry to F.A.						1								

A.W. Holbrook Lt R.E.
for O.C. 77th Field Coy R.E.

1875 Wt. W593/826 1,000,000 4/15 J.B.C. & A. A.D.S.S./Forms/C. 2118.

August 1917.

Instructions regarding War Diaries and Intelligence Summaries are contained in F. S. Regs., Part II. and the Staff Manual respectively. Title pages will be prepared in manuscript.

WAR DIARY
or
~~INTELLIGENCE SUMMARY.~~
(Erase heading not required.)

77th Field Coy R.E.

Army Form C. 2118.

Vol 25

Place	Date	Hour	SHEET NO. (72) Summary of Events and Information	Remarks and references to Appendices
COY H.Q. EFFIE TRENCH	1.8.17		Company employed on deep dugouts in Support line & new Communication Trenches.	
HORSE LINES	2.8.17		— do — " " " " " " " "	
G.16a.9.9.	3.8.17		— do —	
SHEET 51B.N.W.	4.8.17		— do —	
	5.8.17		— do —	Commenced
			Work on strong Pts behind Support line	
	6.8.17		— do —	
	7.8.17		— do —	
	8.8.17		— do —	
	9.8.17		— do —	
	10.8.17		— do — ; Reserve Line (H 6 b & d) wired with double apron fence.	
	11.8.17		— do —	
	12.8.17		— do —	
	13.8.17		— do —	
	14.8.17		— do —	
	15.8.17		— do —	

[illegible signature]

A5834 Wt. W4973/M687 750,000 8/16 D. D. & L. Ltd. Forms/C.2118/13.

Aug 1917

Instructions regarding War Diaries and Intelligence Summaries are contained in F. S. Regs., Part II. and the Staff Manual respectively. Title pages will be prepared in manuscript.

WAR DIARY

or

~~INTELLIGENCE SUMMARY.~~

(Erase heading not required.)

77th Field Coy. R.E.

Army Form C. 2118.

Place	Date	Hour	SHEET NO (73) Summary of Events and Information	Remarks and references to Appendices
Coy Hd Qrs EFFIE TRENCH	16 8/17		Coy employed on deep dugouts in Support line; main C.T. – fire stepping etc. of Strong Pts behind Support line	
HORSE LINES	17 8/17		— do —	
F16a 9.9	19 8/17		— do —	
Sheet 57B N.W.	20 8/17		— do — Commenced digging Reserve Line.	
	21 8/17		— do —	
	22 8/17		— do —	
	23 8/17		— do —	
	24 8/17		— do —	
	25 8/17		— do —	
	26 8/17		— do —	
	27 8/17		— do —	
	28 8/17		— do —	
	29 8/17		— do —	
	30 8/17		— do —	
	31 8/17		— do —	

[illegible] Major R.E.

A5834 Wt. W4973/M687 750,000 8/16 D. D. & L. Ltd. Forms/C.2118/13.

August 1917. 77th Field Coy R.E.

Instructions regarding War Diaries and Intelligence Summaries are contained in F. S. Regs., Part II. and the Staff Manual respectively. Title pages will be prepared in manuscript.

WAR DIARY
or
INTELLIGENCE SUMMARY.
(Erase heading not required.)

Army Form C. 2118.

Place	Date	Hour	SHEET NO (74) Summary of Events and Information	REINFORCEMENTS All Ranks	Horses Mules	CASUALTIES Killed	Wounded	Hospital	Evac	Died	CASUALTIES Killed	Wounded	Hospital	Evac C.	Died	Remarks and references to Appendices
Coy H.Q.	1.8.17		4 O.R rejoined from leave to U. Kingdom. 2nd Lt Barlow reverted to "Sgt" rate of E. Pay													
EFFIE	3.8.17		Sappers Gibbons, Poole and Fish to be 4/U.P.L.C.													
TRENCH.	4.8.17		Dr Harrison evacuated (Leave to United Kingdom						1							
HORSELINES	5.8.17		3 O.Rs from 3rd Army Rest Camp 2 O.Rs to 3 Army Rest Camp, Capt Moncrieff 2 O.R + 2 Horses rejoined from C.E. 3rd Army, 6 O.Rs													
G.16.a.9.9.	6.8.17		Capt Moncrieff to ~~[illegible]~~ C.R.E.s as ADJT. 2 O.R to C.R.E.s command. 1 O.R from C.R.E. attached													
SHEET 51.B. N.W.	8.8.17		Spr Grant to F.A.					1								
	9.8.17		2 O.R reinforcement from No 4 Coy R.E.	2												
	10.8.17		64173 Taylor 1 month leave & bounty, retained in the service AO 209 of 1916. Spr Marland wounded				1									
	11.8.17															
	12.8.17		9 O.R leave to United Kingdom. Spr Peasey to F.A. Spr Young to F.A.					2								
	13.8.17		Spr Barry D from F.A. L/Cpl Saunders G. att C.R.E. 17th Div.													
	14.8.17		Spr Young evac						1							
	15.8.17		3 O.R joined from No 1 Wing R.E. Base depot. Spr Sim married without leave	3												
	16.8.17		Pnr Mathews 7 days F.P. No 1.													
	17.8.17		Lt Slaman H.O to 9th C.C.S.													
	18.8.17		6 O.R leave to United Kingdom 3 O.Rs joined from No 2 Reinforcement Coy, Dr Lane rejoined Unit	3												
	19.8.17		Spr Grant G from Hosp. 1 O.R to 3rd Army Rest Camp. 2 O.Rs from 3rd Army Rest Camp.													
	20.8.17		L/Cpl Fish E.H. S.S. F.A.					1								
	21.8.17		1 L.D. horse died												1	
	22.8.17		Spr Pascoe H rejoined from No 3 Stat Hosp	1												
	23.8.17		Spr Greenwood to F.A. 5 O.Rs joined 4 from No 4 Reinforcement Coy 1 from R.E. Base depot. Spr Peasey from F.A.	5				1								
	24.8.17		9 Sgt Sheb extended service to 12 years colours													
	25.8.17		4 O.Rs leave to U. Kingdom. Spr Whitcroft accidentally injured to F.A.					1								
	26.8.17		Capt H O Slaman evac to England sick						1							
	27/8/17		1 O.R leave to U Kingdom. Spr Finch 7 days F.P No 1													
	28/8/17		S/Smith Peasey to R.E. Base for dentures. Sprs Pascoe & Hawkins to F.A.					2	1							
	29/8/17		Spr Newell deprived 7 days pay, 1 day R.V.													
	31.8.17		Cpl Parker to F.A.					1								

A5834 Wt. W4973/M687 750,000 8/16 D. D. & L. Ltd. Forms/C.2118/13.

September 1917

Instructions regarding War Diaries and Intelligence Summaries are contained in F. S. Regs., Part II. and the Staff Manual respectively. Title pages will be prepared in manuscript.

WAR DIARY
or
~~INTELLIGENCE SUMMARY.~~
(Erase heading not required.)

Army Form C. 2118.

77th Field Coy RE

Vol 26

SHEET NO (75)

Place	Date	Hour	Summary of Events and Information	Remarks and references to Appendices
EFFIE TRENCH AND CAM VALLEY	1st		Improving Communications, Constructing Strong Points in Support & Reserve Lines. etc	[illegible]
HORSE LINE G.S.T. NICHOLAS G 16.d 9.9. SHEET 51 B.N.W.	2nd		— do —	[illegible]
	3rd		— do —	[illegible]
	4th		— do —	[illegible]
	5th		— do —	[illegible]
	6th		— do —	[illegible]
	7th		— do —	[illegible]
	8th		— do —	[illegible]
	9th		— do —	[illegible]
	10th		— do —	[illegible]
	11th		— do —	[illegible]
	12th		— do —	[illegible]
	13th		— do —	[illegible]
	14th		— do —	[illegible]
	15th		— do —	[illegible]

[illegible signature] Major RE

(A7092). Wt. W12839/M1293. 750,000. 1/17. D. D. & L., Ltd. Forms/C.2118/14.

September 1917

Instructions regarding War Diaries and Intelligence Summaries are contained in F. S. Regs., Part II. and the Staff Manual respectively. Title pages will be prepared in manuscript.

WAR DIARY
or
INTELLIGENCE SUMMARY.
(*Erase heading not required.*)

77th Field Coy RE

Army Form C. 2118.

Place	Date	Hour	Summary of Events and Information	Remarks and references to Appendices
			Sheet No 76	
	16th		Improving Communications; Constructing S.P. in Support & Reserve lines. 1 Officer 11 men took section [illegible] in a raid on the enemy's trenches S of ARRAS – DOUAI RLY in which they blew up 2 dug outs, 1 T.M. Empt & a dump of T.M. Ammunition. 3 men were given M.M. for gallantry displayed.	[initials]
	17th		Improving Communications, Constructing S.Pts in Support & Reserve Lines &c	[initials]
	18th		—— do ——	[initials]
	19th		—— do ——	[initials]
	20th		—— do ——	[initials]
	21st		—— do ——	[initials]
	22nd		—— do ——	[initials]
	23rd		—— do ——	[initials]
	24th		—— do —— . Handed over to 478 Coy (51st Div) & marched to ARRAS.	[initials]
LE HAMEAU	25th		Left ARRAS 9am Arrived LE HAMEAU 1pm [illegible]	[initials]
IVERGNY	26th		Left LE HAMEAU & arrived IVERGNY 11am [illegible]	[initials]
"	27th		In Billets Training	[initials]
"	28th		—— do ——	[initials]
"	29th		—— do ——	[initials]
"	30th		—— do ——	[initials]

[signature] Major RE

(A7092). Wt. W12839/M1293. 750,000. 1/17. D. D. & L., Ltd. Forms/C.2118/14.

September 1917 77th Field Coy R.E.

Army Form C. 2118.

WAR DIARY
or
INTELLIGENCE SUMMARY.
(Erase heading not required.)

Instructions regarding War Diaries and Intelligence Summaries are contained in F. S. Regs., Part II. and the Staff Manual respectively. Title pages will be prepared in manuscript.

Sheet No (17)

Place	Date	Hour	Summary of Events and Information	Reinforcements: All Ranks	Reinforcements: Horses & Mules	Casualties Officers, N.C.O.s & Men: Killed	Wounded	Died	Hosp	Evac	Casualties Horses & Mules: Killed	Died	Hosp	Wounded	Evac	Remarks and references to Appendices
H.Q EFFIE TRENCH	1.9.17		Capt Dunlop leave to U.K. 2.O.R leave to U.K. S Smith Stephens to F.A. Sapper Fish from F.A.						1							
HORSELINES	2.9.17		3.O.R from R.E Base Depot. 1.O.R from 3rd Army Rest Camp 3.O.R to 3rd Army Rest Camp 1.O.R to F.A.	3					1							
ST NICHOLAS	-do-		Sp Bowman att. 17th Div Depot awaiting commission. Sp Hawkins & Pascoe evac							2						
G.16.a.9.3																
SHEET 51.B.N.W	6.9.17		Sp Thomas to R.E Base for dentures 1.O.R joined from R.E. Base Depot. Sp Wheatcroft evac sick	1						2						
	7.9.17		3.O.R leave to U. Kingdom. Sp Greenwood evac sick							1						
	8.9.17		Pnr Mathews wounded S Smith Stephens evac sick				1			2						
	9.9.17		1.O.R leave to U. Kingdom II Lt Swindells joined from R.E Base	1												
	10.9.17		3.O.R -do- " Pnr Davidson wounded by shell fire 4.O.R. joined from No 2 Reinforcement Coy	4			1			1						
	11.9.17		4.O.R -do- " Sp Halstead, Fish and Gibbons to be Ta L/Cpls. Sp White to F.A.						1							
	12.9.17		1.O.R -do- " Pnr Stewart joined from 3rd Canadian Stat Hosp II Cpl Fitzgibbon joined	2												
	13.9.17		Sp Crook rejoined without leave													
	14.9.17		3.O.R and II Lt Bergman leave to U Kingdom, 3.O.R from and 3.O.R. to 3rd Army Rest Camp. Sp Gilkes to F.A.						1							
	15.9.17		II Cpl Harrison to R.E Base depot for transfer to England in exchange							1						
	16.9.17		1.O.R leave to U Kingdom 2.O.R joined from R.E Base Depot, Sergt Gibbons to F.A. Sp Harris Wounded	2			1		1	2						
	17.9.17		Sergt Gibbons evac sick L/Cpl II Lt Simpkin to England							1						
	18.9.17		Sp Hawkins from No 8 C.C.S.	1												
	19.9.17		3.O.R leave to U. Kingdom. Sp Day evac sick							1						
	20.9.17		Dr Holland to F.A., Sp Mills W. to F.A.						2							
	21.9.17		Dr Holland from F.A., Cpl Hughes from 17th Divl ~~Depot~~ Reinf.													
	22.9.17		Sp Campbell transferred from 78th Field Coy R.E., Sp Smith from Hosp England	1												
	23.9.17		L/Cpl Longe, Sprs Massey & Marsland awarded M. M.													
	24.9.17															
	27.9.17		Sp Mills & White from XVII C.R.S													
	27.9.17		Pnr Grimley joined, L/Cpl Saunders from C.R.E 17th Div Sp Nicol, Gibbon & Grant from 3rd A.R.C	1												
	27.9.17		Cpl Crumpler to be A/Sergt II Cpls Goff & Griffin to be A/Cpls L/Cpls Roberts & Longe to be A/II Cpls.													
	28.9.17		Sp Holbrook leave to U.K. 1 Mule evac												1	
	29.9.17		Sp Pascoe rejoined from No 3 Canadian STAT Hosp	1												
	30.9.17		Sergt Kirkman to Veterinary School													

(A7092). Wt. W12839/M1293. 750,000. 1/17. D. D. & L., Ltd. Forms/C.2118/14.

October 1917

Instructions regarding War Diaries and Intelligence Summaries are contained in F. S. Regs., Part II. and the Staff Manual respectively. Title pages will be prepared in manuscript.

WAR DIARY 77th Field Company R.E.

or

~~INTELLIGENCE SUMMARY.~~

(Erase heading not required.)

Army Form C. 2118.

Vol 27

Place	Date	Hour	SHEET (48) Summary of Events and Information	Remarks and references to Appendices
IVERGNY	1-10-17		Training	
"	2-10-17		do	
"	3-10-17		Company moved by train via MONDICOURT to PROVEN	
"	4-10-17		Arrived PROVEN at 12 noon, marched to SALEM CAMP.	
SALEM CAMP	5-10-17		Company training.	
"	6-10-17		" " and working for Commandant of Staging Area.	
"	7		do do	
"	8		do do	
"	9		do do	
"	10		do do	
"	11		Company moved to ELVERDINGHE. Dismounted sections by train, transport by road. Dismounted	
CANAL BANK.			sections moved by road to billets in canal bank at C.13.d.3.9. (Sheet Belgium 28 NW)	
	~~12~~		3 officers and 150 O.R. infantry attached to coy for work. Took over work from 1/3rd	
	~~12~~		London Field Coy R.E. of 29th Div.	
do.	13		Started work in line. Laying duckboard track from U.22.b.4.1. (Sheet 20) forwards.	

(A7092). Wt. W12839/M1293. 750,000. 1/17. D. D. & L., Ltd. Forms/C.2118/14.

October 1917

Instructions regarding War Diaries and Intelligence Summaries are contained in F. S. Regs., Part II. and the Staff Manual respectively. Title pages will be prepared in manuscript.

WAR DIARY or ~~INTELLIGENCE SUMMARY.~~ 77th Field Coy RE

(Erase heading not required.)

Army Form C. 2118.

Place	Date	Hour	Summary of Events and Information SHEET (79)	Remarks and references to Appendices
CANAL BANK	13·10·17		Work in line continued. Transport lines moved from ONDANK to ELVERDINGHE	[illegible]
"	14·10·17		"	[illegible]
"	15·10·17		"	[illegible]
"	16·10·17		" Duckboard track completed U12c 6.2.	[illegible]
"	17·10·17		Work under CRE 14th Corps troops. Erecting Nissen hut camp (ROSE CAMP) at C.12. BELGIUM Sheet 28	[illegible]
"	18·10·17		do do	[illegible]
"	19·10·17		do do	[illegible]
"	20·10·17		do do Started COLDSTREAM CAMP at	[illegible]
"	21·10·17		do do continued.	[illegible]
"	22·10·17		do do do	[illegible]
"	23·10·17		do do do Took over work on HUDDLESTONE CAMP from RE of 34th DIV. at	[illegible]
"	24·10·17		Continued work on these camps.	[illegible]
"	25·10·17		ditto	[illegible]
"	26·10·17		Coy moved by rail to PROVEN. P.5 area. PATAGONIA CAMP.	[illegible]
PROVEN	27th to 31st		Coy in rest in Patagonia Camp.	[illegible]

[illegible] Major RE

(A7092). Wt. W12839/M1293. 750,000. 1/17. D. D. & L., Ltd. Forms/C.2118/14.

October 1917 — 77th Field Company Royal Engineers

Instructions regarding War Diaries and Intelligence Summaries are contained in F. S. Regs., Part II, and the Staff Manual respectively. Title pages will be prepared in manuscript.

WAR DIARY
or
INTELLIGENCE SUMMARY.

(Erase heading not required.)

Army Form C. 2118.

Place	Date	Hour	Summary of Events and Information — SHEET (80)	Reinforcements: All ranks	Reinforcements: Horses	Reinforcements: Mules	Casualties Officers, NCOs + Men: Killed	Wounded	Died	Hosp	Evac	Casualties Horses + Mules: Killed	Wounded	Died	Hosp	Evac	Remarks and references to Appendices
	1-10-17		Dr Taylor C to FA evac sick, 2 OR joined from REBD, S.S. Shepherd joined from Rob Stat Hosp	3						1	1						
	2-10-17		Spr Millig to R.E.B.D. (Returned)								1						
	4-10-17		Spr Gilker from FA														
	5-10-17		Sergt Sheik, Spr Campbell leave to U.K. Pion Wallin Spr Crook to CCS sick, Dr Salmon Spr Marsland to CRS							2	2						
	-do-		L/Cpl Millin rejoined from REBD	1													
	9-10-17		1 OR reinforcement from R.E.B.D. L/Cpl Tresise Spr Ford leave to U.K. Sergt Sheik remained without leave	1													
	11-10-17		Sapr Marsland to C.C.S sick								1						
	12-10-17		Spr Isaac joined from 17th Div Engineers. Dr Salmon from C.R.S.	1													
	13-10-17		Spr Binks joined from R.E.B.D. L/Cpl Saunders to CRE att. Staff Sergt Kirkman from Div School	1													
	14-10-17		Sergt King wounded					1									
	15-10-17		S/Spr Slade " Spr Stacey to FA. Spr Tabbett killed Shell				1	1		1							
	16-10-17		Lt Holbrook to CRE 17th Div Adjt														
	17-10-17		Major Vassey leave to U.K. a/Lt Swindells att 93rd Field Coy Spr Stacey evac sick								1						
	19-10-17		Lt Holbrook to Hospital							1							
	20-10-17		L/Cpl Stone, Millin, Pascoe leave to U.K. Lt Holbrook evac sick								1						
	22-10-17		S/Smith Shepherd wounded (at duty) 1 L.D. horse evacuated					1								1	
	23-10-17		L/Cpl Tongs to XIV Corps Infantry School of Instruction														
	24-10-17		1 Officer 5 O.R. 2 horses att from 17th Div HQ RE for rations														
	25-10-17		Spr Boyle & Pion Wilson leave to U Kingdom 2/Lt Box joined for duty														
	29-10-17																
	30-10-17		1 L.D. horse drawn from 29th M.V.S.		1												

(A7092). Wt. W12839/M1293. 750,000. 1/17. D. D. & L., Ltd. Forms/C.2118/14.

[signature] Major RE
for O.C. 77th Field Coy. R.E.

SHEET (81)

Instructions regarding War Diaries and Intelligence Summaries are contained in F. S. Regs., Part II. and the Staff Manual respectively. Title pages will be prepared in manuscript.

WAR DIARY
or
~~INTELLIGENCE SUMMARY.~~
(Erase heading not required.)

77th Field Coy R.E. Army Form C. 2118.

Vol 28

Place	Date	Hour	Summary of Events and Information	Remarks and references to Appendices
PATAGONIA CAMP PROVEN. SHEET 27 F.17.d.5.3.	1-11-17 ↕		Company working on improvements to camps in P.5 area PROVEN	[initials]
	5-11-17		ditto.	[initials]
	6-11-17. ↕		Company moved to CANAL BANK by train, transport by road and took over work in the line from 505th Coy R.E. 57th Div.	
			Sections billeted at C.19.a.0.2. Transport lines at B.24.c.0.2.	
	14-11-17		Works in the line — Duckboard tracks, Support line, Reserve line and Haymarket Dump.	[initials]
	15-11-17 ↓ 16 11		Temporary bridge made over [illegible] with [illegible] other work [illegible] as above	[initials]
	17 11		Work continued as before, [illegible] started	[initials]
	18 11		ditto	[initials]
	19 11		Bridge made over BROOMBEEK [illegible]	[initials]
	20 11		ditto	[initials]
	21 11		Bridge over STEENBEEK [illegible]	[initials]

A5834 Wt. W4973/M687 750,000 8/16 D. D. & L. Ltd. Forms/C.2118/13.

SHEET. (82)

Instructions regarding War Diaries and Intelligence Summaries are contained in F. S. Regs., Part II. and the Staff Manual respectively. Title pages will be prepared in manuscript.

WAR DIARY
or
INTELLIGENCE SUMMARY.
(Erase heading not required.)

77th Field Coy R.E.

Army Form C. 2118.

Place	Date	Hour	Summary of Events and Information	Remarks and references to Appendices
	22.11.17.		Work continued on [illegible] line, Reserve line and duckboard tracks.	[illegible]
	23rd		ditto	[illegible]
	24th		ditto	[illegible]
	25th		New Weldon Trestle bridge built over STEENBEEK with [illegible] completed. Other work as on 24th.	[illegible]
	26th		ditto	[illegible]
	27th		ditto	[illegible]
	28th		ditto	[illegible]
	29th		ditto	[illegible]
	30th		ditto	[illegible]

[illegible] Capt R.E. [?]
for O.C. 77th Coy R.E.

A5834 Wt. W4973/M687 750,000 8/16 D. D. & L. Ltd. Forms/C.2118/13.

SHEET (83) 77th Field Coy R.E.

Instructions regarding War Diaries and Intelligence Summaries are contained in F. S. Regs., Part II. and the Staff Manual respectively. Title pages will be prepared in manuscript.

WAR DIARY
or
~~INTELLIGENCE SUMMARY.~~
(Erase heading not required.)

Army Form C. 2118.

Place	Date	Hour	Summary of Events and Information	Reinforcements All Ranks	Reinforcements Animals	Casualties Officers NCOs & Men Killed	Wounded	Died	Hosp.	Evac.	Casualties Horses and Mules Killed	Wounded	Died	Hosp.	Evac.	Remarks and references to Appendices
PATAGONIA	1-11-17		Cpl Cooper to F.A.						1							
CAMP	2-11-17		Spr Duncombe to F.A., Spr Greenwood from No 6 Stat Hosp, Spr Morgan from C.R.E.	1					1							
PROVEN	3-11-17		2 Lt Bergman to CE 3rd Army on transfer. 6 O.Rs reinforcements from 17th Divl Depot Batt. Cpl Cooper &	6						2						
SHEET 27	4-11-17		Spr Garrod leave to U.K. (Sapper Duncombe evac to 63 CCS)													
E.17.a.5.4	5-11-17															
Siderow al	6-11-17		Sergt Glennie awarded D.C. Medal. Pnr Wilson to F.A. England (whilst on leave to UK)													
Canal Bank	7-11-17		3 O.Rs leave to U.K. 6 O.Rs reinforcements from R.E Base	6												
C.19.a.0.2.	8-11-17															
Transport	9-11-17															
B.24.c.0.2	10-11-17		1 O.R leave to U.K. Dr Gill to F.A. (from R E Base)						1							
SHEET 28 N.W.	11-11-17		1 O.R leave to U.K. Cpl Cooper rejoined. Spr Creasey wounded 2 O.R wounded at duty. 2 Lt Lewis joined	2			3			1						
	12-11-17		Spr Ball to F.A. Spr Creasey died from wounds. Spr Ball evac sick					1	1	1						
	13-11-17															
	14-11-17		L/Cpl Jones to No 4 Vet Hosp (course of instruction)													
	15-11-17		Spr Black joined from R.E Base. Cpl Barlow to 51st Brigade School	1												
	16-11-17		2 O.Rs leave to U.K. Major Vasey to 9 CRE. Spr Dunkley to XIX CRS						1							
	17-11-17		Cpl Hughes, Spr Spares to 17th Divl Depot for transfer to England for commissions							2						
	18-11-17		Sergt King rejoined from R.E Base	1												
	19-11-17		Spr Munslow to R E Base for transfer to England as "Sha ploughman". 1 O.R wounded. 2 O.Rs wounded at duty				3			2						
	20-11-17		2 O.R leave to U.K. 1 O.R "missing believed killed". Cpl Murphy wounded. Major Vasey from 9 CRE.			1	1			2						
	21-11-17		Spr Garrod to R E Base for transfer to England as Sha ploughman							1						
	22-11-17		2 O.Rs wounded, 1 O.R wounded at duty. Spr Laycock to F.A.				3		1							
	23-11-17															
	24-11-17		1 O.R from R.E.B.D. 1 O.R from Boulogne Reinforcement Camp. L/Cpl Lange from XII Corps School	2												
	25-11-17															
	26-11-17		Spr Dawes leave to U.K. (Pnr Hardy evac sick)													
	27-11-17		Spr Black wounded. 1 L.D Mule evac to 29th M.V.S. 1 Riding horse transferred to 78th Coy R.E				1			2					2	1 Mule 1 Horse
	28-11-17		Capt Dunlop to 9 Adjt 17th Div.													
	29-11-17		Sergt Balmer awarded Military Medal.													
	30-11-17		1 O.R wounded				1									

[illegible signature]

December 1917

WAR DIARY
or
INTELLIGENCE SUMMARY.
(Erase heading not required.)

11th Field Company Royal Engineers

Army Form C. 2118.

Instructions regarding War Diaries and Intelligence Summaries are contained in F. S. Regs., Part II. and the Staff Manual respectively. Title pages will be prepared in manuscript.

Place	Date	Hour	Summary of Events and Information	Remarks and references to Appendices
SHEET 28 BELGIUM	1.12.17		Work in the line continued. Support Line, Reserve Line, Duckboard tracks etc.	
BILLETS C.19.a.0.2 Transport B.24.c.0.9	5-12-17		ditto.	
	6.12.17		Coy moved from Canal Bank to PARDO CAMP, PROVEN. Dismounted by train. Transport by road.	
	7-12-17		Coy. resting.	
PARDO. CAMP PROVEN.	8.12.17		Transport moved to WOLVERDINGE with the transport of 51st Bde. Group.	
	9-12-17		" " " HOCQUINGHEN, Dismounted sections moved by train from PROVEN to AUDRICQUES	
HOCQUINGHEN.			and then by road to HOCQUINGHEN.	
do.	10-12-17		Coy. resting in HOCQUINGHEN.	
WESTROVE	11.12.17		Coy left Hocquinghen 10 AM, route marched to WESTROVE, arrived WESTROVE 2.30	
	12.12.17		Coy at WESTROVE. LEFT WESTROVE 8 A.M. ROUTEMARCHED TO WIZERNES Station. ENTRAINED FOR BAPAUME	
			ARRIVED BAPAUME MIDNIGHT. MARCHED TO BARASTRA CAMP.	
BARASTRA.	13.12.17	"	RESTING AT BARASTRA CAMP	
	14.12.17	"	" "	
	15.12.17	"	" "	
	16.12.17	"	" "	
LECHELLE	17.12.17		LEFT BARASTRA CAMP, MARCHED TO LECHELLE, ARRIVED LECHELLE 11.30. AM	

(A7092). Wt. W12839/M1293. 750,000. 1/17. D. D. & L., Ltd. Forms/C.2118/14.

Instructions regarding War Diaries and Intelligence Summaries are contained in F. S. Regs., Part II. and the Staff Manual respectively. Title pages will be prepared in manuscript.

WAR DIARY
or
INTELLIGENCE SUMMARY.
(Erase heading not required.)

77 Fd Coy RE

Vol 29

Army Form C. 2118.

Place	Date	Hour	Summary of Events and Information	Remarks and references to Appendices
LECHELLE	18.12.17		RESTING AT LECHELLE, WEST RAILWAY CAMP	
	19.12.17		" " "	
	20.12.17		" "	
	21.12.17		Left LECHELLE 10 AM, ROUTE MARCHED TO HAVRINCOURT, ARRIVED HAVRINCOURT 1.30pm	
	22.12.17		AT WORK; deepening + WIDENING CLARGES STREET C.T., and Hindenburg Support, IMPROVING HORSELINES	
	23.12.17		" " " " "	
	24.12.17		deepening, + widening CLARGES STREET C.T. and Hindenburg Support; improving HORSELINES	
	25.12.17		"	
	26.12.17		"	
	27.12.17		Deepening + widening CLARGES STREET C.T. and HINDENBURG SUPPORT. IMPROVING	
	28.12.17		WIRING NEW SUPPORT LINE; CPL BROWN SICK, TO FIELD AMBULANCE; SAPPER [illegible]	
	29.12.17		SAPPER [illegible] KILLED, SAPPER HUTCHINSON WOUNDED SHELL, SAPPER JEFFERY WOUNDED SHELL	
	30.12.17		CORPORAL FITZGIBBON WOUNDED, SHELL	
	31.12.17		MAJOR VASEY WOUNDED, SHELL	

A.A. Dunlop Capt R.E.

(A7092). Wt. W12859/M1293. 750,000. 1/17. D. D. & L., Ltd. Forms/C.2118/14.

December 1917 — 77th Field Company Royal Engineers

WAR DIARY
or
~~INTELLIGENCE SUMMARY.~~
(*Erase heading not required.*)

Army Form C. 2118.

Instructions regarding War Diaries and Intelligence Summaries are contained in F. S. Regs., Part II. and the Staff Manual respectively. Title pages will be prepared in manuscript.

Place	Date	Hour	Summary of Events and Information	Reinforcements: All Ranks	Reinforcements: Animals	Casualties Officers/Other Ranks: Killed	Wounded	Died	Hosp	Evac	Animals: Killed	Wounded	Died	Hosp	Evac	Remarks and references to Appendices
			SHEET 86													
SHEET 28	1.12.17		Sp Pragnell + Brooks from R.E.B.D	2												
BELGIUM	2.12.17															
BILLETS	3.12.17		4 O.Rs [illegible] to U Kingdom													
C.19.a.0.2	4.12.17		Sp Herbert to F.A.						1							
Transport	5.12.17		Dr Jones to F.A.						1							
	6.12.17		Sp Evans to England for commission, 2nd Cpl Barlow from 51st Brigade School							1						
B.24.c.0.2	7.12.17															
PARDOE CAMP PROVEN	8.12.17		Spr Morgan, Perkins, Walls + Shefford to F.A.						4							
	9.12.17		6 O.Rs leave to U Kingdom, Sp Guyatt to F.A.						1							
WULVERDINGHE	10.12.17		Sp Littlewood to F.A.						1							
HOCQUINGHEM	11.12.17		3 O.Rs joined from Base Sp Littlewood evacuated	3						1						
	12.12.17															
	13.12.17		Sp Shefford + Walls from F.A.													
	14.12.17															
	15.12.17		6 O.R. 1 Officer leave to U Kingdom													
	16.12.17		Sp Poole to F.A. Sp Stanley to F.A. 2/Lt Lewis evac sick Sp Poole evac						2	2						
	17.12.17															
	18.12.17		Sp Spinder to C.C.S							1						
	19.12.17		— do — evacuated													
	20.12.17															
	21.12.17		5 O.R. leave to U.K. 2nd Cpl Clark to F.A.						1							
	22.12.17		2 O.R. — do — Sp Nicol to F.A. Dr Jones from F.A. Sp Dunkley from F.A.						1							
	23.12.17															
	24.12.17		1 L.D. horse evac to 29th M.V.S												1	
	25.12.17															
	26.12.17		Sp Hindle to F.A. Dr Howard to F.A. Dr Howard evac						2	1						
	27.12.17		2nd Cpl Barlow to F.A. Sp Effery wounded Sp Perkins from C.R.S 1 Bdy horse evac.				1		18						1	
	28.12.17		Sp Garfold killed, Sp Wilkinson wounded Sp Bowman for Eng for Commission			1	1									
	29.12.17		2/Lt Fotheringham wounded				1									
	30.12.17		Major Vasey wounded 2/Lt Stokes joined 1				1									
	31.12.17		Capt Pearce att from 78th Fld Coy R.E.													

(A7092) Wt. W12839/M1293 750,000. 1/17. D. D. & L., Ltd. Forms/C.2118/14.

January 1918

77th Field Coy R.E.

Army Form C. 2118.

WAR DIARY
or
INTELLIGENCE SUMMARY.
(Erase heading not required.)

Instructions regarding War Diaries and Intelligence Summaries are contained in F. S. Regs., Part II. and the Staff Manual respectively. Title pages will be prepared in manuscript.

Vol 30

Place	Date	Hour	Summary of Events and Information	Remarks and references to Appendices
			Sheet 28	
Spoil Heap	15.1.18		Kg 78 Digging and [illegible]: Trench [illegible] dugouts in [illegible] Rd [illegible]. Accommodation at Coy HQ. Drainage of HUNT, BULLEN and ALBAN. Revetting, Dugouts, barricade [illegible]	[illegible]
	16.1.18		Kg Drainage of Hughes Switch, Crosse Av. Front line barricade [illegible] Dugouts [illegible]. Horselines improvements. [illegible] Nation	[illegible]
	17.1.18		Duckboard tracks, Drainage of trenches, Sandbag barricade across Canal, [illegible] Dugouts [illegible]	[illegible]
	18.1.18		do	
	19.1.18		Duckboarding; [illegible] Dugouts [illegible]: Digging Carry Trench, Sandbag barricade [illegible]	
	20.1.18		do	
	21.1.18		do	
	22.1.18		do	
	23.1.18		Carry Trench Digging; Drainage & duckboarding of HUNT [illegible]	
	24.1.18		do and [illegible]	
	25.1.18		Carry Trench Digging &c. Drainage of HUNT AV. & CROSSE AV [illegible]	[illegible]
	26.1.18		do BULLEN & CROSSE AV [illegible] BYE OP Digging Road	
	27.1.18		do	
	28.1.18		do	
	29.1.18		do	
	30.1.18		Carry Trench Digging and [illegible] Drainage [illegible] Post Box [illegible]	[illegible]
	31.1.18		[illegible]	

[illegible signature]
77 Field Coy R.E.

(A7092). Wt. W12839/M1293. 750,000. 1/17. D. D. & L., Ltd. Forms/C.2118/14.

January 1918 ~~December 1917~~

17th Field Company Royal Engineers

WAR DIARY
or
INTELLIGENCE SUMMARY.

(*Erase heading not required.*)

Army Form C. 2118.

Instructions regarding War Diaries and Intelligence Summaries are contained in F. S. Regs., Part II. and the Staff Manual respectively. Title pages will be prepared in manuscript.

Place	Date	Hour	Summary of Events and Information SHEET 87	Remarks and references to Appendices
Havring court	1.1.18		Hindenburg Support Line: Widening and deepening trench. Strengthening [illegible] & Removing wire from parados [illegible]	[initials]
	2.1.18		——— Do ———	[initials]
	3.1.18		——— Do ———	[initials]
	4.1.18		Company accommodation at Horselines & Spoil Heap, Wire [illegible] in Support line	[initials]
	5.1.18		Making Horse Standings, Spoil Heap accommodation; Salvaging timber at Havring court	[initials]
	6.1.18		——— Do ——— Making Concertina wire at Hermies	[initials]
	7.1.18		——— Do ———	[initials]
Spoil Heap K 2 [illegible]	8.1.18		——— Do ———	[initials]
	9.1.18		Wiring support line, Company Accommodation & Improving Horselines	[initials]
	10.1.18		Wiring support line Cross Bullen; Making Shelter for R.A.P. K9c8.0. BDE Soup Kitchen K20a 8.4. Improvements to Billets	[initials]
	11.1.18		Digging new support line ——— Do ———	[initials]
	12.1.18		K9a Wiring Support Line K9a Fire stepping Cross Avenue K9d Wiring Support line K9d Digging support line & [illegible]	[initials]
	13.1.18		K9a Wiring Support line, K9d Do & digging Watson's support line K9c[illegible] Shelter near R.A.P. completed K20a 8.4 Soup Kitchen completed K9a cutting fire steps in Support line. Horselines and Camp.	[initials]
	14.1.18		K9a Wiring support line, K9d Do and digging support line: K20 [illegible] and extending accommodation in Coy billets	[initials]

(A7092). Wt. W12839/M1293. 750,000. 1/17. D. D. & L., Ltd. Forms/C.2118/14.

77th Field Company R.E. January 1918

Army Form C. 2118.

Instructions regarding War Diaries and Intelligence Summaries are contained in F. S. Regs., Part II. and the Staff Manual respectively. Title pages will be prepared in manuscript.

WAR DIARY
or
~~INTELLIGENCE SUMMARY.~~

(Erase heading not required.)

Place	Date	Hour	Summary of Events and Information	Reinforcements: All Ranks	Reinforcements: Animals	Casualties All Ranks: Killed	Wounded	Died	Hosp	Evac	Casualties Animals: Killed	Wounded	Died	Hosp	Evac	Remarks and references to Appendices
HAVRINCOURT SHEET 57C. K.28 a.2.4.	1-1-18															
	2-1-18															
	3-1-18		Sp Dumpley, Dunley & Higgins joined from 17th Divl [illegible] Batt	3												
	4-1-18		Sr Holland to F.A. 7 O.R. leave to U.K.						1							
	5-1-18		Capt Pearse rejoined 78th Fld Coy R.E. Sp Morgan from F.A.													
	6-1-18		Sp Dempsey to F.A.						1							
	7-1-18		Lt McGuinness joined from 93rd Fld Coy R.E., Sr Holland from F.A.	1												
Spoil Bank K.20 central	8-1-18															
	9-1-18		3 O.Rs leave to U. Kingdom													
	10-1-18															
	11-1-18		30 O.Rs att from 51st Brigade "Supply platoon" 1 O.R. joined from R.E. Base	1												
	12-1-18															
	13-1-18		Sp Dempsey from F.A.													
	14-1-18		Cpl [illegible], Sp Hart, Sr Burbridge to F.A.						3							
	15-1-18		4 O.Rs leave to U.K. 2 O.Rs joined from Base 3 O.Rs to F.A.	2					3							
	16-1-18		Sp Isaac to F.A.						1							
	17-1-18		L/Cpl Avery to F.A. Lt McGuinness rejoined 93rd Fld Coy R.E. 1 L.D. mule shot. 3 O.Rs to F.A.						3	1	1					
	18-1-18		Sp Hall to F.A. Sp Belben to F.A. [illegible] to F.A. 19th 2 O.R. Evacuated (evacuated)						2	2						
	19-1-18		Sp Davies from F.A. Sr Harrison & Cross to F.A. Mr Hardy joined from Base 1 L.D. Mule	1					3						1	
	20-1-18															
	21-1-18		Sp Collinson to F.A.						1							
	22-1-18		Sp Lindsay to F.A. Sp Hart from F.A.						1							
	23-1-18		Sr Hargreaves & Rogerson to C.R.S.						2							
	24-1-18		1 O.R. from F.A.													
	25/1/18		2/Lt Davies joined from Base 3 O.R. from F.A.	1												
	26-1-18		1 O.R. leave to U.K. Cp Smith to F.A.						1							
	28/1/18		1 O.R. from F.A.													
	29/1/18		6 O.Rs leave U.K. 5 O.R. leave to U.K. [illegible] 1 Riding [illegible] to M.V.S. 1 Riding 2 L.D. [illegible] drawn		3										1	
	30/1/18		Sr Williams joined from 93rd Fld Coy R.E.	1												

Transport Lines at P.17.a.4.4.

[signature] Major R.E.

COMMDG. 77th (FIELD) COY. R.E.

(A7092). Wt. W12839/M1293. 750,000. 1/17. D. D. & L., Ltd. Forms/C.2118/14.

77th Field Coy RE

Instructions regarding War Diaries and Intelligence Summaries are contained in F. S. Regs., Part II. and the Staff Manual respectively. Title pages will be prepared in manuscript.

WAR DIARY
or
INTELLIGENCE SUMMARY.
(Erase heading not required.)

February 1918 77th Fd Coy RE Vol 31

Army Form C. 2118.

Place	Date	Hour	Summary of Events and Information (Sheet 90)	Remarks and references to Appendices
Spoil Heap, Sheet 57c K.21. central	1st		Digging, draining and duckboarding forward trenches. Improving horse lines.	WHCS
	2nd		Wiring, digging, draining and duckboarding forward trenches. Improving horse lines.	WHCS
	3rd		Work in forward trenches as on 2nd. Improvements to horse lines. Taping out new support line. Making communication trench. Coy billets moved to Broken Houses. K.35.d.	WHCS
	4th		Wiring, digging, draining and duckboarding forward trenches. Improvements to Horse lines.	WHCS
Broken Houses	5th		Wiring and digging Hermies defences. Digging front line of battle zone. Work on test bores. Digging forward trenches.	WHCS
K.36.d.	6th		Digging front line of battle zone, Wiring Hermies Defences & Yorkshire Bank. Supervision of dug out construction.	WHCS
	7th		wiring front line of battle zone do	WHCS
	8th		Digging Hermies Defences & Yorkshire Bank defences, also forward trenches. Wiring Hermies defences & front line of battle zone.	WHCS
	9th		Digging Hermies Defences & Yorkshire Bank. Wiring Hermies defences.	WHCS
	10th		Digging & wiring Hermies Defences. Making Shelters in Yorkshire Bank. Work on test bores.	WHCS
	11th		do	WHCS
	12th		As on 11th. Erecting shelters for electric cells & wireless station	WHCS
	13th		do	WHCS
	14th		Digging Hermies defences, front line of battle zone & forward trenches. Duckboarding Hermies defences. Erecting Shelters for electric cells & wireless. Shelters in Yorkshire Bank	WHCS
	15th		As on 14th. Wiring Hermies defences & front line of battle zone	WHCS
	16th		Digging & wiring Hermies Defences. Digging & duckboarding front line of battle zone. Shelters for wireless & Electric light. Shelters in Yorkshire Bank. Test bores.	WHCS

77th Field Coy RE

WAR DIARY
or
INTELLIGENCE SUMMARY.
(Erase heading not required.)

February 1918

Army Form C. 2118.

Instructions regarding War Diaries and Intelligence Summaries are contained in F. S. Regs., Part II. and the Staff Manual respectively. Title pages will be prepared in manuscript.

Place	Date	Hour	Summary of Events and Information	Remarks and references to Appendices
			Sheet 57	
Broken Houses Sheet 57c. H36.d	17		Digging and duckboarding front line of battle zone. Wiring Hermies defences. Erecting Shelters for Wireless & Electric Light. Shelters in Yorkshire bank. Test box.	WHCS
	18		As on 17th. Wiring gun positions.	WHCS
	19		Work on front line of battle zone. Wiring gun positions. Hermies defences	WHCS
	20		Work on front line of battle zone & Hermies defences.	WHCS.
	21		——— do ———	WHCS
	22		——— do ——— Digging forward trenches.	WHCS
	23		As on 21st.	WHCS
	24		— do —	WHCS
	25		— do —.	WHCS
	26		Work on front line of battle zone, Hermies & Havrincourt defences.	WHCS.
	27		—— do ——	WHCS
	28		—— do ——	WHCS

[signature]
MAJOR, R.E.
COMMDG. 77th (FIELD) COY. R.E.

(A7092). Wt. W12839/M1293. 750,000. 1/17. D. D. & L., Ltd. Forms/C.2118/14.

77th Field Coy R.E. February 1918

WAR DIARY
or
INTELLIGENCE SUMMARY.

(*Erase heading not required.*)

Army Form C. 2118.

Instructions regarding War Diaries and Intelligence Summaries are contained in F. S. Regs., Part II. and the Staff Manual respectively. Title pages will be prepared in manuscript.

Place	Date	Hour	Summary of Events and Information	Reinforcements: All ranks	Reinforcements: Animals	Casualties All Ranks: Killed	Wounded	Died	Hosp	Evac	Casualties Animals: Killed	Wounded	Died	Hosp	Evac	Remarks and references to Appendices
			Sheet 92													
	1st		Sp Barry to II C.R.S						1							
	2nd		1 O.R wounded				1									
	3rd								x							
	4th		Sp Miller to F.A						1							
	5th															
	6th		Sp Smith joined from 1st Special Coy RE	1												
	7th															
	8th		Sp Brooks to F.A 1 Riding horse drawn		1				1							
	9		Sp Paterson, Pnr Day, Sr Williams to F.A						3							
	10		1 O.R leave to U.K. II Lt Codling from V Corp HQ. Sr Williams evac sick							1						
	11		1 O.R leave to U.K. Sp Woodman & Pragnell to F.A						2							
	12		3 O.R -do-													
	13		Sp Paterson from F.A. (att 337 R.P.C RE)													
	14		2 O.R leave to U.K Pnr Day from F.A. Sp Smith Ellis from F.A 11th Swindell													
	15		Sp Brooks evacuated to C.C.S							1						
	16		1 O.R leave to U.K. 1 O.R evac sick							1						
	17		3 O.R leave to U.K Sp Dawes to F.A 3rd Army Dental Centre						1							
	18		Sp Woodman from F.A. (1 O.R to F.A)													
	19		1 Riding horse evacuated sick. Sp Sutton to 37th S.S att. 2 O.R killed & 1 O.R wounded			2	1								1	
	20		1 O.R wounded at duty													
	21		3 O.R leave to U.K 1 O.R att to 8 Pontoon Park 1 O.R att 17th Div Bath													
	22		Cpl Edwards to R.E B.O II Lt Codling to 326 Field Coy R.E													
	23		2 O.R att V Corp School													
	24		10 O.R leave to U.K. 1 O.R att V Corp Gas School 1 O.R from 3rd Army Dental Centre													
	25															
	26		1 L.D mule to 29th M.V.S sick												1	
	27															
	28		1 O.R att from 352nd E & M Coy													

[signature] MAJOR, R.E. COMMDG. 77th (FIELD) COY. R.E.

(A7092). Wt. W12839/M1293. 750,000. 1/17. D. D. & L., Ltd. Forms/C.2118/14.

17th Div.

77th FIELD COMPANY, R.E.

M A R C H

1 9 1 8

Army Form C. 2118. 17

WAR DIARY

~~or~~

~~INTELLIGENCE SUMMARY.~~

(*Erase heading not required.*)

77th Field Coy R.E. Sheet No. 93

Vol 32

Instructions regarding War Diaries and Intelligence Summaries are contained in F. S. Regs., Part II. and the Staff Manual respectively. Title pages will be prepared in manuscript.

Place	Date March	Hour	Summary of Events and Information	Remarks and references to Appendices
	1.3.18		Digging and wiring HERMIES and HAVRINCOURT defences and Front Line Battle Zone	
	2.3.18		-do-	
	3.3.18		-do-	
	4.3.18		-do-	
	5.3.18		-do-	
	6.3.18		-do-	
	7.3.18		-do-	
	8.3.18		-do-	
	9.3.18		-do-	
	10.3.18		-do-	
	11.3.18		-do-	
	12.3.18		-do-	
	13.3.18		-do-	
	14.3.18		-do-	
	15.3.18		-do-	
	16.3.18		-do-	
	17.3.18		-do-	
	18.3.18		-do-	
	19.3.18		-do-	
	~~20.3.18~~			

D. D. & L., London, E.C.
(A8004) Wt W177/M2031 750,000 5/17 Sch. 52 Forms/C2118/14

Instructions regarding War Diaries and Intelligence Summaries are contained in F. S. Regs., Part II. and the Staff Manual respectively. Title pages will be prepared in manuscript.

WAR DIARY

~~or~~

~~INTELLIGENCE SUMMARY.~~

(Erase heading not required.)

Army Form C. 2118.

Sheet No. 94

Place	Date	Hour	Summary of Events and Information	Remarks and references to Appendices
	20·3·18		Company and attached Infy. worked on HERMIES defences.	
	21·3·18		Company and attached Infy stood to all day in billets. O.C. visited 52nd Infy Bde. H.Q. to arrange for orders etc. for demolition of bridges across CANAL du NORD and of water points in HERMIES and VELU.	
	22·3·18		Transport moves from RUYAULCOURT to BEAULENCOURT Company and attached Infy. less 2 sections R.E. moved to 3rd line system and took up a position across CANAL du NORD at P.4.a. The trench occupied was dug out to full depth for a length of 300 yards. 2 Sections R.E. under 2/Lt. STONE R.E. detailed for demolition of bridges etc. reported to 52nd Infy. Bde. H.Q. for orders.	
	23·3·18·		Transport at BEAULENCOURT moves in afternoon to new position 500 yards NORTH WEST. On receipt of orders from G.O.C. 52nd Infy Bde. The following bridges were demolished:— Railway trestle bridge at K.26.c.8.2. at 4.00 a.m. Canal culvert at J.32.a.1.7. at 1.45 p.m. Light railway trestle bridge at J.30. Central 11.30 a.m. Road bridge across canal at J.35.b.8.0 at 1.00 p.m. Canal ramp at J.36.b.9.4. at 12.00 noon. Water point in canal at J.36.a.5.1. at 11.30 a.m. Water point canal at P.4. central at P.4. central at 11.30 a.m. Water point VELU wood at 4.00 a.m. Company and attached Infy. moved from P.4. to BEAULENCOURT arriving at 11.30 a.m. O.C. went with C.R.E to reconnoitre a defensive line between O.8.a. and O.14.b. At night this line was dug out in a series of Platoon Posts by Company and attached Infy.	

(A7092). Wt. W12839/M1293. 750,000. 1/17. D. D. & L., Ltd. Forms/C.2118/14.

Instructions regarding War Diaries and Intelligence Summaries are contained in F. S. Regs., Part II. and the Staff Manual respectively. Title pages will be prepared in manuscript.

WAR DIARY

~~or~~

~~INTELLIGENCE SUMMARY.~~

(*Erase heading not required.*)

Army Form C. 2118.

Sheet No 395

Place	Date	Hour	Summary of Events and Information	Remarks and references to Appendices
	24.3.18		Transport moves to point 700 yards WEST of LE SARS and again at 6.00 p.m. moves to LAVIEVILLE. Lt BOX. evac. sick. Company and attached Infy. under orders of O.C. 7th Y and L took up a defensive position N.E. of GUEDECOURT at 8.30 a.m. At 11.00 a.m. Company and attached Infy. moved to a line between BEAULENCOURT and TILLOY facing EAST. At 3.00 p.m. Company and attached Infy. ordered to a line FLERS. GUEDECOURT to cover withdrawal of 51st Infy. Bde. At 11.00 p.m. Company and attached Infy. formed a rearguard to cover the withdrawal of 50th Infy. Bde. from GUEDECOURT to FLERS. When FLERS was reached. Company and attached Infy. marched with 50th Infy. Bde. to EAUCOURT L'ABBAYE and under orders of 50th Infy. Bde. took up a line thru M.30 on left of 63rd DIV.	
	25.3.18		Transport arrives at LAVIEVILLE at 1.30 a.m. At 9.00 a.m. enemy attacked and was held till 11.00 a.m. when a withdrawal was ordered to COURCELETTE. Company retired ~~thru~~ from COURCELETTE thru 2nd. DIV. In this action 2/Lt. STOKES was killed and 12 O.R. wounded. Capt. SWAN (attached.) wounded.	
	Through?			
	26.3.18		Transport moves at 12.00 noon from LAVIEVILLE to VADENCOURT. At 6.00 p.m. transport moves from VADENCOURT to PUCHEVILLERS via HARPONVILLE. VARENNES. FORCEVILLE and ACHEUX. Company and attached Infy. concentrated at HENENCOURT. Attached Infy. returned to Battalions. Company marched to billets in SENLIS.	

(A7092). Wt. W12839/M1293. 750,000. 1/17. D. D. & L., Ltd. Forms/C.2118/14.

Instructions regarding War Diaries and Intelligence Summaries are contained in F. S. Regs., Part II. and the Staff Manual respectively. Title pages will be prepared in manuscript.

WAR DIARY

~~or~~

~~INTELLIGENCE SUMMARY.~~

(Erase heading not required.)

Army Form C. 2118.

96

Sheet. No 4.

Place	Date	Hour	Summary of Events and Information	Remarks and references to Appendices
	27·3·18		Transport arrives at PUCHEVILLERS at 7.00 a.m. and at 12.00 noon moved to new camp 500 yards away. Company dig defensive line of posts in front of SENLIS will thru V.24.a – V.12.C. with assistance of 50 Pioneers.	//
	28·3·18		Transport moves from PUCHEVILLERS at 7.00 p.m. arrives CONTAY at 11.00 p.m. Company took over work of 78th (Field) Coy. R.E. and extended posts dug by them thru D.6.a – V.30.C. O.C. visited 51st Infy. Bde. and was asked to assist 7th LINCOLN'S REGT. to dig in on a new line thru W.25 and E.1. this work was carried out and the whole battalion dug in before daylight.	//
	29·3·18		Work continued on line thru V.30.C and D.6.a.	//
	30·3·18		– do –	//
	31·3·18		– do –	//

[illegible] Lt. R.E.

for O.C. 77th (Field) Coy. R.E.

A5834 Wt. W4973/M687 750,000 8/16 D. D. & L. Ltd. Forms/C.2118/13.

77th Field Coy. R.E. — March 1918

Instructions regarding War Diaries and Intelligence Summaries are contained in F. S. Regs., Part II. and the Staff Manual respectively. Title pages will be prepared in manuscript.

WAR DIARY
or
~~INTELLIGENCE SUMMARY.~~
(Erase heading not required.)

Army Form C. 2118.

Sheet No 5. 97

Place	Date	Hour	Summary of Events and Information	Reinforcements All Ranks	Reinforcements Animals	Casualties All Ranks Killed	Wounded	Died	Hosp.	Evac	Casualties Animals Killed	Wounded	Died	Hosp.	Evac	Remarks and references to Appendices
	1		Spr Pascoe to F.A. Spr Barry rejoined from C.R.S.						1							
	2		Spr Redfern to C.R.S. Cpl Fisk to Hospl. 1. L.D. Horse evac. sick						2						1	
	3		Spr Putt from R.E.B.D. Sgt Thain to F.A.	1					1							
	4		1. L.D. Horse evacuated sick												1	
	5		Cpl Cooper from R.E.B.D. Spr Smith & Miller from F.A. Sgt Thain evacuated	1						1						
	6		Spr Dunkley to F.A.						1							
	7		2. O.R. leave to U. Kingdom.													
	8		Spr Pascoe evacuated							1						
	9		Spr Redfern from Hospl. Cpl Fisk evacuated							1						
	10		Cpl Goff to Corps School of instruction													
	11		Spr Barry & Wood to F.A.						2							
	12		6. O.R. leave to U Kingdom. Dr Jones to F.A.						1							
	13		4. O.R. leave to U Kingdom Spr Dunkley & Shepherd evacuated							2						
	14		L.Cpl Ford to Corps School of instruction. Cpl [illegible] & Spr Webb from Corps School													
	15		9. O.R. leave to U. Kingdom													
	16		Spr Whitley from R.E.B.D. Cpl Newman granted increase of E.P.	1												
	17		Dr Jones rejoined from F.A. Spr Cosgrove ~~to~~ from School of Cookery													
	18		Spr Williams to F.A. Spr Wood from F.A. Spr Barry evacuated. Spr [illegible] to School of Cookery						1	1						
	19		1. L.D. Horse evac sick												1	
	20		Dr Hammond to Hospl						1							
	21		Spr Higgins to F.A. wounded				1									
	22		Spr Dunkley from F.A. Spr Williams evacuated							1						
	23		C.S.M. Livingston to III Army School. Sergeants [illegible] wounded. 2. O.R. to F.A. [illegible] rejoined. 1. L.D. Horse killed 1. Mule	1			2		2		2	2				1 L.D. Horse [illegible] L/Cpl [illegible] from R.E.B.D.
	24		Lt Box to F.A. L/Cpl Ford rejoined from Corps School Spr Butterworth rejoined from F.A.						1							
	25		Spr [illegible] rejoined from Divnl Baths. Spr [illegible] to F.A. 9. O.R. wounded 1. Officer 1. O.R. missing believed killed	2			9		1							
	26															
	27		Dr Hammond evacuated. 1. Horse Rider missing. Spr Higgins evacuated							1						
	28		Spr Butterworth A. to F.A.						1							
	29		Spr Butler & Smith to F.A. Spr Wright, Thain & Dr Evans evacuated						2	3						
	30		Spr Dutton rejoined from 37 S. Section													
	31		Spr Pelling to Hospl						1							

[illegible] for Season 11 R.E.
for O.C. 77th (Field) Coy. R.E.

(A7092). Wt. W12839/M1293. 750,000. 1/17. D. D. & L., Ltd. Forms/C.2118/14.

17th Divisional Engineers

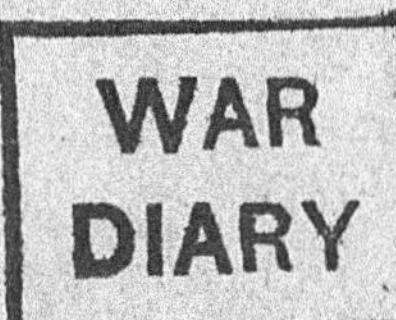

77th FIELD COMPANY R. E.

APRIL 1918

Army Form C. 2118.

Instructions regarding War Diaries and Intelligence Summaries are contained in F. S. Regs., Part II. and the Staff Manual respectively. Title pages will be prepared in manuscript.

WAR DIARY
or
~~INTELLIGENCE SUMMARY.~~

(Erase heading not required.)

77th (Field) Coy. R.E.
April 1918
Sheet No 1.

Vol 33

Place	Date	Hour	Summary of Events and Information	Remarks and references to Appendices
	1.4.18		Transport lines at CONTAY. Forward billets at SENLIS. Wiring and digging on Front Line System at E.82-70 to E.82.75.	
	2.4.18		Company moved to HÉNENCOURT.	
	3.4.18		Wiring and digging on MILLENCOURT Line.	
	4.4.18		-do-	
	5.4.18		-do-	
	6.4.18		No work done.	
	7.4.18		Company and Transport moved to BONNEVILLE	
	8.4.18		Company and Transport moved to ST. HILAIRE	
	9.4.18		Company Training.	
	10.4.18		-do-	
	11.4.18		Company and Transport moved to La VICOGNE	
	12.4.18		Company and Transport moved to ACHEUX. 100 Attached Infantry joined	
	13.4.18		Digging fire trench and C.T. in FORCEVILLE Line.	
	14.4.18		Digging platoon posts and C.T. in FORCEVILLE Line.	
	15.4.18		Transport moved to CLAIRFAYE Farm. Took over work from 249 (Field) Coy. R.E. 2 Sections and 21 Attached Infy. moved to ENGLEBELMER. 2 Sections and 79 Attached Infy. moved to FORCEVILLE.	

D. D. & L., London, E.C. (A8004) Wt W1771/M2031 750,000 5/17 Sch. 52 Forms/C2118/14

Instructions regarding War Diaries and Intelligence Summaries are contained in F. S. Regs., Part II. and the Staff Manual respectively. Title pages will be prepared in manuscript.

WAR DIARY

~~or~~

~~INTELLIGENCE SUMMARY.~~

(Erase heading not required.)

Army Form C. 2118.

Sheet No. 2.

Place	Date	Hour	Summary of Events and Information	Remarks and references to Appendices
	16.4.18		Digging and Wiring Intermediate Line and building shelters in Q.25.c.2.7 and P.36.b.9.1 Sheet 57.d.S.E.	
	17.4.18		do	
	18.4.18		do	
	19.4.18		do	
			-do- No. 3 Section moved from ~~[illegible]~~ to ENGLEBELMER	
	20.4.18		to SHELTERS in P.36.b.9.1. 21 Attached Infy moved from ENGLEBELMER to FORCEVILLE No. 1 Section from FORCEVILLE to P.36.b.9.1. No. 2 Section from ENGLEBELMER to FORCEVILLE.	
	21.4.18		Digging on Intermediate Line contd.	
	22.4.18		-do-	
	23.4.18		Digging and wiring on Intermediate Line contd.	
	24.4.18		-do- No. 2 Section moved from FORCEVILLE to P.36.b.9.1	
			No. 3 Section moved from P.36.b.9.1 to FORCEVILLE.	
	25.4.18		Digging and wiring on Intermediate Line Contd.	
	26.4.18		-do-	
	27.4.18		-do-	

D. D. & L., London, E.C.
(A8204) Wt W1771/M2031 750,000 5/17 Sch. 52 Forms/C2118/14

Instructions regarding War Diaries and Intelligence Summaries are contained in F. S. Regs., Part II. and the Staff Manual respectively. Title pages will be prepared in manuscript.

WAR DIARY

or

~~INTELLIGENCE SUMMARY.~~

(Erase heading not required.)

Army Form C. 2118.

Sheet No 3.

Place	Date	Hour	Summary of Events and Information	Remarks and references to Appendices
	28.4.18		Digging and wiring on Intermediate Line contd.	"
			No. 4 Section moved from P.36 b.9.1 to FORCEVILLE. No. 3 Section moved from FORCEVILLE to P.36.b.9.1 Sheet 57d. S.E.	"
	29.4.18		Digging and wiring on Intermediate Line contd.	"
	30.4.18		do.	"

[illegible] Lt. R.E.
for O.C. 97th (Field) Coy. R.E.

D. D. & L., London, E.C.
(A8204) Wt W1771/M2031 750,000 5/17 Sch. 52 Forms/C2118/14

44th Field Coy Royal Engineers

Instructions regarding War Diaries and Intelligence Summaries are contained in F. S. Regs., Part II. and the Staff Manual respectively. Title pages will be prepared in manuscript.

WAR DIARY
or
~~INTELLIGENCE SUMMARY.~~
(Erase heading not required.)

April 1918

Army Form C. 2118.

Sheet No. 4

Place	Date	Hour	Summary of Events and Information	Reinforcements: All Ranks	Reinforcements: Animals	Casualties All Ranks: Killed	Wounded	Died	Hospital	Evacuated	Casualties Animals: Killed	Wounded	Died	Hospital	Evacuated	Remarks and references to Appendices
	1/4/18		Sprs: Bedlern, & Dutton wounded, Cpl Goff wounded, L/Cpl Jewells &				3									
			Sapper Green killed, C S M Livingstone rejoined from III Army School			2										
			2nd Lieut Davis wounded				1									
	2/4/18		Sapper Lee to Hospital England													
	3		A/Sgt Edwards reported to Hospital							1						
	4															
	5															
	6		L/Cpl Baggaley to F A							1						
	7															
	8															
	9		Sappers Renward & Morris to F A							2						
	10		Sapper Griffiths to F A. II Lieuts A J Herdon & A Schofield joined from R.E Base Depot	2						1						
	11															
	12															
	13		3 Mules & 3 Horses arrived from 29 M.V.S.		6											
	14		Sapper Lee rejoined from Hospital in England													
			Sapper Cosham G. rejoined from 8th Pontoon Park													
	15		13 Reinforcements arrived from R.E Base Depot	13												
	16		Sapper Blay to F A Sick							1						
	17		2 L.D. Mules arrived from 29th M.V.S.	~~2~~	2											
	18		1 Reinforcement. II Cpl Procter 21/R att: Wounded. Sgt Belmont & Cpl Roberts wounded remained with Unit							1						
	19		Spr: Smith Hospital England, Spr Duncan to Base Auth: DAG. CR No 81907 of 14/4/18							1						
	20		II Lieut Swindles rejoined from 337 R.C. Coy. R.E													
	21		Sprs: Hughes & Ketteridge to F A							2						
	22															
	23		Sgt: Edwards & 22 Reinforcements from R.E. Base Depot	23												
	24															
	25		A/Sgt Griffin reverts to Cpl. Sprs Keys & Spr Dunkley to C.C.S. Spr Wright wounded							3						
	26		Major R B Dunlop awarded Bar to Military Cross, L/Cpl Binks & Sappers Campbell, Jenkins & Pickering the M.M.													
	27															
	28		L/Cpl Nicol to 5th Corps Gas School,													
	29															
	30															

[illegible] for OC 44th Field Coy R.E

D. D. & L., London, E.C.
(A8204) Wt W1771/M2031 750,000 5/17 Sch. 52 Forms/C2118/14

Instructions regarding War Diaries and Intelligence Summaries are contained in F. S. Regs., Part II. and the Staff Manual respectively. Title pages will be prepared in manuscript.

WAR DIARY

or

~~INTELLIGENCE SUMMARY.~~

(Erase heading not required.)

Army Form C. 2118.

77th (Field) Coy. R.E. Sheet No. 1.

WO 34

Place	Date	Hour	Summary of Events and Information	Remarks and references to Appendices
	1.5.18.		No. 1.2.3 Sections at P.36.b.9.4. No. 4 Section and Attached Infy at FORCEVILLE Horse Lines at CLAIR FAYE FARM. No. 3 Section working forward under Brigade. Company working on Intermediate System.	
	2.5.18.		No. 4 Section relieved No. 1 Section in forward billets. Company working on Intermediate System	
	3.5.18		2/Lt. R.H. OATRIDGE 7 Y.&L. attached. Work as above	
	4.5.18		-do-	
	5.5.18		Attached Infy moved from FORCEVILLE to billets at V.5.b.8.4. Work as above.	
	6.5.18		do.	
	7.5.18		do.	
	8.5.18		Company and Transport moved to LA VICOGNE arrived 5.30 p.m. Attached Infy rejoined units	
	9.5.18		Company started training Physical Drill Company Drill and Rifle Practice	
	10.5.18		do.	
	11.5.18		do.	
	12.5.18		do.	

D. D. & L., London, E.C.
(A8004) Wt W1771/M2031 750,000 5/17 Sch. 52 Forms/C2118/14

Army Form C. 2118.

Instructions regarding War Diaries and Intelligence Summaries are contained in F. S. Regs., Part II. and the Staff Manual respectively. Title pages will be prepared in manuscript.

WAR DIARY
or
~~INTELLIGENCE SUMMARY.~~
(Erase heading not required.) 77th (Field) Coy. R.E.

Sheet No. 2

Place	Date	Hour	Summary of Events and Information	Remarks and references to Appendices
La VICOGNE	13.5.18		Company Training. Physical Drill. Company Drill. Rifle Practice	
	14.5.18		do	
	15.5.18		do	
	16.5.18		Inspection by Corps Commander at TALMAS	
	17.5.18		General Training	
	18.5.18		Company and Transport left La VICOGNE arrived BEAUQUESNE	
BEAUQUESNE	19.5.18		General Training	
	20.5.18		do	
	21.5.18		do	
	22.5.18		do	
	23.5.18		do	
	24.5.18		do	
	25.5.18		do	
	26.5.18		Company and Transport left BEAUQUESNE. Company to billets at P.12.b.9.9 Transport to O.G.C. Central. Attached Infy. joined company at P.12.b.9.9. Took over work from 70th (Field) Coy. R.E.	

D. D. & L., London, E.C.
(A8004) Wt W1771/M2031 750,000 5/17 Sch. 52 Forms/C2118/14

Instructions regarding War Diaries and Intelligence Summaries are contained in F. S. Regs., Part II. and the Staff Manual respectively. Title pages will be prepared in manuscript.

WAR DIARY

~~or~~

~~INTELLIGENCE SUMMARY.~~

(Erase heading not required.) - 77th (Field) Coy R.E   Sheet No. 3

Army Form C. 2118.

Place	Date	Hour	Summary of Events and Information	Remarks and references to Appendices
P.12.b.9.9	27.5.18		Company and Attached Infy digging and wiring in left Bgde. Sector on defences of AUCHONVILLERS. No. 1 Section working forward under Brigade orders.	"
	28.5.18		do	"
	29.5.18		do	"
	30.5.18		do	"
	31.5.18		do Major DUNLOP wounded by Shell fire	"

[illegible] Lt R.E
O/C 77th (Field) Coy R.E

D. D. & L., London, E.C.
(A8004) Wt W1771/M2031 750,000 5/17 Sch. 52 Forms/C2118/14

44th Field Coy Royal Engineers

Instructions regarding War Diaries and Intelligence Summaries are contained in F. S. Regs., Part II. and the Staff Manual respectively. Title pages will be prepared in manuscript.

WAR DIARY
or
INTELLIGENCE SUMMARY.
(*Erase heading not required.*)

May 1918

Army Form C. 2118.

Sheet No 4

Place	Date	Hour	Summary of Events and Information	Reinforcements All Ranks	Reinforcements Animals	Casualties All Ranks Killed	Wounded	Died	Hospital	Evacuated	Casualties Animals Killed	Wounded	Died	Hospital	Evacuated	Remarks and references to Appendices
Blairfaye Farm Coy at Forceville	1/5/18		Sapper Taylor J.R. to F.A sick						1							
	2/5/18															
	3/5/18		Sapper Blackwell J. wounded M.G. Bullet to F.A				1									
	4/5/18		" Pritchard L. to F.A sick, Sapper Benstead F.A wounded (S)				1		1							
			Lieut Swindells to 834th Artisan Coy. R.E.													
	5/5/18		Spr Trout to Hospital (sick), L/Cpl Proctor to 3rd Northern G. Hos: Sheffield						1	1						
	6/5/18		L/Cpl Nicol J.M. rejoined Unit from V Corps Gas School													
	7/5/18		Dr Marlow on Special Leave to U.K. II Cpl Halstead & Dr Dunn to Hospital, Sapper Pritchard rejoined Unit from D.R.S													
La Vicogne	8/5/18															
	9/5/18		Dr Southgate to Canadian C.C.S. sick, Sprs Day & Morse to						3							
	10/5/18	→	F.A (sick) Cpl Perry to 5th Corps Gas School. 8 O/R to													
	11/5/18		51st Bde as Instructors (temporary) 2nd Lieut Marriott													
			& 8 O/R joined Unit from R.E.B. Depot, Spr Taylor rejoined	9												
			Unit from F.A													
	12/5/18															
	13/5/18		8 O/R returned from 51st Brigade													
	14/5/18		L/Cpl Lewis H.J. to be A/II Cpl													
	15/5/18															
	16/5/18	L/Cpl	Shaw to C.C.S (sick)							1						
	17/5/18		1 L.D. Horse (sick) to 29th M.V.S.												1	
Beauquesne	18/5/18		3 O/R to F.A (sick)							3						
	19/5/18															
	20/5/18		1 Rider (sick) to 29th M.V.S.												1	
	21/5/18		A/Cpl Halstead rejoined Unit from D.R.S. Cpl Perry from Gas School													
	22/5/18		Sapper Woods W.J. to C.C.S. (sick)						1							
	23/5/18		Sgt Spiers J. to C.C.S. (sick) 1 O/R joined Unit from R.E.B.D	1					1							
	24/5/18		II Cpl Barlow to 51st Infantry Bde. School													
	25/5/18		(Rest Camp)													
Coy at P12-b 9.9 Horselines at C.6. c (central)	26/5/18		Cpl Halstead to 5th Corps Gas School, L/Cpl Cosgrove to 17 Div													
	27/5/18		2 O/R to C.C.S (wounded) Spr Morse rejoined from D.R.S.							2						
	28/5/18		Dr Baxter to C.R.E. on Command													
	29/5/18		1 O/R joined from R.E Base Depot	1												
	30/5/18		2 O/R to F.A (wounded) 1 O/R to F.A (sick)						3							
	31/5/18		Major B.B. Dunlop to C.C.S. (wounded)						1							

7th Brigade [illegible] of R.E.
c/o 97th (Field) Coy R.E.

D. D. & L., London, E.C.
(A8004) Wt W1771/M2031 750,000 5/17 Sch. 52 Forms/C2118/14

Instructions regarding War Diaries and Intelligence Summaries are contained in F. S. Regs., Part II. and the Staff Manual respectively. Title pages will be prepared in manuscript.

77th Field Company R.E.

June 1918.

11

WAR DIARY
or
~~INTELLIGENCE SUMMARY.~~
(Erase heading not required.)

Army Form C. 2118.

Vol 35

Place	Date	Hour	Summary of Events and Information	Remarks and references to Appendices
BEAUSSART	1-10 6/18		Company + att^{d} infantry digging + wiring in Left Bde Sector AUCHONVILLERS defences.	
	10 6/18		Captain Harman R.E joined + took over command of the Company	
	11-22 6/18		Digging + wiring Auchonvillers defences.	
	22 6/18		Relieved by 249th Coy R.E. - moved to TOUTENCOURT	
	23-6		Company moved to ~~[illegible]~~ Sh. T5 A 6.5	
T5 A 6 5 57D.	24th 25th		Cleaning up, cleaning wagons, kit inspections	
	26th to 30th		Company training, Physical training, Drill musketry, shooting on range	

G. Harman Major RE
OC 77th Coy RE

(A7092). Wt. W12839/M1293. 750,000. 1/17. D. D. & L., Ltd. Forms/C.2118/14.

Army Form C. 2118.

77th Field Company R.E.

WAR DIARY

or

~~INTELLIGENCE SUMMARY.~~

(Erase heading not required.)

Instructions regarding War Diaries and Intelligence Summaries are contained in F. S. Regs., Part II. and the Staff Manual respectively. Title pages will be prepared in manuscript.

JUNE 1918

Place	Date	Hour	Summary of Events and Information	Reinforcements: All Ranks	Reinforcements: Animals	Casualties All Ranks: Killed	Wounded	Died	Hospl	Evacuated	Casualties Animals: Killed	Wounded	Died	Hospl	Evacuated	Remarks and references to Appendices
TRANSPORT at O.6.c. Central	1st		Lt R. MacGregor MacQuarrie left Horse Lines for forward Billets to take charge Coy													
	2nd		450469 Spr Palmer A.J. wounded, 506700 Spr Morse G. 98436 Spr Holroyd A to F.A.				1		2							
Corpl. P.12.b.9.9.	3rd		160396 Spr Poole A & 98430 Spr Holroyd A to F.A. & evacuated						2	2						
〃 - P.5.a.5.0	4th		Coy moved Billets to P.5.a.5.0 on account of heavy Shelling at P.12b.9.9 BEAUSSART													
	5th															
	6th															
	7th															
	8th															
	9th		57215 L/Cpl Hammett & Spr Duncan A to III Army Rest Camp													
	10th		19293 Sgt Shiels J rejoined from RE Base Depot. Sgt Harman joined from 84th Coy	2												
	11th		51435 Spr Morgan J to Hospl						1							
	12th		398847 Spr Rhodes J & 165002 Spr Hood A to III Army School of Cookery. 4 O.R. Evacuated. 311753 Spr Rontledge [illegible]							4						
	13th		441094 Spr Harrison J 442642						1							
	14th		Cpl Smith Dr Fireash & Dr Baxter to Hospl. Office moved from Horse Lines to forward Billets						3							
	15th		II Lt H.C. Swindells transferred to 834th Emp Artizan Coy.													
	16th		Dr Holland R wounded in G. Bullet. 6 O.R. rejoined from Base. Spr Walker J.S. to Hospl	6			1		1							
	17th															
	18th		Cpl Roberts W. & II Cpl Ithor H.J. wounded. L/Cpl Saunders takes over Pay duties				2									
	19th		II Cpl Fres. H. died of wounds 18th. 1 L.D. Horse evac. 1 Horse wounded Off charge. 3 O.R. rejoined from Hospl					1				1			1	
	20th		3 O.R. joined from RE B.D. 2 L.D. Horses drawn from M.V.S. 1 O.R. to Hospl. Capt Edwards transferred [illegible]	3	2				1							
	21st		Spr Harrison evacuated 3 O.R. to Hospl						3	1						
	22nd		Coy left BEAUSSART P.5a.5.0 for TOUTENCOURT at T.6.a.2.3													
	23rd		2 O.R. to Hospl. Spr Cook C. to III Army Rest Camp. II Cpl Barlow rejoined from Army School						2							
	24th		Spr Hood joined from III Army School. II Lt Schofield joined from C.R.A.s 2 O.R. from RE B.D.	2												
	25th		Coy left TOUTENCOURT T.6.a.2.3 for HERISSART T.5.a.6.5													
	26th		Cpl Petty W. to Hospl						1							
	27th		Dr Smith G. rejoined from Hospl	1												
	28th		Lt C.W. Box joined from RE B.D.	1												
	29th		Spr Very, Spr Morgan F.A. and Spr Rossmond joined from RE B.D.	3												
	30th		Coy Sports were held													[illegible] Major, R.E. Comdg. 77th (Field) Coy. R.E.

D. D. & L., London, E.C. (A8364) Wt W1771/M2031 750,000 5/17 Sch. 52 Forms/C2118/14

Army Form C. 2118.

Instructions regarding War Diaries and Intelligence Summaries are contained in F. S. Regs., Part II. and the Staff Manual respectively. Title pages will be prepared in manuscript.

WAR DIARY
or
~~INTELLIGENCE SUMMARY.~~
(*Erase heading not required.*)

July 1918

77th (Field) Coy R.E.

VR 36

Place	Date	Hour	Summary of Events and Information	Remarks and references to Appendices
HERISSART.	1st to 9th		Company resting and training near HERISSART. 2 sections living and working forward in Corps lines under C.E. V Corps. These withdrawn on 8th inst. Coy sports held on 29th ult.	
V.2.d.6.3	10th		Coy relieved 69th (Field) Coy RE 12th Div. as reserve company in AVELUY Sector V Corps Front. Coy billets North of SENLIS. Horselines U.11.c.5.7. near HARPONVILLE	
	17th		Capt. A. Moncrieff. M.C. RE. joined as 2nd i/c from Adjt RE 17th Div.	
P.36.a.1.9.	20th		Div Front extended north. Taking over half 38th Div Front. 3 Bdes in the line. Company billets moved to South of ENGLEBELMER. and working with 52nd Inf. Bde in the line in MESNIL Sector. No 2 Section left in billets at V.2.d.6.3 working with 305th Battln U.S. Engineers.	
	27th		Major E. Hayman. RE proceeded on leave. Capt. A. Moncrieff. RE a/O.C Company. One platoon U.S. Pioneers 1-320th Inf. Regt. U.S.A. under II Lieut Cole U.S.R. attached for billets & work. Also 1 Platoon U.S Engineers. 305th Battln attached for work under Lieut Lebeck U.S.R. Company at present disposed for work as follows. No 2 Section under Lieut Box RE working under Bde in Advanced forward zone. No 1 & 3 Sections under II Lt Hedden RE working, wiring & digging in Intermediate line localities.	
	29th		Lt Stone RE No 2 Section rejoined Company, & commenced digging new billets.	
	30th		Lt Stone RE II Lt Schofield RE attached RE. moved to billets with company at P.36.a.1.9. No 2 Section completed their accomodation.	
	31st		No 2 Section working with No 1 & 3 in Main Forward Zone digging & wiring localities	

Alan Moncrieff Capt RE
a/O.C 77th Coy RE

D. D. & L., London, E.C.
(A8004) Wt W1771/M2031 750,000 5/17 Sch. 52 Forms/C2118/14

77th Field Coy. R. E.

Army Form C. 2118.

WAR DIARY
or
~~INTELLIGENCE SUMMARY.~~
(*Erase heading not required.*)

Instructions regarding War Diaries and Intelligence Summaries are contained in F. S. Regs., Part II. and the Staff Manual respectively. Title pages will be prepared in manuscript.

July 1918.

Place	Date	Hour	Summary of Events and Information	Reinforcements: All Ranks	Reinforcements: Animals	Casualties All Ranks: Killed	Wounded	Died	Hosp.	Evac.	Casualties Animals: Killed	Wounded	Died	Hosp.	Evac.	Remarks and references to Appendices
Company at T5 a 6.5	1st		Drill & General Training. L/Cpl Millins from Hospl.													
	2nd		do Spr Mills & Spr Sims A.E. to Hospl. Dvr Cook E. to Hospital & Evac.						3	1						
	3rd		do Spr Mills & Spr Sims evac.							2						
	4th		do 5. O.R. admitted to Hospl. & Evac.						5	5						
	5th		do 8 O.R. joined from R.E.B.D.	8												
	6th		do 1 Officer & 1 O.R. to R.E.I.S. Rouen.													
	7th		do 3 O.R. joined from R.E.B.D.	3												
	8th		do Spr Dudley to Hospl & Evac.						1	1						
Transport Lines	9th		do													
at U 11 c 5.7.	10th		Company left Herrissart area T5 a 6.5 & proc. to V2 d 6.3													
Coy at V2 d 6.3	11th		Dvr Davies joined from 87th Field Coy	1												
	12th		1 O.R. admitted to Hospl & Evac.						1	1						
	13th		1 O.R. do do. 1 Rider Evac & 1 L.D. Horse Killed						1	1	1				1	
	14th		1 O.R. joined from R.E.B.D.	1												
	15th															
	16th		2 O.R. from CRE 17 Divn.	2												
	17th		1 O.R. to Hospl & Evac. {Capt Moncrieff joined from C.R.E. 17 / Lieut Morris to 78th Fd Coy.	1												
	18th		1 O.R. rejoined from Hospl.	1												
	19th		3 L.D. & 1 Rider evacuated to 29th M.V.S.												4	
P36 a 1.9.	20th		2 O.R. joined from R.E.B.D. 2 O.R.s wounded. Coy. move from V2 d 6.3 to P36 a 1.9. Transport. No 2 Section remains at V2 d 6.3 at same place.	2			2			1						
Transport at	21st		1 O.R. to III Army Rest Camp.													
U 11 c 5.7.	22nd		1 O.R. rejoined from III Army Rest Camp: 1 Rider from 29 M.V.S.		1											
	23rd															
	24th		1 O.R. rejoined from Hospital	1												
	25th		1 O.R. to Hospital & Evac. 1 O.R. to Hospl. 1 O.R. wounded & evac.				1		2	2						
No 2 Plon "B" Coy 1st Bn 305th U.S.E. att for work	26th		1 O.R. to Hospl. 1 O.R. from III Army Vet. School (rejoined)						1							
	27th		1 Off & 46 O.R. att. from 2 Plon 320 Inf. American Army arrived & lodg themselves in. Relieved by this unit from 30-7-18													
	28th		Major Norman proceeds on leave. Capt. Moncreiff assumes command. 2 O.R. wounded & evac.				2			2						
	29th		1 O.R. to III A. School of Cookery. 1 O.R. to Hospl. No 2 Section rejoin Coy at P36 a 1.9						1							
	30th		1 O.R. to Hospital													
	31st															

Alan Jamieson
Captain R.E.
O/C. 77th Field Coy R.E.

D. D. & L., London, E.C.
(A8004) Wt W1771/M2031 750,000 5/17 Sch. 52 Forms/C2118/14

17th Divl.
Engineers

77th FIELD CO.,

ROYAL ENGINEERS,

A U G U S T 1 9 1 8.

77th Field Co. R.E.

Army Form C. 2118.

Vol 37

WAR DIARY
or
~~INTELLIGENCE SUMMARY~~
(Erase heading not required.)

Instructions regarding War Diaries and Intelligence Summaries are contained in F. S. Regs., Part II. and the Staff Manual respectively. Title pages will be prepared in manuscript.

24

August 1918.

Place	Date	Hour	Summary of Events and Information	Reinforcements All Ranks	Reinforcements Animals	Casualties All Ranks Killed	Wounded	Died	Hosp.	Evac.	Animals Killed	Wounded	Died	Hosp.	Evac.	Remarks and references to Appendices
Company at P36.a.1.9. Transport at U11.C5.7.	1st		1 O.R. to Hosp. evacuated, 3 O.R's evacuated						1	4						
	2nd		1 O.R. " " "						1	1						
	3rd		1 Officer + 46 O.R's attached from 320th U.S.A. rejoined Regt.													
			2 L.D. Horses evacuated. 1 O.R. to Hospital						1						2	
	4		1 O.R. to Hospital, 1 O.R. to V Corps Gas School.						1							
	5		1 O.R. "						1							
	6		1 Officer + 1 O.R. to R.E. Training Sch. Rouen + 1 O.R. to III Army Rest Camp.													
			1 " + 1 O.R. rejoined from R.E. Training Sch. + 3 O.R's joined from R.E.B.D	3												
TOUTENCOURT.			Company moved from P36.a.1.9 to Toutencourt, Horse lines T6.d.9.9.													
	7		1 Rider from 29th M.V.S.		1											
DAOURS	8		Coy. moved from Toutencourt to Daours. Transport lines same place.													
	9		" " Daours " J26.d.9.7 " " "													
	11		2 O.R's to Hospital						2							
	12		1 O.R. "						1							
	13		Coy. moved from J.26.d.9.7. Coy. H.Qrs, Nos 3 & 4 Sections & Transport lines at P.6.d.9.3. Nos 1 & 2 Sections at O.20.b.6.6. 4 L.D. Horses from 29 M.V.S. Major Harman rejoins from leave & resumes Command of Coy.		4											
FOUILLOY.	16		Nos 1 & 2 Sections rejoin Coy at P6.d.9.3 & Coy. moves to O.10b.4.9. Transport lines at same place. 1 Officer + 1 O.R. to 4th Bn. VI Corps.													
VECQUEMONT.	17		Coy. moved from O.10b.4.9 to Vecquemont H.6.c.9.4													
	18		1 O.R. to Hospital						1							
HERRISART	18/19		Coy moved from H.6.c.9.4 to Herrisart. Transport lines same place.													
			1 O.R. joined from 6 Siege Co. R.E., 1 O.R. rejoined from V Corps Gas School.	1												
			5 O.R's rejoined from Hospital, 5 O.R's joined from R.E.B.D	5												
	20		1 O.R. to Hospital. 1 O.R. rejoined from III Army Rest Camp.													
TOUTENCOURT	21		Coy moved from Herrisart to Toutencourt													
	"		" " Toutencourt to P.27.d.6.8. 1 O.R. to Hosp. evacuated						1	1						
	23		1 O.R. rejoined from Hospital													
	24		Coy moved from P27.d.6.8 to Q.2.c.9.8. 1 O.R. rejoined from III Army Corps Sch. 7 O.R's joined from R.E.B.D	7												
	25		Coy moved from Q.2.c.9.8 to R.32.b.1.9. Transport lines same place.													
	28		" " " R.32b.1.9 to M.19.d.2.2. " " remain at R.32b.1.9. 2 L.D. Horses from 29 M.V.S.		2											
	29		Transport lines move from R.32b.1.9 to M.19.d.2.2.													
	30		1 O.R. rejoined from Hosp. No. 3 Section moves to													
	31		1 O.R. to Hospital wounded. 2 Horses Killed				1		1		2					

Harman
MAJOR, R.E.
COMMDG. 77th (FIELD) COY. R.E.

Instructions regarding War Diaries and Intelligence Summaries are contained in F. S. Regs., Part II. and the Staff Manual respectively. Title pages will be prepared in manuscript.

WAR DIARY
or
~~INTELLIGENCE SUMMARY.~~

(Erase heading not required.)

Army Form C. 2118.

77th (Field) Coy RE

August:-

Place	Date	Hour	Summary of Events and Information	Remarks and references to Appendices
ENGLEBELMER	1st		Company working on digging & wiring localities in main forward zone.	
	1st–6th		No 4 Section Forward with 52nd Infy. Bde	
TOUTENCOURT	6th		Coy Relieved by 124th (Field) Coy RE & moved to TOUTENCOURT.	
DAOURS	8th		Coy in G.H.Q. reserve moved to DAOURS	
VAUX-SUR-SOMME	9th		Coy " " " " VAUX-SUR-SOMME	
"	10th		Company standing by dressing	
" "	12th		Took over from 10th Australian (Field) Coy.	
GAILLY	13th		Coy moved to GAILLY. H.Q. No 3 & 4 sections & Horselines in camp there. No 1 & 2 Section at Q.20 b.0 (Sheet 62d) Work commenced on SOMME bridges.	
	13–16th		Work, maintaining communication across the Somme	
FOUILLOY	16th		Relieved by No 8 Coy A. Engineers, moved to FOUILLOY	
	17th		Moved to VECQUEMONT	
HERISSART	18th		Moved to HERISSART into V Corps	
	20th		Moved to TOUTENCOURT	
	21st		Moved to FORCEVILLE, standing by in reserve	
	24th		Moved to MAILLY-MAILLY	
	25th		Built bridge for 1st line transport across R. ANCRE at Q18 c 7.4	
R 32 b 1.9.	26th–28th		Moved to R 32 b 1.9 Work on roads	
	28th		Moved to COURCELETTE	
Courcelette	28th–31st		Work on roads	

E Marman(?) Major RE

A5834 Wt. W4973/M687 750,000 8/16 D. D. & L. Ltd. Forms/C.2118/13.

September 1918 — 77th Fld Coy RE

Army Form C. 2118.

Instructions regarding War Diaries and Intelligence Summaries are contained in F. S. Regs., Part II. and the Staff Manual respectively. Title pages will be prepared in manuscript.

WAR DIARY
or
INTELLIGENCE SUMMARY.
(Erase heading not required.)

VR 38

Place	Date	Hour	Summary of Events and Information	Remarks and references to Appendices
COURCELETTE	3rd		Company moved to ROCQUIGNY. No 2 Section detailed to work with Advd guard of the Divn + to maintain communications.	
	5th		Commenced work bridging the Canal du Nord at ETRICOURT. Design of bridge – timber plate girder total span 108' divided into 3. 2 crib piers	
	6-9th		Work continued – bridge opened for lorry traffic at 7.30 pm 9th	
	11th		Relieved by 151 Coy RE	
	11-17th		In Rest.	
	17th		Moved to neighbourhood of Heudicourt	
	18th		Attack on positions opposite Gauche wood etc	
	19th-24th		Consolidating in front of GOUZEAUCOURT	
	25th		Relieved by 97th Coy RE + move back to Transport Lines	
	25th-30th		In rest	

G. Harmens
Major RE

A5834 Wt. W4973/M687 750,000 8/16 D. D. & L. Ltd. Forms/C.2118/13.

September 1918

WAR DIARY
or
~~INTELLIGENCE SUMMARY.~~
(Erase heading not required.)

Army Form C. 2118.

Instructions regarding War Diaries and Intelligence Summaries are contained in F. S. Regs., Part II. and the Staff Manual respectively. Title pages will be prepared in manuscript.

Place	Date	Hour	Summary of Events and Information	Reinforce: OR	Reinforce: Animals	Casualties, All Ranks: Killed	Wounded	Sick	Hosp.	Evac	Animals: Killed	Wounded	Sick	Hosp.	Evac	Remarks and references to Appendices
M19d 2.2	3rd		Coy move from M19d 2.2 to O26d 7.5. 1 No 2 Section to P25 a 0.2 Transport N30 a 2.5.													
O26d 7.5	4th		1 OR (Forward Section) Wounded				1			1						
	6th		No 2 Section move to V3c 1.7.													
V7b 7.6	7th		Coy move to V7b 7.6. 2 Section to V4d 1.7. 4 OR from REBD 1 OR from Hos.	5												
Transport at	9th		4 OR's from REBD. 1 Absentee rejoined. 1 OR to F.A. (Sick)	4					1	1						
V1a 0.4	10th		1 OR to Hospital (Sick)						1	1						
	11th		Relieved by 151 Coy RE. Remain in same location. No 2 Section rejoins Coy.													
	12th		Lt Stace MC rejoins from RE [illegible]													
	15th		1 LD Horse from 29 MVS		1											
	16th		2 OR's proceed on Leave to UK.													
V6c 5.4.	17th		Coy moves to V6c 5.4. Transport remains V1a 0.4.													
W9c 9.3.	18th		" " " W9c 9.3. " " "													
	21st		3 OR's wounded. 1 OR rejoined from No 5 Port Park. 1 OR from REBD.	1			3			3						
	22nd		2 OR's Killed. 2 OR's wounded.			2	2			4						
	23rd		1 OR Killed. 1 LD Horse Evac Sick. 1 LD Horse destroyed. 3 OR's wounded (remain at duty). 1 OR rejoined from Spec. Duties Course WAIL			1	3			3	1			1	2	
	24th		1 OR. wounded.				1			1						
U6b 6.7	25th		Coy relieved by 97th Coy & move to U6b 6.7. Transport at same place. Sapper Promoted L/Cpl Pd & 1 Unpaid.													
	28th		1 OR att'd CRE. 1 OR rejoined Coy from CRE. 2 OR to F.A.						2							
	30th		1 OR Evac to CCS.						1	1						

COMMDG. 7th [illegible]

A5834 Wt. W4973/M687 750,000 8/16 D. D. & L. Ltd. Forms/C.2118/13.

16

Instructions regarding War Diaries and Intelligence Summaries are contained in F. S. Regs., Part II. and the Staff Manual respectively. Title pages will be prepared in manuscript.

WAR DIARY

~~or~~

~~INTELLIGENCE SUMMARY.~~

(Erase heading not required.)

77th Fd Coy RE

Army Form C. 2118.

October 1918. Sheet No 1.

Vol 39

Place	Date	Hour	Summary of Events and Information	Remarks and references to Appendices
V.1.a.0.4 57.C.S.E.	1.10.18		Company in training.	
	2.		-do-	
	3. 4.		-do-	
H.6.C.4.9. 57.C.S.E.	5.		Company and transport move to H.6.C.4.9. one section with 51st: Infy. Bgde.	
	6.		Company under orders to move forward.	
	7.		-do-	
X.3.a.80.15 57.C.S.E.	8.		Company less One Section move to X.3.a. 80.15.	
N.27.c.8.7. 57.b.S.W.	9.		Company and transport move to N.27.C.8.7. Company filling in mine craters.	
J.21.c.central 57.b.	10.		Company and transport move to J.21.C. central. One sections with forward brigade. 3 sections filling in mine craters.	
	11.		-do- -do-	
	12.		-do- -do- O.C. wounded on reconnaissance of River SELLE.	
	13.		Erecting temporary heavy bridges at dump.	
	14.		-do- Reconnaissance made of River SELLE	
	15.		-do- Foundations of temporary tank bridge made at K.1.C.6.7. (57.b.)	
	16.		-do- -do- Marking out cross country tracks.	

A5834 Wt. W4973/M687 750,000 8/16 D. D. & L. Ltd. Forms/C.2118/13.

Instructions regarding War Diaries and Intelligence Summaries are contained in F. S. Regs., Part II. and the Staff Manual respectively. Title pages will be prepared in manuscript.

WAR DIARY

~~or~~

~~INTELLIGENCE SUMMARY.~~

(Erase heading not required.)

Army Form C. 2118.

October 1918.

Sheet No. 2.

Place	Date	Hour	Summary of Events and Information	Remarks and references to Appendices
~~K.1.c.6.7~~ J.21.c. Central (57.b.)	17.10.18		Marking out cross country tracks.	[illegible]
	18.10.18		Digging ramp and laying foundations to temp. tank bridge at K.1.c.6.7.	[illegible]
	19.10.18		Erecting temp. tank bridge at K.1.c.6.7.	[illegible]
J.17.c.7.7. (57.b.)	20.10.18		Company less transport lines move to J.17.c.7.7. Company converting temp. tank bridge at K.1.c.6.7 into transport bridge, and — Erecting tank bridge at K.8.a.1.6.	[illegible]
	21.10.18		-do-	[illegible]
	22.10.18		-do-	
	23.10.18		Company in camp under ½ hours notice to move	[illegible]
J.20.d.05.05 (57.b.)	24.10.18		Company and transport move to AUDENCOURT. J.20.d.05.05.	[illegible]
	25.10.18		Company in camp under ½ hours notice to move.	[illegible]
VENDEGIES	26.10.18	16-00	Company proceed by march route to VENDEGIES and billet at F.7a.5.0	
	27.10.18	10.00	O.C. accompanies CRE. round line of posts in front of POIX DU NORD.	a.c.m.
		NIGHT.	Company at work on consolidation on Main Zone Defence Line in front of ~~[illegible]~~ POIX DU NORD.	a.c.m.
	28.10.18	NIGHT.	Company at work on consolidation on Main Zone Defence Line in front of POIX du NORD.	a.c.m.
NEUVILLY	29.10.18	14.30	Company proceeded by march route to NEUVILLY J.8.B.6.6.	a.c.m.
	30.10.18		Company training. cleaning up and fatigues.	
	31.10.18		Company training. cleaning up.	

A.C. Mitchell Major R.E.

O.C. 77 Field Co. R.E.

A5834 Wt. W4973/M687 750,000 8/16 D. D. & L. Ltd. Forms/C.2118/13.

October 1918.

Army Form C. 2118.

WAR DIARY
or
~~INTELLIGENCE SUMMARY.~~
(Erase heading not required.)

Instructions regarding War Diaries and Intelligence Summaries are contained in F. S. Regs., Part II. and the Staff Manual respectively. Title pages will be prepared in manuscript.

77th (FIELD) COMPANY ROYAL ENGINEERS No. .... Date

Casualties

Place	Date	Hour	Summary of Events and Information	Reinf. all Ranks	Reinf. Animals	All Ranks: Killed	All Ranks: Wounded	All Ranks: Died	All Ranks: Hospital	All Ranks: Evac.	Animals: Killed	Animals: Wounded	Animals: Died	Animals: Hospital	Animals: Evac.	Remarks and references to Appendices
U6b 6-7	1st.		1 O.R. to Hospital.						1							
	2nd.		2 O.R. to CRE 17th Divn. 1 OR rejoined from CRE 17 Divn													
	3rd.		1 Officer & 3 O.R. Leave to UK. 2 L.D. Horses from 29 MVS		2											
	4th.		1 OR. from F.A. 1 OR. to F.A. & Evac.						1	1						
W6 c 4.9.	5th.		Coy. move to W6 c 4.9. 1 O.R. Leave to UK. 1 OR to CofS Rouen.													
	6th.		1 OR. to Hospital & Evac.						1	1						
X3a 80.15	8th.		No 1 Section move forward with Brigade. Coy (less No 1) to X3a 80.15													
			1 Rider from 29 MVS. 2 OR from RE B.D.	2	1											
N27c 8-7	9th.		Coy move to N27c 8-7. 3 & 4 Sections forward													
J21c cent.	10th.		Coy less 1, 3 & 4 Sections to J21c Central. 3 & 4 Sections rejoin													
	12th		1 OR. wounded at duty. Maj Harman wounded & Evac.				2			1						
	13th.		No 1 Section rejoins Coy at J21c central. 1 OR to Hosp. 8 OR from REBD	8					1	1						
	14th.		2 OR. Leave. 1 OR rejoins from Hosp.	1					[illegible]							
	15th.		1 L.D. Horse to 29 MVS.												1	
	18th.		2 OR's Leave to UK.													
	19th.		1 OR. wounded & Evac				1			1						
J17c 7-7	20th.		Coy (less Transport) move to J17c 7-7.													
	21st.		3 OR's Leave to UK.													
	23rd.		1 Officer to Hosp.						1							
J20d 05.05	24th.		Coy (with Transport – move to J20d 0.5.05 (AUDENCOURT).													
	25th.		2 OR's Leave to UK. 1 OR to Hosp & Evac.						1	1						
			Maj Mitchell MC. joins to command	1												
F7a 5.0.	26th.		Coy move to VENDEGIES F7a 5.0.													
	27th		3 OR's leave to UK.													
J8b 6-6.	29th.		Coy move to NEUVILLY J8b 6-6. 1 OR to F.A. 1 Rider from MVS.		1											
	31st.		1 O.R. rejoins from RE B.D.	1												

A5834 Wt. W4973/M687 750,000 8/16 D. D. & L. Ltd. Forms/C.2118/13.

MAJOR, R.E.
COMMDG. 77th (FIELD) COY. R.E.

Instructions regarding War Diaries and Intelligence Summaries are contained in F. S. Regs., Part II. and the Staff Manual respectively. Title pages will be prepared in manuscript.

WAR DIARY
~~or~~
~~INTELLIGENCE SUMMARY.~~
(Erase heading not required.)

77 Field Co. R.E.

November 1918

Army Form C. 2118.

Sheet No 1.

Vol 4

Place	Date	Hour	Summary of Events and Information	Remarks and references to Appendices
NEUVILLY. ENGLEFONTAINE	1.11.18		Company Training. Company proceeded to VENDEGIES and located F13 a 8.7. O.C. Reported to C.R.E. 21st Division and work commenced on Assembly Trenches X24c40 to X24c43 and X24c44 to X24c47. First task completed throughout. 3 casualties due to shelling.	A.C.H.
"	2.11.18		Work resumed on Assembly Trenches as follows X24c40 to X24c43, X24c44 to X24c47, X24c95 to S19d23. Second task completed throughout.	A.C.H.
VENDEGIES	3.11.18		Moved out of CHATEAU and bivouacked. O.C. attended Conference at H.Q.R.E. Weather - wet.	A.C.H.
Poix du NORD.	4.11.18		Attack on MORMAL FOREST commenced. O.C. directing work of 77 Field Co. R.E. 93 Field Co. R.E. Two Companies of Pioneer Batt:	A.C.H.
		0830	LIEUT MARRIOT proceeded forward on Road reconnaissance.	
		0950	O.C. proceeded forward with Officer from Pioneer Batt: to inspect road. 10 50 a.m. 93 Field Co. & one Company 7th Y.o.L. moved forward and commenced work on Craters at S20 d 21. Capt MACQUARRIE moved necessary transport and stores up from Corps Dumps. Enemy demolition & traps discovered at culverts on BAVAI Road and pointed out to Tunnelling Coy officer. Company billeted at Spinning Mill. The two companies R.E. & two Companies pioneers continued work after dark & maintenance party left by 77 Field Co.	A.C.H.
	5.11.18		Work continued on BAVAI Road and Craters at S20 d.21.	
LOCHNIGNOL 5	~~6~~.11.18		Weather - Very wet. Company proceeded by march route to LOCHNIGNOL and bivouacked in field. / 6.11.18 CAPT. MACQUARRIE proceeded	A.C.H.
6	~~7~~.11.18	1900	with transport to Timber Dump in MORMAL FOREST and thence to Crater on road between LOCHNIGNOL and BERLAIMONT.	A.C.H.
BERLAIMONT 7	~~8~~.11.18	0700	At LOCHNIGNOL - Moved to BERLAIMONT. Heavy rain. Reconnaissance of road.	A.C.H.
	8.11.18		Company moved to billets near BACHANT. Reconnaissance of roads by O.C., LIEUTS BOX and MARRIOT. Afternoon - LIEUT. SCHOFIELD through Weldon Trestle bridge across stream at LIMONT-FONTAINE. No 3 Section completed bridge over crater near LIMONT-FONTAINE	A.C.H.
	9.11.18		Three sections engaged bridging three culverts in neighbourhood of LIMONT-FONTAINE. O.C. reconnoitring roads to DAMOUSIES. Three Sections billeted at LIMONT-FONTAINE.	A.C.H.
	10.11.18		Company moved into Billets at BEAUFORT. Road reconnaissance round DAMOUSIES and WATTIGNIES carried out by 2/Lieut MARRIOTT.	A.C.H.
	11.11.18		Hostilities ceased at 11.00 hrs. Company moved to BERLAIMONT. Repaired pontoon bridge over SAMBRE at BERLAIMONT.	A.C.H.
	12.11.18		Washing wagons. Maintenance work on bridges across SAMBRE and road leading therefrom. LIEUT L.C. ROBERTSHAW joined unit.	A.C.H.
	13.11.18		Maintenance of roads & bridges as above. LIEUTS MARRIOT & SCHOFIELD proceeded on leave.	A.C.H.
	14.11.18		Company proceeded by march route to ENGLEFONTAINE via LOCQUIGNOL.	A.C.H.
TROISVILLES	15.11.18		Company proceeded by march route to TROISVILLE. 1600 O.C. attended conference at C.R.E. office.	A.C.H.
	16.11.18		LIEUT BOX proceeded to AMIENS for Canteen Supplies	A.C.H.
	17.11.18		United Thanksgiving Church Parade Service at TROISVILLE. O.C. attended Education Conference at H.Q. 51st Brigade.	A.C.H.
	18.11.18		C.R.E. visited unit. Lecture given on Education & demobilization	A.C.H.
	19.11.18		Cleaning transport. C.R.E. visited unit. Lecture on demobilization. Football.	A.C.H.
	20.11.18		Cleaning transport. Football. 1630. O.C. attended Conference at C.R.E. Office. Interviewing all ranks re Education	A.C.H.

A5834 Wt. W4973/M687 750,000 8/16 D. D. & L. Ltd. Forms/C.2118/13.

Instructions regarding War Diaries and Intelligence Summaries are contained in F. S. Regs., Part II. and the Staff Manual respectively. Title pages will be prepared in manuscript.

WAR DIARY

~~or~~

~~INTELLIGENCE SUMMARY.~~

(*Erase heading not required.*)

Army Form C. 2118.

77th (Field) Coy. R.E.

November. 1918.

Sheet. No 2.

Place	Date	Hour	Summary of Events and Information	Remarks and references to Appendices
TROISVILLES	21.11.18		Cleaning Transport. Company training. Football. Interviewing all ranks re education	[illegible]
	22.11.18		Cleaning Transport. Company training.	[illegible]
	23.11.18		Cleaning Transport. Company training. Football.	[illegible]
	24.11.18		Church Parade.	[illegible]
	25.11.18		C.R.E's inspection of company and transport. O.C. went to Div Hd. Qrs as a/C.R.E.	[illegible]
	26.11.18		G.O.C. Division inspection of Brigade group	[illegible]
	27.11.18		Company training.	[illegible]
	28.11.18		Company training.	[illegible]
	29.11.18		Company training. 14.30 a/O.C. attended conference at Bgde. Hd. Qrs.	[illegible]
	30.11.18		Company training.	[illegible]

[illegible] Capt R.E.
a/O.C. 77th (Field) Coy. R.E.

A5834 Wt. W4973/M687 750,000 8/16 D. D. & L. Ltd. Forms/C.2118/13.

Army Form C. 2118.

~~WAR DIARY~~

~~or~~

~~INTELLIGENCE SUMMARY.~~

(Erase heading not required.)

Instructions regarding War Diaries and Intelligence Summaries are contained in F. S. Regs., Part II. and the Staff Manual respectively. Title pages will be prepared in manuscript.

Place	Date	Hour	Summary of Events and Information	Reinforcements: Ranks	Reinforcements: Animals	Casualties – All Ranks: Killed	Casualties – All Ranks: Wounded	Casualties – All Ranks: Died	Casualties – All Ranks: Hospl	Casualties – All Ranks: Leave	Casualties – Animals: Killed	Casualties – Animals: Wounded	Casualties – Animals: Died	Casualties – Animals: Hospl	Casualties – Animals: Leave	Remarks and references to Appendices
VENDEGIES.	1st.		Coy move to F 8a 8.7. Transport E 18 b 3.5						5	5						
	2nd.		Moved into bivouacs at E 18 b 3.5. 6 men leave.						1	1		2			2.	
POIX DU NORD	4th															
	5th.		Coy move to LOCQUIGNOL area. Bivouacs	1					1	1						
LOCQUIGNOL.	6th.		1 OR. rejoined from R.E.T.S. ROUEN. 1 O.R. to ditto									1			1	
BERLAIMONT	7th.		Coy move to U 21 c 2.5.		1											
BACHANT	8th.		Coy move to U 17 b 5.9. Transport U 17 b 3.7.													
	9th.		Nos 1, 2, & 4 Sections to LIMONT FONTAINE.													
BEAUFORT.	10th.		Coy move W 15 a 3.7 (1 & 4 Sections join at latter place)													
			Transport W 15 a 5.0: No 2 Section LIMONT FONTAINE.													
			12 men leave to U.K: 1 OR to III A. Cookery School													
BERLAIMONT.	11th.		Coy move to U 21 c 5.6. Transport U 21 c 40.55.	1												
	12th.		1 Officer joined. 2 Officers on leave. 2 O.R. Hospl.	1					2	2.						
ENGLEFONTAINE	14th.		Coy. move to F 6 a 75.70.													
TROISVILLES	15th.		2 O.R.'s Joined from R.E.B.D. Coy move to J 35 b 2.2.	2.												
	17th.		1 O.R. transferred to 2?7th Coy. R.E. 1 O.R. Hospl. 1 O.R. leave						1	2						
	18th.		6 O.R. leave to U.K. 1 O.R. died U.K.							1						
	21st.		1 O.R. Special leave U.K.													
	26th.		O.C. and 2 O.R. to C.R.E. 17th Div. O.C. Acting C.R.E.													
	28th.		1 N.C.O. reverts to ranks.													
	30th.		4. O.R.'s leave to U.K.													

[signature] Capt.
for MAJOR, R.E.
COMDG. 77th (FIELD) COY. R.E.

D. D. & L., London, E.C.
(A8094) Wt W1771/M2031 750,000 5/17 Sch. 52 Forms/C2118/14

Instructions regarding War Diaries and Intelligence Summaries are contained in F. S. Regs., Part II. and the Staff Manual respectively. Title pages will be prepared in manuscript.

WAR DIARY

~~or~~

~~INTELLIGENCE SUMMARY.~~

(Erase heading not required.)

Army Form C. 2118.

77th Fld Coy R.E. Sheet No. 1.

V8 41

Place	Date	Hour	Summary of Events and Information	Remarks and references to Appendices
TROISVILLE	1-12-18		Company Church Parade.	
"	2-12-18		Company Physical training and drill	
"	3-12-18		-do- Transport and cyclists proceed by route march to BAILLEUL. arrive Les VIGNES - 13.45 hours.	
"	4-12-18		Company training. Transport and cyclists left Les VIGNES 09.00 hours arrive MANANCOURT 15.00 hours.	
"	5-12-18		-do- Transport and cyclists left MANANCOURT 09.00 hours arrive camp near ALBERT 16.30 hours.	
"	6-12-18		Dismounted portion of company left TROISVILLE 08.00 hours en route for BAILLEUL. entrained at CAUDRY - 09.00 hours detrained at AMIENS 24.00 hours. Transport and cyclists left ALBERT arrive PONT NOYELLES 16.00 hours	
PICQUIGNY	7-12-18		Dismounted portion of company left AMIENS 01.00 hours bus to PICQUIGNY. arrive. 03.00 hours. Transport and cyclists left PONT NOYELLES 08.30 hours. arrive PICQUIGNY 12.00 hours	
BAILLEUL	8-12-18		Company and transport left PICQUIGNY 09.30 hours arrive BAILLEUL 16.00 hours Horse lines at BELLIFONTAINE.	
	9-12-18		Company cleaning up and washing wagons.	
	10-12-18		-do-	

A5834 Wt. W4973/M687 750,000 8/16 D. D. & L. Ltd. Forms/C.2118/13.

Army Form C. 2118.

WAR DIARY

~~or~~

~~INTELLIGENCE SUMMARY.~~

(*Erase heading not required.*)

Instructions regarding War Diaries and Intelligence Summaries are contained in F. S. Regs., Part II. and the Staff Manual respectively. Title pages will be prepared in manuscript.

Sheet No. 2.

Place	Date	Hour	Summary of Events and Information	Remarks and references to Appendices
BRAY les MAREUIL	11.12.18		Company and transport moved to BRAY les MAREUIL arrive 14 00 hours. Reconnaissance of villages LIERCOURT. BAILLEUL. BELLIFONTAINE. EPAGNE. EPAGNETTE and EAUCOURT made for hutting scheme and water supply. Hutting started at BAILLEUL and LIERCOURT.	[initials]
	12.12.18		Hutting and erecting accomodation at BAILLEUL and LIERCOURT.	[initials]
	13.12.18		-do- - Reconnaissance made of villages of CROUY. SOUES. Le MESGE for hutting etc.	[initials]
	14.12.18		Hutting and accomodation at BAILLEUL and LIERCOURT.	[initials]
	15.12.18		-do-	[initials]
	16.12.18		Hutting and accomodation at LIERCOURT and EPAGNE. 9 O.R. attached to 155 A.F.A at CROUY for work.	[initials]
	17.12.18		— do — Dismantling hut at BAILLEUL. Remainder of No. 1 Section attached to 155 A.F.A at CROUY for work on Hutting stables etc.	[initials]
	18.12.18		Hutting and accomodation at LIERCOURT. EPAGNETTE and EPAGNE. dismantling hut at BAILLEUL. No. 1 Sect. attached 155 A.F.A. at CROUY.	[initials]
	19.12.18		Hutting and accomodation at LIERCOURT. EPAGNETTE. EPAGNE and BRAY. dismantling hut at BAILLEUL. No. 1 Sect. attached 155 A.F.A. at CROUY.	[initials]

A5834 Wt. W4973/M687 750,000 8/16 D. D. & L. Ltd. Forms/C.2118/13.

Instructions regarding War Diaries and Intelligence Summaries are contained in F. S. Regs., Part II. and the Staff Manual respectively. Title pages will be prepared in manuscript.

WAR DIARY

~~or~~

~~INTELLIGENCE SUMMARY.~~

(Erase heading not required.)

Army Form C. 2118.

Sheet No 3.

Place	Date	Hour	Summary of Events and Information	Remarks and references to Appendices
BRAY les MAREUIL	20.12.18		Hutting and accomodation at LIERCOURT. EPAGNETTE. EPAGNE and BRAY. No 1 Section attached 155 A.F.A at CROUY	
	21.12.18		-do- -do-	
	22.12.18		Sunday. Company Inspection.	
	23.12.18		Hutting and accomodation at LIERCOURT. EPAGNETTE. EPAGNE and BRAY No 1 Section ~~returned to BRAY~~ attached 155 A.F.A at CROUY	
	24.12.18		-do- No 1 Section returned to BRAY	
	25.12.18		Christmas Day. Company visited by Brig. Gen. DUDGEON of 51st. Inf. Bgde. Major MITCHELL. R.E. a/C.R.E. went round company dinners.	
	26.12.18		Company Inspection. Inter-section football in afternoon.	
	27.12.18		Hutting and accomodation at LIERCOURT. EPAGNETTE. EPAGNE and BRAY 10. O.R. returned to CROUY for work with 155. A.F.A.	
	28.12.18		Hutting and accomodation at LIERCOURT. EPAGNETTE. EPAGNE. EAUCOURT and BRAY. 10. O.R. attached 155 A.F.A. at CROUY.	
	29.12.18		-do- -do-	
	30.12.18		-do- -do-	
	31.12.18		-do- -do- Lt. F.F. MARRIOTT joined his section at CROUY.	

[illegible] Capt. R.E.
o/c 77th (Field) Coy. R.E.

A5834 Wt. W4973/M687 750,000 8/16 D. D. & L. Ltd. Forms/C.2118/13.

Instructions regarding War Diaries and Intelligence Summaries are contained in F. S. Regs., Part II. and the Staff Manual respectively. Title pages will be prepared in manuscript.

WAR DIARY
or
INTELLIGENCE SUMMARY.
(Erase heading not required.)

Army Form C. 2118.

Place	Date	Hour	Summary of Events and Information	Reinforcements All Ranks	Casualties – All Ranks: Killed	Wounded	[illegible]	Hosp'l	Evac.	Casualties – Animals: Killed	Wounded	[illegible]	Hosp'l	Evac.	Remarks and references to Appendices
TROISVILLE.	1-12-18		1 O.R. to Hospital Sick					1	1						
	2-12-18		1 OR to Hospital Sick					1	1						
	3-12-18		Transport & Cyclists proceed by March Route to BAILLEUL. Arrived LESVIGNES 15 hrs.												
	4-12-18		Transport left LESVIGNES 9 am. Arr. MANANCOURT 15 hrs.												
	5-12-18		Transport left MANANCOURT 9 am Arr ~~[illegible]~~ NR ALBERT 18 hrs. 5 men Leave.												
TRANSPORT - PONT NOYELLES	6-12-18		Dismounted Section less Transport by Train to AMIENS. Joined												
	7-12-18		Transport at PECQUINY on 7-12-18.												
BAILLEUL.	8-12-18		Coy arrives at BAILLEUL. 5 men on Leave. Transport Line												
	9-12-18		established at BELLIFONTAINE.												
BRAY-LÉS-MAREUIL	10-12-18	14 hrs.	Coy. complete with Transport moved to BRAY-LÉS-MAREUIL.												
	13-12-18		1 OR. to Hospital. 22 Infantry attached for rations.					1	1						
	14-12-18		1 O.R. rejoined from RETS. 11 OR's Joined from R.E.B.D. 1 OR. from Hosp'l.	11											
	15-12-18		5 O.R. proceed on Leave. 1 O.R. att'd CRE.												
	18-12-18		1 OR. to C of J. DREUIL-LÉS-MAREUIL												
	22-12-18		1 OR. to Hosp'l & Evacuated.					1	1						
	23-12-18		1 OR. to Hosp'l & Evacuated. 2 OR's on Leave.					1	1						
	24-12-18		1 OR. rejoined from R.E.B.D. 2 OR's Joined from R.E.B.D. 1 OR from Hosp'l	3.											
	30-12-18		8 men on Leave. to UK	1											
	31-12-18		5 men on Leave UK.												

E. [illegible] Capt R.E.
O/C. 77th (Field) Coy. R.E.

17

Army Form C. 2118.

WAR DIARY
or
INTELLIGENCE SUMMARY.
(Erase heading not required.)

77th (Field) Coy. R.E.
Sheet No. 1. January 1919.

43

Instructions regarding War Diaries and Intelligence Summaries are contained in F. S. Regs., Part II. and the Staff Manual respectively. Title pages will be prepared in manuscript.

Place	Date	Hour	Summary of Events and Information	Remarks and references to Appendices
BRAY	1-1-19		Hutting and repairing billets at LIERCOURT. EPAGNE. EPAGNETTE and BRAY. 1/Lt MARRIOTT and 9. O.R. attached 155 A.F.A.	
	2-1-19		- do - - do -	
	3-1-19		- do - - do - and FONTAINE, - do -	
	4-1-19		- do - - do - - do -	
	5-1-19		- do - - do - - do -	
	6-1-19		- do - - do - - do -	
	7-1-19		Hutting & repairing billets at LIERCOURT. EPAGNE. EPAGNETTE. BRAY & FONTAINE. Erecting theatre at EAUCOURT. 1/Lt MARRIOTT and 9. O.R. attached 155 A.F.A. 1/Lt HERDON and 3. O.R. attached PONT REMY saw mills	
	8-1-19		- do - - do - 1/Lt MARRIOTT and 10 O.R. attached 155 A.F.A. 1/Lt HERDON and 5. O.R. attached PONT REMY saw mills	
	9-1-19		- do - - do - - do -	
	10-1-19		- do - - do - - do -	
	11-1-19		- do - - do - - do -	
	12-1-19		Company Inspection	
	13-1-19		Hutting & repairing billets at LIERCOURT EPAGNE EPAGNETTE. BRAY & FONTAINE. Erecting theatre at EAUCOURT 1/Lt MARRIOTT and 10 O.R. attached 155 A.F.A. 1/Lt HERDON and 5 O.R. attached PONT REMY saw mills	
	14-1-19		- do - - do - do Lt BOX and 7. O.R. attached HANGEST [illegible] camp.	
	15-1-19		- do - - do - - do -	

D. D. & L., London, E.C. (A8204) Wt W1771/M2031 750,000 5/17 Sch. 52 Forms/C2118/14

Instructions regarding War Diaries and Intelligence Summaries are contained in F. S. Regs., Part II. and the Staff Manual respectively. Title pages will be prepared in manuscript.

WAR DIARY

or

~~INTELLIGENCE SUMMARY.~~

(*Erase heading not required.*)

Army Form C. 2118.

Sheet No. 2.

Place	Date	Hour	Summary of Events and Information	Remarks and references to Appendices
BRAY	16-1-19		Hutting & repairing billets at LIERCOURT. EPAGNE. EPAGNETTE. BRAY & ERONDELLE. Erecting theatre at EAUCOURT.	
			ii Lt. MARRIOTT and 10 O.R. attached 155 A.F.A.	
			ii Lt. HERDON and 5 O.R. attached PONT REMY saw mills	
			Lt. BOX and 7 O.R. attached HANGEST reception camp.	
	17-1-19		- do - - do - - do -	
	18-1-19		- do - - do - - do -	
	19-1-19		Erecting theatre at EAUCOURT. - do -	
	20-1-19		Hutting & repairing billets at LIERCOURT EPAGNE EPAGNETTE. BRAY. ERONDELLE and FONTAINE. Erecting theatre at EAUCOURT.	
			ii Lt. MARRIOTT and 10 O.R. attached 155 A.F.A.	
			ii Lt. HERDON and 4 O.R. attached PONT REMY saw mills	
			Lt. BOX and 6 O.R. attached HANGEST reception camp	
	21-1-19		- do - - do - - do -	
			ii Lt MARRIOTT demobilised.	
	22-1-19		- do - - do -	
			9 O.R. attached 155 A.F.A	
			ii Lt. HERDON and 4 O.R. attached PONT REMY saw mills	
			Lt. BOX and 6 O.R. attached HANGEST reception camp	
	23-1-19		- do - - do - - do -	
			Lt. BOX and party return from HANGEST.	
	24-1-19		Hutting & repairing billets at LIERCOURT. EPAGNETTE and BRAY. Erecting theatre at EAUCOURT.	
			9 O.R. attached 155 A.F.A.	
			ii Lt. HERDON and 4 O.R. attached PONT REMY saw mills	
	25-1-19		- do - - do - - do -	
	26-1-19		Company inspection	

A5834 Wt. W4973/M687 750,000 8/16 D. D. & L. Ltd. Forms/C.2118/13.

Army Form C. 2118.

Sheet No 3.

* Instructions regarding War Diaries and Intelligence Summaries are contained in F. S. Regs., Part II. and the Staff Manual respectively. Title pages will be prepared in manuscript.

WAR DIARY
~~or~~
~~INTELLIGENCE SUMMARY.~~
(Erase heading not required.)

Place	Date	Hour	Summary of Events and Information	Remarks and references to Appendices
BRAY.	27-1-19.		Hutting and repairing billets at LIERCOURT & EPAGNETTE. Erecting theatre at EAUCOURT. 7 O.R. attached 155 A.F.A. 2/Lt. HERDON and 4 O.R. attached PONT REMY saw mills	[illegible]
	28-1-19		-do- -do- and EPAGNE. -do-	[illegible]
	29-1-19		-do- -do- -do- -do-	[illegible]
	30-1-19		-do- -do- -do- -do-	[illegible]
	31-1-19		-do- -do- -do- -do-	[illegible]

[illegible] Capt R.E.
a/O.C. 77th (Field) Coy R.E.

Instructions regarding War Diaries and Intelligence Summaries are contained in F. S. Regs., Part II. and the Staff Manual respectively. Title pages will be prepared in manuscript.

WAR DIARY
or
~~INTELLIGENCE SUMMARY.~~
(Erase heading not required.)

Army Form C. 2118.

Place	Date	Hour	Summary of Events and Information	Reinforcements all Rank	Casualties All Rank: Hosp.	Evacuated	Demobilised	Animals: Evacuated	Remarks and references to Appendices
BRAY-LES-MAREUIL	2-1-19		1 O.R. attached 7 Border Regt (work at Pont Remy Sawmills)						
	4-1-19								
	5-1-19		1 Officer + 1 O.R. att'd 7 Border Regt (work at Pont Remy Sawmills)						
	6-1-19		2 Horses E.D. to 29 M.V.S					2	
	7-1-19		1 O.R. to Hospital (injured)		1				
	8-1-19		1 O.R. att'd 7 Border Regt (work Pont Remy Sawmills)						
	10-1-19		1 Officer and 1 O.R. from R.E.B.D	2					
	11-1-19		4 O.R. Leave to U.K. 1 O.R. to Hospital Evac			1			
	13-1-19		6 O.R. left unit for Demobilization in UK				6		
	16-1-19		1 O.R. rejoined from 7 Border Regt.						
	18-1-19		1 O.R. transferred to 497 Field Coy R.E.						
	21-1-19		1 Officer + 18 O.R. left unit for Demob'n 1 Officer Leave to UK				19		
	22-1-19		1 O.R. to Hospital One O.R. Leave to U.K.						
	24-1-19		5 O.R. Leave to U.K. 1 Horse Evac to 29 M.V.S					1	
	25-1-19		1 O.R. Leave to U.K.						
	26-1-19		1 O.R. Leave to U.K. 3 O.R. rejoined from 155 Bde AFA						
	27-1-19		16 O.R. left unit for Demobilization				16		
	31-1-19		2 O.R. rejoined from 1?5 Bde [illegible]						

Capt R.E.
O/C 77th Field Coy, R.E.

3 Lac Lucien Lac Ing [illegible] Capt. R.E.
a/O.C. 77 the Field Coy R.E.

D. D. & L., London, E.C.
(A8004) Wt W1771/M2031 750,000 5/17 Sch. 52 Forms/C2118/14

Instructions regarding War Diaries and Intelligence Summaries are contained in F. S. Regs., Part II. and the Staff Manual respectively. Title pages will be prepared in manuscript.

WAR DIARY
or
~~INTELLIGENCE SUMMARY.~~
(Erase heading not required.)

Sheet (1)

Army Form C. 2118.

77 FIELD. CO. RE.

FEBRUARY 1919

Vol 43

Place	Date	Hour	Summary of Events and Information	Remarks and references to Appendices
BRAY-LES-MAREUIL	1-2-19		Hutting at LIERCOURT EAUCOURT, EPAGNE, EPAGNETTE Workshop at BRAY. Repairs in 155 A.F.A. area – Running PONT. REMY SAW MILLS	a.c.h
	2.2.19	09.30	Ceremonial Parade.	a.c.h
	3.2.19		Hutting, stabling + repairs as above in villages in 51st BRIGADE Area. Workshop at BRAY. 155 A.F.A. + SAW MILLS as above	a.c.h
	4.2.19		do do do do do do. do: PONT REMY Party returned to BRAY.	a.c.h
	5.2.19		do do do do do do do.	a.c.h.
	6.2.19		Hutting and repairs in villages in 51st BRIGADE AREA and 155 A.F.A. Area. do. Cleaning wagons.	a.c.h.
	7.2.19		do do do do do.	a.c.h
	8.2.19		do do do do do.	a.c.h
	9.2.19	09.30	Ceremonial Parade – Repairing hall for Concert party at EPAGNE.	a.c.h.
	10.2.19		Hutting and repairs in villages in 51st Brigade area and 155 A.F.A. Area do.	a.c.h
	11.2.19		do do. do. do. do. MAJOR A.C. MITCHELL rejoined unit from Leave	a.c.h
	12.2.19	1700	do do do do. LIEUTS C.W. BOX + ROBERTSHAW left unit for demobilization. O.C. attended conference at C.R.E. HALLENCOURT do. Workshop at BRAY.	a.c.h.
	13.2.19		do do do do	a.c.h.
	14.2.19		do do do do O.C. proceeded to 78 Field Co. R.E. WIRY as President of Court of Inquiry.	a.c.h.
	15.2.19		Cleaning wagons – repairs in workshop.	a.c.h.
	16.2.19	0930	Ceremonial Parade.	a.c.h.
	17.2.19		G.O.C. 51st Brigade at BRAY. Cleaning up and checking stores.	a.c.h
	18.2.19		Cleaning up and checking stores.	a.c.h
	19.2.19		CAPT. E. McGREGOR MACQUARRIE proceeded to LONGPRÉ in charge of detachment repairing huts.	a.c.h.
	20.2.19		Cleaning up and checking stores. Repairing huts at LONGPRÉ.	a.c.h.
	21.2.19		do do do.	a.c.h.
	22.2.19		do do. do.	a.c.h.
	23.2.19	0930	Ceremonial Parade.	a.c.h.
	24.2.19		Cleaning up and checking stores. do.	a.c.h
	25.2.19		do do do.	a.c.h
	26.2.19		CAPT. E. McGREGOR MACQUARRIE and detachment from LONGPRÉ returned to unit at BRAY.	a.c.h
	27.2.19		Cleaning up and checking stores	a.c.h
	28.2.19		do. do.	a.c.h

A.C. Mitchell Major R.E.
O.C. 77 Field. Co. R.E.

A5834 Wt. W4973/M687 750,000 8/16 D. D. & L. Ltd. Forms/C.2118/13.

Army Form C. 2118.

Instructions regarding War Diaries and Intelligence Summaries are contained in F. S. Regs., Part II. and the Staff Manual respectively. Title pages will be prepared in manuscript.

FIELD COMPANY No. ... ROYAL ENGINEERS

WAR DIARY
or
~~INTELLIGENCE SUMMARY.~~

(Erase heading not required.)

Place	Date	Hour	Summary of Events and Information	All Ranks: Demobilized	Evacuated	Hospital	Dead	Wounded	Killed	Reinforcements	Animals: Demobilized	Evacuated	Hospital	Dead	Wounded	Killed	Reinforcements	Remarks and references to Appendices
Longpré-le-Corps-Saints	1.5.19		1 OR despatched as Watford Detail															
"	4.5.19		8 O.R. despatched for Dispersal	8														
"	5.5.19		O/C Leave to U.K.															
"	6.5.19		1 OR rejoin from leave in UK															
"	7.5.19		3 " —— " ——															
"	13.5.19		1 " —— " ——															
"	14.5.19		1 " —— " ——															
"	17.5.19		1 " attached to 52 Bde H.Q. for re-posting to A of O															
"	18.5.19		2 Officers + 39 O.R. entrain for Le Havre en route for Sandling Kent for disposal + disbandment of Unit															
	19.5.19		1 O.R. from Cadre after arrival at Le Havre sent to 39 General Hospital V.D.G.			1												
	23.5.19		2 Officers 38 O.R. embark for Southampton en route to Sandling, Kent England for demobilization															

A.C. Mitchell.
MAJOR, R.E.
COMMDG. 77th (FIELD) COY. R.E.

D. D. & L., London, E.C.
(A10266) Wt W5300/P713 750,000 2/18 Sch. 52 Forms/C2118/16.

Sheet (1)

Casualties

Instructions regarding War Diaries and Intelligence Summaries are contained in F. S. Regs., Part II. and the Staff Manual respectively. Title pages will be prepared in manuscript.

WAR DIARY

~~or~~

~~INTELLIGENCE SUMMARY.~~

(Erase heading not required.)

Army Form C. 2118.

Place	Date	Hour	Summary of Events and Information	All Ranks: Demob'd	Evacuated	Hospital	Died	Wounded	Killed	Reinf'ments	Demob'd	Evacuated	Hosp't	Died	Killed	Remarks and references to Appendices
BRAY-LES-MAREUIL																
"	1-2-19		14 OR Demob'd, 2 Sherwoods rejoin their Bn. 1 OR posted to T.F. Depot	14												
"	2-2-19		1 OR rejoin Coy from Pont Remy Sawmills													
"	3-2-19		1 OR promoted, 1 OR attached to 155 Bde A.F.A. 1 OR to Hosp			1										
"			19 OR Infantry rejoin their Bns													
"	4-2-19		1 Officer and 2 OR rejoin Coy from Pont Remy Sawmills													
"	5-2-19		1 OR rejoined Coy from Det' with 155 Bde A.F.A													
"	6-2-19		8 OR Demobilized	8												
"	7-2-19		3 OR — " — 2 OR leave to U.K.	3												
"	8-2-19		1 OR Demobilized	1												
"	9-2-19		1 OR rejoined from C. of S. 1 OR from leave. 2 horses to 29 M.V.S										2			
"	10-2-19		8 Horses Evac' to Corps Horse Camp (Demob'd) 3 OR rejoin								8					
"			from leave. 1 OR S.O.S													
"	12-2-19		8 OR + 2 Officers Demob'd, 1 OR att'd to CRE, surplus Bicycles	10												
"			handed in to ~~A.O.D.~~, 1 OR rejoins from leave													
"	13-2-19		2 OR Demob'd, 1 OR rejoin from leave	2												
"	14-2-18		1 OR — " — 2 — " —	1												
"	15-2-18		1 OR from leave, 1 OR + 2 Horses rejoin from C.R.E. H.Q													
"			1 OR att'd to CRE 17 Divn													
"	16-2-19		1 Horse Demob'd (to Corps Horse Camp)								1					
"	17-2-19		3 Horses + 4 Mules to 29 M.V.S										7			
"	19-2-19		1 Officer + 17 OR. att'd to Area Cmdt Longpré (2 Mules 4 Horses)													
"	20-2-19		20 Horses to Corps Horse Camp Demobilized								20					
	21-2-19		1 OR promoted.													
	22-2-19		1 OR rejoins from Hospital													
	26-2-19		1 Officer and 11 OR rejoined from Longpré													
			3 OR Demobilized	3												

A C Mitchell

MAJOR, R.E.

COMMDG. 77th (FIELD) COY. R.E.

(A8504) Wt W1771/M2031 750,000 5/17 Sch. 53 Forms/C2118/14

Instructions regarding War Diaries and Intelligence Summaries are contained in F. S. Regs., Part II. and the Staff Manual respectively. Title pages will be prepared in manuscript.

WAR DIARY

or

~~INTELLIGENCE SUMMARY.~~

(Erase heading not required.)

Army Form C. 2118.

77 FIELD. COY. R.E.

MARCH. ~~FEBRUARY~~ 1919

44

Place	Date	Hour	Summary of Events and Information	Remarks and references to Appendices
BRAY-LES-MAREUILS.	1.3.19		Work in Saw Mills PONT REMY. CAPT. E.M. McQUARRIE M.C. proceeds on leave. Reclassification of horses.	a.c.m.
	2.3.19	10.00	Ceremonial Parade	a.c.m.
	3.3.19		O.C. Scheduling huts and stores in 51st Brigade Area. C.R.E. called in afternoon.	a.c.m.
	4.3.19	11.00.	O.C. attended conference at C.R.E. HALLENCOURT. Heavy rain	a.c.m.
	5.3.19		Cleaning up and overhauling stores.	a.c.m.
	6.3.19		O.C. at 51st Brigade Headquarters. Heavy rain.	a.c.m.
	7.3.19		O.C. and CAPT. MORRIS Adj. R.E. proceeded to inspect billeting at HANGEST. reported to C.R.E. at HALLENCOURT.	a.c.m.
	8.3.19		Farewell Race Meeting of 17 Division at HANGEST.	a.c.m.
	9.3.19	09.30	Ceremonial Parade.	a.c.m.
	10.3.19		O.C. moves to HANGEST with advance party of unit. Arrangements for billeting three Field Co. put in hand.	a.c.m.
HANGEST-SUR SOMME.	11.3.19		At work in connection with billeting at HANGEST. Orderly room staff arrived in HANGEST.	a.c.m.
	12.3.19.		78 Field Co. R.E. arrived at HANGEST. LIEUT. S.R. BALL proceeded on leave to U.K.	a.c.m.
	13.3.19		93 Field Co. R.E. & remainder of 77 Field Co. R.E. arrived in HANGEST.	a.c.m.
	14.3.19		C.R.E. visited Company in HANGEST.	a.c.m.
	15.3.19		O.C. visited detachment at LONGPRÉ. CAPT. E.McG. McQUARRIE M.C. posted to 93 Field Co. R.E.	a.c.m.
	16.3.19		CAPT. E. McG. McQUARRIE M.C. returned from leave & reports to 93 Field Co. R.E. a.m. Ceremonial Parade	a.c.m.
	17.3.19		LIEUT. S.R. BALL posted to 93 Field Co. R.E.	a.c.m.
	18.3.19		O.C. going into Company matters with CAPT. McQUARRIE M.C.	a.c.m.
	19.3.19		O.C. assumes command of 78 Field Co. R.E.	a.c.m.
	20.3.19		O.C. exercises animals. Takes over stores etc of 78 Field Co. R.E. 1/Lieut A.J. HERDON at BRAY.	a.c.m.
	21.3.19		O.C. exercises animals.	a.c.m.
	22.3.19		Parades of 77 + 78 Field Cos. combined.	a.c.m.
	23.3.19	09.30	Ceremonial parade.	a.c.m.
	24.3.19		O.C. hands over command of 78 Field Co. R.E. to LIEUT. MALCOLM.	a.c.m.
	25.3.19		O.C. proceeds to ABBEVILLE by motor lorry for Canteen stores.	a.c.m.
	26.3.19		Adjutant R.E. visits company at HANGEST.	a.c.m.
	27.3.19		77 + 78 Field Cos. Combine their canteens.	a.c.m.
	28.3.19		Animal accounts checked. O.C. proceeds to HALLENCOURT to take over from CAPT. E.G. MORRIS D.S.M.	a.c.m.
	29.3.19		1/Lieut A.J. HERDON takes command of 77 Field Co. O.C. takes over C.R.E. work.	a.c.m.
	30.3.19		A/C.R.E. visits company.	a.c.m.
	31.3.19		CAPT. McQUARRIES X horse transferred to 93 Field Co. R.E.	a.c.m.

A.C. Mitchell Major R.E.
O.C. 77 Field Co. R.E.

A5834 Wt. W4973/M687 750,000 8/16. D. D. & L. Ltd. Forms/C.2118/13.

Instructions regarding War Diaries and Intelligence Summaries are contained in F. S. Regs., Part II. and the Staff Manual respectively. Title pages will be prepared in manuscript.

WAR DIARY

~~or~~

~~INTELLIGENCE SUMMARY.~~

(Erase heading not required.)

Army Form C. 2118.

Place	Date	Hour	Summary of Events and Information	All Ranks: Demobilized	Evacuated	Hospital	Died	Wounded	Killed	Reinforcements	Animals: Demobilized	Evacuated	Hospital	Died	Killed	Reinforcements	Remarks and references to Appendices
Hangest - Sur - Somme	1/3/19		1 Officer leave to UK 5 OR att'd Cadre Park Longpré														
	2.3.19		3 Horses to No 7 Vet' Hosp								4		3				
	4.3.19		3 Mules " 29 M.V.S Cocquerel										3				
	5.3.19		1 OR leave to Paris														
	6.3.19		5 Mules to 33rd M.V.S Hornoy								5						
	7.3.19		2 OR att'd 7 Border Regt working at Pont Remy Sawmills														
	— " —		1 — " — rejoined from leave.														
	8.3.19		1 OR demobilized	1													
	9.3.19		1 OR despatched as Watford Detail to T.G.K.C. Watford														
	" — "		3 OR leave to UK.														
	11.3.19		1 OR rejoined from C of. D														
	12.3.19		1 Officer leave to UK. 12 OR demobilized	12													
	13.3.19		1 Horse to I Corp. Horse Camp Boudon								1						
	— " —		4 OR att'd 17 Divn Cadre Park Longpré														
	14.3.19		3 " — " —														
	15.3.19		1 OR leave to UK. 1 Officer Posted to 93 Field Coy RE														
	16.3.19		1 " rejoined from leave.														
	17.3.19		1 Officer Posted to 93 Field Coy RE														
	18.3.19		2 OR leave to UK.														
	20.3.19		1 Mule to 5th V.E.S Montières								1						
	21.3.19		2 Horses to I Corps Horse Camp, 1 Horse to 29 M.V.S														
			5 OR att'd CRE H.Q. 17 Divn														
	22.3.19		1 Mule to 29 M.V.S								1						
	23.3.19		23 OR re-Posted to 93 Field Coy RE for A of O														
	24.3.19		1 Mule to 29 M.V.S.								1						
	26.3.19		1 OR rejoined from CRE 17 Div. 1 OR attd Cadre Park.														
	27.3.19		1 OR leave to UK.														
	28 ~~30~~.3.19		1 Officer and 1 OR attd CRE HQ 17th Div														
	30.3.19		1 OR Posted from 93rd Field Coy. 1 OR attached from 93rd Fd Coy RE							1							A. C. Mitchell. Major R.E. Commdg. 77th Field Coy.
	31.3.19		1 OR leave to UK. 1 OR and 1 Horse attached CRE 17th Divn														
	31.3.19		1 Horse transferred to 93rd Field Co RE														

A5834 Wt. W4973/M687 750,000 8/16 D. D. & L. Ltd. Forms/C.2118/13.

Army Form C. 2118.

Instructions regarding War Diaries and Intelligence Summaries are contained in F. S. Regs., Part II. and the Staff Manual respectively. Title pages will be prepared in manuscript.

WAR DIARY
or
~~INTELLIGENCE~~ SUMMARY.
(Erase heading not required.)

77 FIELD COY. R.E.
APRIL 1919

VR 45

Place	Date	Hour	Summary of Events and Information	Remarks and references to Appendices
HANGEST SUR SOMME	1.4.19		A/C.R.E. visits Company	[initials]
	2.4.19.		Repairs to windows in 50th Bde Men billets.	[initials]
	3.4.19.		Camp fatigues. Pay Parade ~~[illegible]~~	[initials]
	4.4.19		A/C.R.E. visits company	[initials]
	5.4.19.		2/Lt. A.J. HERDON proceeds to LONGPRE to pay cadre Park Det	[initials]
	6.4.19.	0930	Ceremonial Parade	[initials]
	7.4.19		Lt Malcolm took over command of 77th Field Coy. 2/LT. A.J. Herdon proceeds on leave to U.K. Camp fatigues.	[initials]
	8.4.19.		6 x mules to V Corps Horse Camp.	[initials]
	9.4.19		Camp fatigues.	[initials]
	10.4.19		Camp fatigues, pay parade	[initials]
	11.4.19		Repairing brick wall, LT N MALCOLM demobilized. Camp fatigues. 2/Lt. MILLER took over company.	[initials]
	12.4.19		1 Ride for Army Animal Coll. Stn. Candas.	[initials]
	13.4.19		Ceremonial Parade.	[initials]
	14.4.19		Camp fatigues.	[initials]
	15.4.19		Camp fatigues.	[initials]
	16.4.19		Camp fatigues.	[initials]
	17.4.19		Camp fatigues 2/Lt. HERDON retd. leave. Pay parade. 77th COY. taken over by 2/Lt. HERDON	[initials]
	18.4.19		camp fatigues repairing wall in settlement of claim.	
	19.4.19.		Camp fatigues.	

A.J. Herdon 2/Lt. R.E. AJH

MAJOR, R.E.
COMMDG. 77th (FIELD) COY. R.E.

A5834 Wt. W4973/M687 750,000 8/16 D. D. & L. Ltd. Forms/C.2118/13.

Instructions regarding War Diaries and Intelligence Summaries are contained in F. S. Regs., Part II. and the Staff Manual respectively. Title pages will be prepared in manuscript.

WAR DIARY
or
INTELLIGENCE SUMMARY.

(Erase heading not required.)

Army Form C. 2118.

Place	Date	Hour	Summary of Events and Information	Remarks and references to Appendices
HANGEST SUR SOMME	20.4.19.	09.30	Ceremonial Parade.	AHH
	21.4.19.		Camp Fatigues. Combined Canteen closed and Coy Canteen opened	AHH
	22.4.19		Camp fatigues.	
	23.4.19.		Camp fatigues.	AHH
	24.4.19.		Coy moved to Longpré.	AHH
LONGPRÉ.	25.4.19.		Camp Fatigues. Work at Cadre Park. Pay parade 14.30 hrs.	AHH
	26.4.19		Camp fatigues. Work at Cadre Park	AHH
	27.4.19	10.00	Ceremonial Parade.	AHH
	28.4.19.		Work at Cadre Park. Inspection of unserviceable stores by O.O.	AHH
	29.4.19.		Camp fatigues.	AHH
	30.4.19.		Camp Fatigues.	AHH

[signature] Heldon
1.5.19

MAJOR, R.E.
COMDG. 7th (FIELD) COY. R.E.

A5834 Wt. W4973/M687 750,000 8/16 D. D. & L. Ltd. Forms/C.2118/13.

Instructions regarding War Diaries and Intelligence Summaries are contained in F. S. Regs., Part II. and the Staff Manual respectively. Title pages will be prepared in manuscript.

WAR DIARY
or
~~INTELLIGENCE SUMMARY.~~

(*Erase heading not required.*)

Army Form C. 2118.

Place	Date	Hour	Summary of Events and Information	Casualties – All Ranks: Demob'd	Evacuated	Hospital	Died	Wounded	Killed	Reinf's	Animals: Demob'd	Evacuated	Hospital	Died	Wounded	Remarks and references to Appendices
Hanglest-sur-Somme	1.4.19		4 OR leave to UK. 10 OR from 93 Field Coy RE in lieu of 9 from Coy Demobilized & 1 to make up strength													
	2.4.19		1 OR leave to UK													
	5.4.19		9 OR demobilized	9												
	6.4.19		8 " proceed on leave to UK. 1 Officer leave to UK													
	7.4.19		2 " Rejoin from Pont-Remy Sawmills													
	8.4.19		6 Mules to V Corps Horse Camp Boudon								6					
— " —	9.4.19		1 OR att'd CRE Mallencourt.													
	10.4.19		2 " " 17 Div Cadre Park Longpré													
	11.4.19		2 " leave to UK. 1 Rider to A.6. Str Camden								1					
	13.4.19		4 — " — 1 OR rejoin from leave.													
	15.4.19		1 " rejoin from leave													
	16.4.19		1 — " —													
— " —	17.4.19		4 " Leave to UK													
	19.4.19		8 " Promoted to complete Cadre													
	20.4.19		2 " Demob'd	2												
— " —	21.4.19		1 " att'd 17 Div Cadre Park Longpré													
	22.4.19		2 " leave to UK.													
	23.4.19		1 " att'd from 48th Field Coy RE for demobilization.													
Longpré	24.4.19		Coy Cadre move to Longpré (Billet 45) 2 Mules evac'								2					
	25.4.19		9 OR rejoin from CRE's HQ Detachment.													
	26.4.19		4 Bicycles evacuated to O.O., I.G.S													
	27.4.19		3 OR proceed for Repatriation to Winchester 2 OR Demob	5												
	28.4.19		1 " leave to UK. 3 OR rejoin from leave.													
	29.4.19		2 " take over Dump from CRE at Longpré													
	30.4.19		1 " att'd from HQ CRE for demobilization.													

Apperdon [illegible] RE

MAJOR, R.E
COMMDG. 77th (FIELD) COY. R.E

D. D. & L., London, E.C.
(A10266) Wt W5300/P713 750,000 2/18 Sch. 52 Forms/C2118/16.

9881 46 17

Army Form C. 2118.

WAR DIARY
or
~~INTELLIGENCE SUMMARY.~~
(Erase heading not required.)

Instructions regarding War Diaries and Intelligence Summaries are contained in F. S. Regs., Part II. and the Staff Manual respectively. Title pages will be prepared in manuscript.

SHEET No 1. 77 FIELD COY. R.E. MAY. 1919.

Place	Date	Hour	Summary of Events and Information	Remarks and references to Appendices
LONGPRÉ -LE- CORPS-SAINTS	1.5.19.		Work on harness and equipment at Cadre Park.	A.C.M.
	2.5.19		Board of Officers held to audit coy. accounts. HQ R.E. having entrained from England work of C.R.E. taken over by 77th Field Coy R.E.	A.C.M.
	3.5.19.		Camp fatigues, work at cadre Park.	A.C.M.
	4.5.19.	10.00.	Ceremonial Parade	A.C.M.
	5.5.19.		Cleaning area. O.C. proceeds on leave.	A.C.M.
	6.5.19.		Cleaning area, checking of wagon equipment at cadre Park.	A.C.M.
	7.5.19.		Camp fatigues checking of wagon equipment at cadre Park.	A.C.M.
	8.5.19.		Camp fatigues. Pay Parade 14.30 hrs.	A.C.M.
	9.5.19		Work at cadre Park	A.C.M.
	10.5.19		do.	A.C.M.
	11.5.19	10.00	Ceremonial Parade, clean arms inspection.	A.C.M.
	12.5.19		Cleaning and oiling wagons at cadre Park. Surplus stores return to I.O.S	A.C.M.
	13.5.19		do do.	A.C.M.
	14.5.19		Camp fatigues	A.C.M.
	15.5.19		do Pay parade 14.30. hrs.	A.C.M.
	16.5.19		O.C returns from leave. Loading wagons at cadre Park.	A.C.M.
	17.5.19		O.C. closes Imprest account canteen closed. Loading wagons at cadre Park	A.C.M.
LONGPRÉ	18.5.19		Cadre of unit entrains at LONGPRE with O.C. + 2nd LIEUT. A. J. HERDON. Arrived ROMESCAMP 18.50.	A.C.M.
LE HAVRE.	19.5.19		Arrived LE HAVRE early am. and commenced detraining wagons at 6.0 am. Proceeded by lorry and march route to No 3 Wing Reception Camp HARFLEUR. Transferred to Embarkation camp in afternoon.	A.C.M.
HARFLEUR	20.5.19		Cadre remains at HARFLEUR	A.C.M.
	21.5.19		" " " "	A.C.M.

A.C. Mitchell
MAJOR, R.E.
COMMDG. 77th (FIELD) COY. R.E.

D. D. & L., London, E.C.
(A10266) Wt W5300/P713 750,000 2/18 Sch. 52 Forms/C2118/16.

Army Form C. 2118.

Instructions regarding War Diaries and Intelligence Summaries are contained in F. S. Regs., Part II. and the Staff Manual respectively. Title pages will be prepared in manuscript.

WAR DIARY
or
SHEET No 2 INTELLIGENCE SUMMARY. 77 FIELD Co. RE
MAY 1919.

(*Erase heading not required.*)

Place	Date	Hour	Summary of Events and Information	Remarks and references to Appendices
HARFLEUR.	22.5.19		Orders received re embarkation.	ach
	23.5.19		Loading party 1 Officer 12 O.R. proceed to HAVRE DOCKS and loaded wagons on SS. IONNA. Main body of Cadre left camp at 3.30 pm and proceeded to Quay L'ESCAUT for embarkation. Cadre embarked on SS. CAESAREA and left harbour for SOUTHAMPTON at 9 pm.	ach

A C Mitchell.
MAJOR, R.E.
COMMDG. 77th (FIELD) COY. R.E.

D. D. & L., London, E.C.
(A10266) Wt W5300/P713 750,000 2/18 Sch. 52 Forms/C2118/16.

www.ingramcontent.com/pod-product-compliance
Lightning Source LLC
Chambersburg PA
CBHW081359160426
43193CB00013B/2065